Bonus study and revision support available **free**, online

online resource centre
www.oup.com/lawrevision/

Take your learning further:

- Multiple-choice questions
- Revision technique advice
- An interactive glossary

- Outline exam answers
- Flashcards of key cases
- . . . and much more

New to this edition

- Greater depth of information in relation to international sources of law and recent updates in relation to the European Constitution, the new Lisbon Treaty and new institutions of the European Union.

- New sample essay questions on issues related to the various international sources of law.

- Greater depth of information in relation to the secondary sources of law, equity, custom, and recent changes in relation to the doctrine of judicial precedent and the newly constituted Supreme Court.

- New information on books of authority and modern textbooks/journals as sources of law.

- Recent developments included in relation to jury usage and the issue of jury tampering.

- Overview of recent academic research undertaken in conjunction with official government agencies on the operation of criminal juries.

- Updated information on the criminal process reflecting the new updated Code for Crown Prosecutors.

- Updates on recent developments including the continuing implementation of Tribunal Reform and Lord Jackson's proposals for costs reforms.

- Greater range of legal authority, cases/statutory provisions highlighted to support the various chapters.

English Legal System
Concentrate

2nd edition

Tim Vollans

Principal Lecturer, Coventry University

Glenn Asquith

Lecturer, Coventry University

OXFORD
UNIVERSITY PRESS

OXFORD

UNIVERSITY PRESS

Great Clarendon Street, Oxford OX2 6DP

Oxford University Press is a department of the University of Oxford.
It furthers the University's objective of excellence in research, scholarship,
and education by publishing worldwide in

Oxford New York

Auckland Cape Town Dar es Salaam Hong Kong Karachi
Kuala Lumpur Madrid Melbourne Mexico City Nairobi
New Delhi Shanghai Taipei Toronto

With offices in

Argentina Austria Brazil Chile Czech Republic France Greece
Guatemala Hungary Italy Japan Poland Portugal Singapore
South Korea Switzerland Thailand Turkey Ukraine Vietnam

Oxford is a registered trade mark of Oxford University Press
in the UK and in certain other countries

Published in the United States
by Oxford University Press Inc., New York

British Library Cataloguing in Publication Data

Data available

Library of Congress Cataloging in Publication Data

Data available

Typeset by Newgen Imaging Systems (P) Ltd, Chennai, India
Printed in Great Britain
on acid-free paper by
Ashford Colour Press Ltd, Gosport, Hampshire

ISBN 978-0-19-958777-3

10 9 8 7

Contents

#1

Sources of law I: International sources of law

Key facts

- The law of the English legal system has many sources, custom being the oldest with the most modern sources being delegated legislation and international sources of law: European Union (EU) law, and the European Convention on Human Rights and Fundamental Freedoms.

- The European Union has its origins in the 1950s when six Member States signed up to three foundation treaties in order to promote peace and cooperation within Europe following the Second World War. The European Union presently has 27 Members. The UK joined the EU on 1 January 1973 when the provisions of the European Communities Act 1972 came into force. Where EU law conflicts with UK law, EU law prevails and can override domestic forms of law. The legislative ability of the UK Parliament has been limited due to membership of the European Union.

- The primary form of EU law is the treaties – these combined stipulate the objectives of the European Union and create/detail the operation/composition of the various European institutions such as the Commission, Parliament, and Court of Justice. The most recent treaty created is the Lisbon Treaty which was enacted in December 2009.

- The secondary forms of EU law include regulations, directives etc. There are various institutions involved in the creation of these forms of law such as the Commission, Parliament, etc. Courts of Member States if unsure how to implement or interpret EU law can apply for a ruling from the Court of Justice of the European Union. Once a ruling is made then it must be implemented/applied by the court which has requested it.

Key facts

✳✳✳✳✳✳✳✳✳

- The European Convention on Human Rights and Fundamental Freedoms is not a part of European Union law and is thus not enforced or developed by the European Union institutions. The Convention creates numerous rights and freedoms which can be enjoyed by citizens within the various Member States that have signed up to the Convention and its protocols, eg the right to a fair trial, right to life, etc. If these rights and freedoms are breached then a citizen can take a case to the European Court of Human Rights for a remedy against the offending Member State.

- The Human Rights Act 1998, which came into force in 2000, incorporates the Convention into UK law – now if an article is breached then the citizen can enforce their rights and obtain satisfaction direct from UK courts.

Introduction

The law of England has been built up gradually over many centuries. The various sources of law in historical order are:

- custom
- common law
- books of authority
- equity
- legislation
- delegated legislation
- international sources of law – European Union law and the **European Convention on Human Rights and Fundamental Freedoms**.

Historically, the most important way of creating the law was through local customs and then decisions of the judiciary. Alongside the development of the common law, equity was formed remedying the common law defects. Eventually Parliament became the most powerful law creator and statute law became the primary source of law. However, the judiciary still play an important role by interpreting statutes and developing areas of the common law, which are not covered by statutory provisions. During the twentieth century, two new sources of law became important: delegated legislation and European law. All of these sources combined make up the law of the English legal system.

This chapter will focus on the international sources of law: European Union law and the European Convention of Human Rights. Chapter 2 will focus on UK legislation, including the legislative process, legislative interpretation, and delegated legislation. Chapter 3 will focus on the common law, equity, custom law, and books of authority.

Revision Tip

When selecting relevant case law to revise in order to provide support, initially select those cases that have facts that you can easily remember and are of interest to you. Once you have learnt those cases then learn the more difficult cases. The more cases and legal support, eg judicial comment, academic comment, and statutory provisions, that you can provide in any examination question, the more credit you will obtain and the better your answer will generally be.

European Union law

The European Union (EU) has grown dramatically both in terms of the number of members (it started with 6 and is now at 27), and in the scope of its powers. The European Economic Community (as it then was) was set up in 1957 with just six members. Historically the EU was formed after the two world wars and was created to try to maintain peaceful relations between the European states. The origins of the European Union can be traced back to the

European Union law

✳✳✳✳✳✳✳✳✳

foundation treaties created between 1951 and 1957. The first treaty of the European Union, the Treaty of Paris was designed to create political unity within Europe and prevent future conflict between European states. As a result, the European Coal and Steel Community was established by Italy, France, West Germany, Belgium, Luxembourg, and the Netherlands. This placed the production of coal and steel in all Member States under the ambit of one Community organization, indirectly controlling arms production.

In 1957 the Treaty of Rome was created which formed the European Economic Community (EEC). The aim of the EEC, now known as the European Union, was to create a single market in the European continent, which promoted the abolition of restrictions in order to promote the free movement of workers, goods, and money between Member States. It was designed to compete on an economic and political basis with the US and Japan. The resulting single market would be available to producers within all the Member States. It established the European Atomic Energy Community known as Euratom. This organization was designed to promote cooperation in relation to nuclear research and further enhance the profile of the Community.

The EU consists of individual countries (Member States), which have agreed to join and be bound by the rules and laws created by the EU institutions. Each Member State has agreed to concede its own sovereignty in the areas governed by the EU (most of the EU law is to do with trade, though it is expanding to include other areas, such as social areas). Each Member State plays a part in deciding on those laws but is bound by the overall decisions and laws of the European Union. (EU law is deemed to be *supranational* law, ie it sits *above* national law – as opposed to *international* law – agreements *between* States.) Member States have sacrificed their sovereignty in exchange for the economic and social benefits which the EU provides. The common market allows all Member States to trade more freely within each other's territories. Citizens of the Member States are also citizens of Europe and have certain individual rights as a result, eg the right to travel, live, and work in other Member State countries.

The UK joined on the 1 January 1973 following the passing of the European Communities Act 1972. Under s 2:

* All EU regulations and other directly applicable European law (passed before or after the UK joined the EU) are part of English law, and enforceable by the English courts, without any further enactment.

* The Government can implement EU directives by subordinate legislation, without having to go through the full parliamentary process.

* All domestic enactments (passed before or after accession) have effect only subject to directly applicable rules of EU law. This overrides the usual presumption that any later enactment overrides any earlier law inconsistent with it.

Joining the European Union has created a new important source of law which impacts on the English legal system. In *HP Bulmer Ltd v J Bollinger SA (No 2)* [1974] Lord Denning stated that the EU law is 'like an incoming tide. It flows into the estuaries and up the rivers. It cannot be held back.'

Membership of the EU has reduced the sovereignty of the UK Parliament in the following ways:

* There is now an external body competent to make laws affecting the UK, which are applied by the English courts irrespective of the wishes of Parliament.
* The UK is obliged to legislate to implement obligations arising from EU membership.
* Parliament is no longer free to legislate without restriction in areas governed by EU law. The European Court of Justice is in no doubt that Community law overrides any national law that conflicts per *Van Gend en Loos v Netherlands* [1963]. This was confirmed in *R v Secretary of State for Transport ex p Factortame* [1991].

....

R v Secretary of State for Transport ex p Factortame [1991] 3 All ER 769

Spanish fishermen claimed that the UK law as contained within the Merchant Shipping Act 1988 was contrary to EC law. This statute contained provisions under which fishing licences were granted only to boats whose owners and crews were predominantly British. The court held it violated Article 52 EC Treaty. As a result of this ruling the UK Government was obliged to amend the legislation to ensure that there was no conflict with EC law.

....

* All the rights and obligations created by EU law are incorporated by the European Communities Act 1972 into our domestic law, and take precedence even over primary legislation where this is inconsistent.

Changes were due to be made to the operation of the EU and European institutions to cope with the European Union's expanded membership through the passing of a new European Constitution. The Constitution within Part I contained wide-ranging reforms, *inter alia*:

* explicitly stating that EU law had priority over domestic law of Member States
* the Constitution would be the highest form of law
* EU legal instruments would be reclassified to provide a clear hierarchy distinguishing between administrative and legislative forms
* the EU would have stronger political profile with the creation of a Commission President and a Minister of Foreign Affairs
* the number of Commissioners would be reduced to two-thirds the number of Member States
* the European Parliament would be restricted to 750 members and its legislative role would be increased

- the President of the European Council would be appointed for two and a half years rather than six months
- the system of voting within the European Council would be changed.

Part II of the European Constitution contained a Charter of Fundamental Rights. These provisions covered:

- civil rights
- political rights
- economic rights
- social rights.

However, voters in France and the Netherlands rejected the European Constitution. As a result the treaty, signed in Lisbon in December 2007, was drawn up to replace the draft European Constitution. The Lisbon Treaty was initially rejected by Irish voters in a referendum on 12 June 2008. Under EU rules, the treaty could not enter into force if any of the 27 Member States failed to ratify it. The plan was for all 27 to ratify the treaty but by the end of 2008 France's Europe Minister Jean-Pierre Jouyet had spoken of a possible 'legal arrangement' with Ireland at the end of the ratification process. The treaty got overwhelming support in a second referendum in the Irish Republic on 2 October 2009. The treaty was finally ratified by all 27 Members States in November 2009 and came into force on 1 December 2009. The Lisbon Treaty was ratified by the UK on 19 June 2008 under the European Union Amendment Act 2008. The last country to ratify the treaty was the Czech Republic, which completed the process on 3 November 2009. The Constitution attempted to replace all earlier EU treaties and start afresh, whereas the new treaty merely amends the Treaty on European Union and the Treaty Establishing the European Community, without replacing them. It provides the Union with the legal framework and tools necessary to meet future challenges and to respond to citizens' demands. The Lisbon Treaty contains many of the changes the Constitution attempted to introduce.

To realize its full potential, the European Union needed to modernize and reform. The European Union of 27 members was operating with rules designed for an EU of 15. Over the last decade, the European Union had been looking for the right way forward to optimize the instruments at its disposal and reinforce its capacity to act. At the same time, there was increasing support for the EU to work together on issues that affect all Member States, such as climate change and international terrorism. As the EU has grown and its responsibilities changed, it made sense to update the way in which it worked. *Inter alia*, the Treaty of Lisbon:

- explicitly recognized for the first time the possibility of a Member State withdrawing from the Union
- amalgamated the functions of the High Representative for common foreign and security policy (CFSP) with those of a Vice-President of the Commission. (This was designed to

strengthen coherence in external action and raise the EU's profile in the world giving Europe a clear voice in relations with its partners worldwide)

- created the European External Action Service which will provide support to the High Representative

- stipulated new policy objectives designed to tackle the twin challenges of climate change and functioning of the energy market, in particular energy supply, the promotion of energy efficiency and energy saving, and the development of new and renewable forms of energy

- placed freedom, justice, and security at the centre of its priorities – promoting and supporting action in the area of crime prevention and to tackling terrorism through the freezing of assets, and 'Solidarity clauses' indicating that the Union and its Member States shall act jointly in a spirit of solidarity if a Member State is the target of a terrorist attack or the victim of a natural or man-made disaster

- provided a commitment to the development of a common immigration policy

- provided special arrangements for national parliaments to become more closely involved in the work of the Union – within the legislative process consultation by the Commission before a proposal is considered in detail by the European Parliament and the Council of Ministers

- introduced the European Citizens' Initiative – 1 million citizens coming from a significant number of Member States may take the initiative of inviting the Commission to submit any appropriate proposal on matters where citizens consider that a legal act of the Union is required

- increased the number of policy areas where the directly elected European Parliament has to approve EU legislation together with the Council comprising national ministers (the 'co-decision' procedure)

- extended qualified majority voting to new policy areas, in order to adopt a more streamlined approach to decision-making within the EU

- stipulated that the European Parliament is to have a maximum of 751 members

- implemented changes to the term of office of the President of the European Council

- introduced the Charter of Fundamental Rights into European primary law – rights that the EU believed all citizens of the Union should enjoy, giving them legal embodiment in the Union. It preserved existing rights whilst introducing new ones. The six chapters of the Charter covered individual rights related to dignity, freedoms, equality, solidarity, citizenship status, and justice. These rights are drawn essentially from other international instruments, like the European Convention on Human Rights. The institutions of the Union and Member States must respect the rights written into the Charter (especially when legislating). The Court of Justice is given the role of ensuring that the Charter is applied correctly.

 *Looking for extra marks?*

In relation to any question that relates to European Union law and its sources of law you may wish to mention some recent developments – the provisions contained within the Lisbon Treaty and how it differs from the original proposed European Constitution. An excellent source of information on the contents of the Lisbon Treaty can be found at the following websites: <http://europa.eu/lisbon_treaty/glance/> and <http://europa.eu/lisbon_treaty/faq/index_en.htm#8>.

What are the main forms of EU law?

The Commission, Parliament, and Council all play a role in the creation of European Union legislation. Historically the Commission and Council were primarily responsible via the different legislative processes. Parliament's role was purely advisory only. This attracted significant criticism in relation to the perceived democratic deficit. The Parliament was the only institution where citizens of the various Member States elected the individual members who sat. However, it was the institution with the least involvement in the actual creation of law. The role of the Parliament within the various legislative processes was significantly increased by the Single European Act, the Mastricht Treaty, Amsterdam Treaty, and the Lisbon Treaty.

The primary legislative process is the co-decision process, now known as the ordinary legislative process following changes made by the Lisbon Treaty. The co-decision procedure was originally introduced by the Treaty of Maastricht. It gives the European Parliament the power to adopt instruments jointly with the Council. In practice, it has strengthened Parliament's legislative powers. The Treaty of Amsterdam and the Lisbon Treaty simplified the co-decision procedure, making it quicker, more effective, and more transparent, and its use was extended to new areas. Article 294 Treaty on the Functioning of the European stipulates the basic procedure as follows:

1. The Commission formulates a proposal for new legislation.

2. This proposal is sent to the Parliament and the Council for consultation (outline of proposal also sent to national parliaments for consideration).

3. The Parliament will debate the proposal and formulate its opinion.

4. The Parliament's opinion will be sent to the Council.

5. The Council will deliberate on the Commission proposal and the Parliament's opinion. If it agrees with the unamended proposal or to any amendments made by Parliament then it may recommend that the legislative proposal is adopted. If it disagrees with the proposal and amendments it will provide a statement to Paliament as to why it disagrees.

6. This will be sent back to the Parliament for its second reading. The Parliament then has three months to either:

   (a) approve (or refrain from reacting to) the Council's Common Position, in which case it will be adopted and become law

(b) amend the Common Position in which case a Committee is set up. (This Committee consists of equal representatives of the Council and the Parliament who negotiate the amendments which are subsequently adopted or rejected)

(c) reject the Common Position outright in which case the Council can convene the Conciliation Committee and commence negotiations as (b) above.

7. If the Conciliation Committee reaches an agreement and approves the Common Position it becomes law. If the Common Position is rejected by Parliament at this stage by a qualified majority the proposal is lost and does not become law.

Revision tip

When revising the legislative processes and the various forms of law of the European Union ensure that you revise from the most up-to-date sources. For example the European Union has its own website which provides up-to-date information on the forms of law and legislative processes and detailed flowcharts to accompany this information. See <http://ec.europa.eu/codecision/index_en.htm>. Also ensure that you are aware that there are other legislative processes which have existed dependent on the subject matter being considered by the relevant European institutions, eg consultation, assent, etc.

The main forms of EU law are:

- treaties
- regulations
- directives
- decisions.

Treaties

The Treaty of Rome 1957, Single European Act 1985, Treaty of Maastricht 1992, Treaty of Amsterdam 1996, Treaty of Nice 2001, and the Lisbon Treaty are the primary sources of European law. The treaties are superior to all other law, European or domestic, and any amendment or addition to the treaties requires the unanimous agreement of all Member States. The treaties lay down the objectives of the European Union, the creation of the institutions, and the legislative processes that create other forms of EU law and in some circumstances create rights and obligations themselves. The treaties are binding on all Member States, and on all individuals so far as they apply to them. In practice the treaties govern mainly the organization of the Community and relationships between the Member States, but some of them affect individuals directly.

Regulations

These become part of the law of each Member State as soon as they are created: eg Council Regulation 1612/68 sets out principles for promoting the free movement of workers (including students) by abolishing discrimination as regards employment, remuneration, trade union rights, housing, family life, social and tax benefits, and access to training.

Leonesio v Italian Ministry for Agriculture and Forestry [1973] ECR 287

An EU regulation encouraged the reduction of dairy production and provided that a subsidy would be payable to farmers who slaughtered cows and agreed not to produce milk for five years. Leonesio, a farmer, fulfilled this requirement but was refused payment because the Italian constitution required legislation to authorize government expenditure. The European Court of Justice stated that once the claimant fulfilled the relevant stipulations of the regulation, then payment must be made. The Italian Government could not use its own laws to frustrate this right.

Directives

These are designed to harmonize the law throughout the EU. They are aimed at a particular Member State or States and direct them to introduce their own version of the provisions of the directive within a stipulated time period. The directive allows the Member State the choice of how it actually enacts the provisions. Directives in the UK are implemented via an Act of Parliament or by Statutory Instrument. For example, the Product Liability Directive 85/374 was implemented in the UK by the Consumer Protection Act 1987, and the Unfair Contract Terms Directive 93/13 was put into effect (six months after the deadline) by the Unfair Terms in Consumer Contracts Regulations 1994.

If a Member State fails to implement a directive, it is in breach of its obligations and can be called to account by the Commission before the Court of Justice. Where a Member State persistently fails to comply, the European Court of Justice (ECJ) has power to impose a financial penalty. An individual citizen may even be able to claim compensation in relation to a failure to implement a directive.

Van Duyn v Home Office [1974] 1 WLR 1107

The Home Office refused Van Duyn permission to enter the UK, because she was a member of a religious group, the Scientologists, which the Government wanted to exclude from the country at the time. Van Duyn argued her exclusion was contrary to provisions in the Treaty of Rome on freedom of movement. However, the Government highlighted that the treaty allowed exceptions on public-policy grounds. A subsequent directive, however, stated that public policy could only be invoked on the basis of personal conduct. Here Van Duyn had done nothing personally to justify such an exclusion. The ECJ found that the obligation conferred on the Government was clear and unconditional and so created enforceable rights. To hold otherwise would allow Member States to deny individual rights by their own wrongful failure to implement.

Francovich v Italy [1992] IRLR 84

A company went into liquidation but failed to pay its employees arrears of salary. The Italian Government at the time had not implemented the requirements of an EU directive which required a compensation scheme to be put in place to cover such situations. Francovich, one of the company employees, sued the Italian Government. It was held that the Italian Government was required to pay the litigant compensation.

Decisions

These can be addressed to Member States, to corporations, or to individual citizens. A decision is binding only on the person to whom it is directed, eg Commission Decision 84/381 was addressed to United Breweries and the Carlsberg Brewery and granted exemptions from competition rules for particular contracts. Decision 92/213 imposed a fine on Aer Lingus for unfair trading practices and was addressed only to Aer Lingus.

Institutions of the EU

There are, following the Lisbon Treaty, six EU institutions:

* the Commission
* the Council of Ministers
* the European Council
* the European Parliament
* the Court of Justice of the European Union
* the European Central Bank.

The *Commission* has 27 members called commissioners. They are appointed by the relevant Member States for a five-year period. Commissioners do not represent the interests of the national government of their Member State. Their role is to represent the interests of the European Union. The Commission represents EU interests and its relationship with other trading blocs and countries around the world, for instance dealing with accession of new members and negotiating trade agreements. It draws up the budget for the EU and has a role to play in creating European legislation. It is responsible for ensuring Member States uphold the law of the European Union. It brings offending Member States before the European Court of Justice. This is in addition to its role in relation to creating legislation.

The *Council of Ministers/European Council* represent the interests of the individual Member States. Though technically separate institutions they have the same powers. The European Council consists of the 27 heads of state from the various Members States of the

European Union law

✳✳✳✳✳✳✳✳✳✳ ✳

European Union and the President of the Council. This individual is appointed for a term of two and a half years, replacing the six-monthly rotating presidency between the Members States. The present President is Herman Von Rompuy. The members of the Council of Ministers are drawn from each Member State and are chosen by the individual Member State on the basis of the subject matter under discussion. It therefore does not have a permanent membership. The European Council meets at least biannually, whereas the Council of Ministers will meet usually on a weekly basis where it will agree proposals for new policy initiatives for the European Union. They also play a role in the legislative process of the European Union.

Under amendments made by the Lisbon Treaty, the *European Parliament* has a maximum of 751 members known as MEPs. Each Member State is allocated a number of seats within the Parliament on the basis of size of population. MEPs sit within the Parliament on the basis of political grouping. Citizens within each Member State elect them. Such elections are held within the UK every five years. The Parliament is involved in the various legislative processes. It supervises the Commission, which has to submit a budget for its approval. It can appoint and dismiss the Commission as a whole, known as censure. Parliament can, if there has been a purported failure to implement EU law, bring an action against other EU institutions. An ombudsman appointed by the Commission can investigate complaints about maladministration by Union institutions/ MEPs.

The *Court of Justice* of the European Union consists of three courts:

- the European Court of Justice (the ECJ)
- the General Court
- Civil Service Tribunal.

The court of primary importance is the **European Court of Justice**. The Court is situated in Luxembourg. It has 27 judges appointed by the Member States for six years and appointments are renewable. Such individuals will have previously held high judicial office within Member States. They are assisted by eight Advocate Generals who produce opinions on the cases assigned to them. The opinions will highlight the relevant issues and suggest potential conclusions. The Court delivers a single judgment with no indication on the number of judges who dissented.

Proceedings against Member States can be brought by other Member States or by the Commission alleging breaches of EU law. Proceedings against EU institutions may be brought by Member States or other EU institutions because, for instance, treaty powers and procedures have been misused and abused.

Article 267 of the Treaty on the Functioning of the European Union (formerly Article 234) provides that any court or tribunal of a Member State can refer a question on EU law to the ECJ. The **preliminary reference procedure** promotes uniformity of interpretation throughout the EU. The case in the domestic court is adjourned until the European Court of Justice directs the English court on the correct interpretation to be implemented. The domestic court must then apply the ECJ's ruling to the facts of the case before it. A reference must be made if the national court is one from which there is no further appeal, eg the UK Supreme Court (the former House of Lords).

HP Bulmer Ltd v Bollinger SA No 2 [1974] Ch 401

In this case, Lord Denning stated that to save expense and delay no reference should be made where:

- it would not be conclusive of the case and other matters would remain to be decided
- there had been a previous ruling on the same point
- the court considers that point to be reasonably clear and free from doubt
- the facts of the case had not yet been decided.

A Court of First Instance with limited jurisdiction was established in 1988 under Article 225 of the EC Treaty in order to assist and reduce the workload of the European Court of Justice. It is now known as the *General Court* following changes made by the Lisbon Treaty. In order to hear disputes between the European Institutions and its civil servants a new *Civil Service Tribunal* has in addition been created to deal with such matters.

The Lisbon Treaty also officially recognized the *European Central Bank* based in Germany as an institution of the European Union. It is responsible for organizing and coordinating both the monetary and the economic policy of the Member States of the European Union that have adopted the Euro, the single European currency. It is independently responsible for keeping inflation under control and setting interests rates within the Eurozone.

Revision tip

When covering the area of sources of law and the EU institutions ensure you support your points with relevant treaty provisions, regulations, directives, decisions, and case law. In addition, you need to ensure that you highlight the relationship between EU law and UK domestic courts and law-making institutions – again supporting points with relevant statutory provisions, eg the European Communities Act 1972; relevant case law, eg *Factortame*; and even judicial comment on the impact of this form of law.

Human rights law – European Convention on Human Rights and Fundamental Freedoms

The **European Convention on Human Rights and Fundamental Freedoms** (ECHR) is an international treaty. It is *not the same as* and *not part of* EU law although many of the signatories are the same. If a country fails to protect the rights listed in the Convention, then an individual can take the country to the **European Court of Human Rights** for a remedy (but only after having tried and failed to seek a remedy in the offending country). The ECHR protects fundamental civil rights and liberties.

Human rights law

✳✳✳✳✳✳✳✳✳✳

The provisions have subsequently been expanded via the use of protocols. The rights protected by the ECHR include, *inter alia:*

Figure 1.1

Article 2	Right to life
Article 3	Freedom from torture, inhuman, or degrading treatment
Article 4	Freedom from slavery or forced labour
Article 5	The right to liberty and security of the person
Article 6	The right to a fair trial
Article 7	The prohibition of retrospective criminal laws

These rights and freedoms were brought into the domestic law of the UK by the Human Rights Act 1998. Fundamental rights may be subject to limitation for various reasons. Some rights are non-derogable (eg the right not to be tortured or enslaved), but some are subject to exceptions and others are subject to restrictions in time of war or other comparable public emergency. For example, Art 2 European Convention on Human Rights states:

(1) Everyone's right to life shall be protected by law. No one shall be deprived of his life intentionally save in the execution of a sentence of a court following his conviction of a crime for which this penalty is provided by law.

It goes on to state:

(2) Deprivation of life shall not be regarded as inflicted in contravention of this Article when it results from the use of force which is no more than absolutely necessary

  (a) in defence of any person from unlawful violence;

  (b) in order to effect a lawful arrest or to prevent the escape of a person lawfully detained;

  (c) in action lawfully taken for the purpose of quelling a riot or insurrection.

Article 15 European Convention on Human Rights states:

(1) In time of war or other public emergency threatening the life of the nation any High Contracting Party may take measures derogating from its obligations under this Convention to the extent strictly required by the exigencies of the situation, provided that such measures are not inconsistent with its other obligations under international law.

(2) No derogation from Article 2, except in respect of deaths resulting from lawful acts of war, or from Articles 3, 4(1) and 7 shall be made under this provision.

Article 8 European Convention on Human Rights states:

(1) Everyone has the right to respect for his private and family life, his home and his correspondence.

(2) There shall be no interference by a public authority with the exercise of this right except such as is in accordance with the law and is necessary in a democratic society in the interests of national security, public safety or the economic well-being of the country, for the prevention of disorder or crime, for the protection of health or morals, or for the protection of the rights and freedoms of others.

The Human Rights Act 1998 provides that:

- New Acts of Parliament should be checked to confirm they do not breach the ECHR.

- Courts must interpret all Acts so as not to breach the Convention rights – see information in relation to the statutory interpretation later in this chapter.

- Courts are obliged to interpret and develop the common law so as to comply with Convention rights.

- Any public body carrying out a public function can be sued in the UK courts if they breach Convention rights.

- It does not remove the right to take the UK to the European Court of Human Rights if the domestic courts fail to provide a remedy.

An example of case being taken to the European Court of Human Rights following determination by the UK courts is *Laskey, Brown & Jaggard v United Kingdom* (1997).

. . . .

Laskey, Brown & Jaggard v United Kingdom (1997) 24 ECHR 39

A number of men who had engaged in consensual sado-masochism were convicted of unlawful wounding and other offences under the Offences Against the Person Act 1861 and imprisoned for up to six months. They appealed to the House of Lords but their grounds for appeal were dismissed and their conviction upheld. The men subsequently took a case to the European Court of Human Rights arguing a breach of the European Convention Art 8. The Court unanimously rejected Laskey et al's claim that the conviction by the UK court violated their right to privacy under Art 8, and upheld the intervention of the law as justified due to the need to protect health and morals.

. . . .

Revision tip

When dealing with issues of European Union law and human rights law ensure that you revise them separately; this will ensure that you do not get confused between the two areas which is a common fault of students within examinations – though the European Union Constitution would have incorporated such fundamental freedoms and rights into EU law this was rejected by numerous Member States. Therefore, they are still separate areas and sources of law, and are enforced by different courts. Ensure that you are aware of the impact of such sources on the creation and interpretation of UK law.

Key cases

✻✻✻✻✻✻✻✻✻✻

 *Looking for extra marks?*

An excellent discussion on the historical development of EU law and institutions, human rights law, and their relationship with UK law, can be found in the following text: A Gillespie, *The English Legal System* (Oxford University Press, 2009), Chapter 4, pp 89–135 and Chapter 5, pp 138–71. The chapter also provides further information in relation to the operation of certain forms of EU law, such as directives, and highlights a wide range of case law and judicial comment. A detailed list of the provisions of the European Convention and the operation of the Human Rights Act 1998 can be found in G Slapper et al, *The English Legal System*, 11th edn (Routledge & Cavendish, 2010), Chapter 1, pp 21–76.

 *Key cases*

Case	Facts	Ratio/Held
Francovich v Italy [1992] IRLR 84	A company went into liquidation, but failed to pay its employees arrears of salary. The Italian Government at the time had not implemented the requirements of an EU directive which required a compensation scheme to be put in place to cover such situations. Francovich, one of the company employees, sued the Italian Government.	It was held that although the provisions of the directive were not directly effective the Italian Government was required to pay the litigant compensation.
Leonesio v Italian Ministry for Agriculture and Forestry [1973] ECR 287	A regulation designed to encourage reduced dairy production stated that a cash premium should be payable to farmers who slaughtered cows and agreed not to produce milk for five years. Leonesio fulfilled this requirement but was refused payment because the Italian constitution required legislation to authorize government expenditure.	The ECJ stated that once the claimant fulfilled the relevant stipulations of the regulation, then payment must be made; the Italian Government could not use its own laws to frustrate this right.
R v Secretary of State for Transport ex p Factortame [1991] 3 All ER 769	Spanish fishermen claimed that the UK law as contained within the Merchant Shipping Act 1988 was contrary to EC law. This contained provisions under which fishing licences were granted only to boats whose owners and crews were predominantly British.	The Court held it violated Art 52 EC Treaty and the UK Government was obliged to amend the legislation to ensure that there was no conflict with EC law.

Case	Facts	Ratio/Held
Van Duyn v Home Office [1974] 1 WLR 1107	The Home Office refused Van Duyn permission to enter the UK because she was a member of a religious group, the Scientologists, which the Government wanted to exclude from the country at the time. Van Duyn argued her exclusion was contrary to provisions in the Treaty of Rome on freedom of movement. The Government responded by pointing out that the Treaty allowed exceptions on public policy grounds but Van Duyn relied on a later directive which said that public policy could only be invoked on the basis of personal conduct.	The ECJ found that the obligation conferred on the Government was clear and unconditional and so created enforceable rights. To hold otherwise would allow Member States to deny individual rights by their own wrongful failure to implement.

? Exam questions

Essay question 1

Highlight the role and composition of the European Court of Justice and explain the basis upon which the UK domestic courts can request a ruling on European Union law issues.

An outline answer can be found at the end of this book.

Essay question 2

Lord Denning in *HP Bulmer Ltd v J Bollinger SA (No 2)* [1974] described European Union Law as being:

> like an incoming tide. It flows into the estuaries and up the rivers. It cannot be held back.

In light of the above comment highlight the various forms of European Union law, how such forms are implemented within the UK, and the impact on the sovereignty/supremacy of Parliament.

An outline answer is available online at <http://www.oxfordtextbooks.co.uk/orc>.

#2
Sources of law II: Legislation

- The primary source of law is an Act of Parliament; all other forms of law created within the English legal system are secondary sources only, eg custom, common law, delegated legislation, etc. Where an Act therefore conflicts with these secondary sources it will override them.

- Prior to the European Communities Act 1972, Parliament was the supreme law creator within the English legal system; however now law created by Parliament may be nullified if it conflicts with EU law. Parliament may even be required through the issuance of EU directives to actually create an Act to implement EU obligations.

- Parliament when legislating consists of the House of Lords, Commons, and the monarch. The Parliament Acts can be utilized under limited circumstances when the Lords refuses to pass the bill approved by the Commons.

- The courts cannot challenge the validity of an Act. The courts, however, do have significant discretion and can even defeat the intention of Parliament when creating a piece of legislation through the process of statutory interpretation.

- A range of devices and rules can be utilized by the judiciary when interpreting legislation.

- Law-making powers can be delegated by Parliament to other organizations and individuals via an Enabling Act. There are limited methods by which delegated legislation can be controlled by courts and Parliament.

Legislation

The law must adapt if it is to retain the respect of the majority of society. Wide-ranging changes in the law are made by Parliament and the Queen via legislation. Inspiration for this can come from:

- the judiciary
- pressure groups
- political party manifestos
- European Union obligations
- public opinion and media pressure
- official law reform agencies
- private members.

The judiciary: Judges often feel that due to the fact they are not elected representatives of the people, areas of social and moral controversy should be considered by Parliament. For example in response to criticisms in relation to a gap in the criminal law identified in *R v Preddy* [1996], that people who had committed mortgage frauds were not guilty of any offence, Lord Bingham stated:

> there could be no doubt that Preddy had exposed a glaring anomaly in this important area of criminal law…It was to be hoped that appropriate legislation would be enacted with all deliberate speed.

Pressure groups: These can use a variety of different methods to highlight the need for law reform, lobbying MPs, petitions, public demonstrations, etc. The larger the pressure group usually the more effective they are. Such groups include the National Union of Teachers, the Confederation of British Industry, and the League Against Cruel Sports.

Political party manifestos: Some legislative proposals are made in order to enact specific proposals identified in the Government's commitments as highlighted in their manifestos. These proposals are outlined in the state opening of Parliament within the Queen's Speech.

European Union obligations: Legislation may be implemented in order to enact the United Kingdom's legal obligations under European law per the European Communities Act 1972, eg the Product Liability Directive 85/374 was implemented in the UK by the Consumer Protection Act 1987.

Media pressure and public opinion: Members of the public may make their feelings known on particular legal areas by writing to Members of Parliament, government ministers, and to the media. The media can be utilized as a powerful force to inflate public opinion on legal issues.

Official law reform agencies: This is a substantial subject and is dealt with under the separate heading below.

Private members: Reforms can be proposed by back-bench members of either House. An example is the Abortion Act 1967 which was the result of a successful private member's bill proposed by MP David Steel

Official law reform agencies

There are a number of agencies which have been set up by the Government to investigate areas of potential legal reform:

- Law Commission
- Criminal Law Revision Committee
- Royal Commissions
- Law Reform Committee.

Law Commission: This was established by the Law Commission Act 1965. Its duty is to:

> keep under review all the law with which they are respectively concerned, with a view to its systematic development and reform,...Codification, elimination of anomalies, repeal obsolete...enactments, reduction of the number of separate enactments and the simplification...modernisation of the law.

It is a permanent body which comprises members of the judiciary, legal professionals, and academics. The Commission works on reform projects that are:

- referred to it by the Lord Chancellor
- referred by Government departments
- on areas which the Commission itself feels are suitable areas.

The Commission publishes a consultation document, which identifies the area of law in question, its defects, and options for reform. The Commission sets outs its final recommendations in a report which will contain a draft bill. Its recommendations have led to the following enactments: Law Reform (Year and A Day Rule) Act 1996 and the Supply of Goods and Services Act 1982.

Criminal Law Revision Committee: This Committee considers potential reforms of the criminal law. It is responsible to the Home Secretary, and its members include the Director of Public Prosecutions as well as members of the judiciary and leading academics. The Theft Act 1968 codified theft and related offences and was generally thought to be the greatest achievement of this reform agency.

Royal Commissions: These are set up to study particular areas of law reform. They are made up of a wide cross-section of people who have expertise and experience of the legal area concerned. A Royal Commission can commission research and also take submissions from interested parties. It produces a final report, which the Government can choose to act upon. Proposals made by the Royal Commission on Criminal Procedure were enacted within the Police and Criminal Evidence Act 1984. Recommendations made by the Royal

Commission on Criminal Justice were enacted within the Criminal Justice and Public Order Act 1994 and the Criminal Appeal Act 1995.

The Law Reform Committee: This is set up on a part-time basis and considers only small areas of the civil law referred to it by the Government. Its recommendations have been enacted within the Occupiers' Liability Act 1957 and the Civil Evidence Act 1968.

Problems associated with the law reform agencies include, *inter alia*, that:

- The Government has no duty to consult the law reform bodies, set up a Commission or committees when it determines that legal areas are in need of reform.
- The Government has no obligation to follow recommendations and proposals made by the law reform agencies.
- The Government may not enact the recommendation in a way originally proposed and thereby reduce their effectiveness in dealing with problem areas of the law.
- No single ministry is solely responsible for law reform and therefore it is not a priority for the Government.

The legislative process

Legislation is the primary source of English law and is created by Parliament. The original constitutional view was that Parliament was sovereign and the supreme source of law and could make or alter any law it wished. Parliament's ability to create law has been restricted by the United Kingdom's membership of the European Union per European Communities Act 1972. The ECJ in *Van Gend en Loos v Netherlands* [1963] stated that EU law overrides any national law that conflicts with it. In *R v Secretary of State for Transport ex p Factortame* [1991] legislation was found to conflict with EU law. This required the UK Government to amend the legislation in question.

Parliament when legislating consists of the House of Commons, House of Lords, and the monarch. Law created by Parliament is called an Act or statute, eg the Consumer Credit Act 2006 and Companies Act 2006. Parliament creates approximately 50 to 70 Acts each year. The powers of Parliament are extensive. An Act of Parliament can:

- alter the calendar, per the Calendar (New Style) Act 1750
- regulate the date of religious festivals, per the Easter Act 1928
- alter the hours of daylight, per the Summer Time Act 1972
- determine the succession of the monarchy, per the Act of Settlement 1700
- alter its own operation composition and powers, per the Parliament Act 1911, Representation of the People Act 1948, Life Peerages Act 1958, House of Lords Act 1999, and the Parliamentary Standards Act 2009
- have effect outside the United Kingdom, per Continental Shelf Act 1964 and the War Crimes Act 1991

Legislation

✸✸✸✸✸✸✸✸✸✸

- delegate its law-making powers to other individuals and organizations, per the National Trust Act 1933, European Communities Act 1972, Emergency Powers Act 1920, and Local Government Act 1972.

An Act of Parliament will stay in force until it is repealed. However, no Parliament can bind its successors by purporting to make a law that cannot be repealed: in *Godden v Hales* (1686), Herbert CJ stated *obiter*: 'that if an Act of Parliament had a clause in it that it should never be repealed, yet without question the same power that made it may repeal it'.

The House of Lords:

- is involved in the creation of law – statute law
- considers indirect laws – delegated legislation
- examines the work of Government
- holds general debates
- undertakes committee work
- examines European proposals.

The House of Commons undertakes a variety of work, for it:

- makes laws – creation of statutes
- controls Government finance
- examines the work of Government
- controls indirect law-making – delegated legislation
- represents grievances of individual citizens.

An Act of Parliament starts life as a bill. A bill can start the legislative process in the House of Commons *or* Lords. Sometimes the Government will set out its ideas for a bill in a discussion document known as a Green Paper. Organizations send in their comments to the relevant minister concerned with drafting the bill. Firm proposals are produced in a White Paper. Parliamentary Counsel will draft the bill following consultation with the relevant minister, which will be introduced into Parliament. There are various forms of bill:

Public bills: These alter the law throughout England and are intended to apply to all people in any part of the country. A public bill may be:

- a Government bill proposed by a Government minister, and reflects the Government's legislative commitments as highlighted by the Queen during the opening of Parliament; eg the Access to Justice Act 1999, the Disability Discrimination Act 1995, the Theft Act 1968, the Children Act 1989, the Education Act 1996, and the House of Lords Act 1999, were enacted as the result of such bills
  - a private member's bill proposed by an individual back-bench member of either House, eg Murder (Abolition of Death Penalty) Act 1965.

Private bills: These only apply to individuals or certain bodies and are promoted by local authorities, corporations, police, etc, for their own purposes; eg the Lloyds Bank (Merger) Act 1985, Greater Nottingham Light Rapid Transit Act 1994, British Railways Act 1968, and the University College London Act 1996 were enacted as the result of such bills.

Hybrid bills: These contain both public and private provisions; eg the Channel Tunnel Act 1987 and the Cardiff Bay Barrage Act 1993 were enacted as the result of such bills.

Money bills: These contain purely financial provisions that relate to the operation of the country.

Below is a brief summary of the legislative stages:

First reading: The name and main aims of the bill are read out. There is a public announcement that the bill has been introduced into Parliament and copies of the bill are available for inspection. Under the Human Rights Act 1998, the minister must make a statement that the provisions of the bill are compatible with Convention rights, or if he is unable to make such a statement, the Government nevertheless wishes the House to proceed – per s 19.

Second reading: This is a discussion of the general principles of the bill. Once the debates have been concluded the House will undertake a vote in order for the bill to proceed to the next stage of the legislative process.

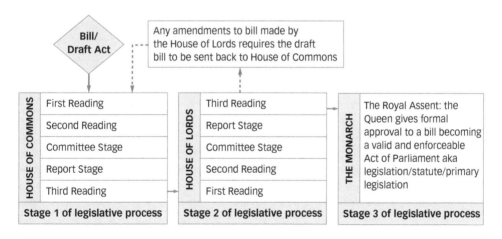

Figure 2.1

Legislation

✳✳✳✳✳✳✳✳✳✳

Committee stage: A detailed examination of the clauses of the bill is undertaken by a committee usually consisting of between 16 and 50 MPs. The Committee members will have a special interest or knowledge of the subject of the bill. Amendments can be made to the bill.

Report stage: The House reviews and accepts or rejects the amendments made by the Committee. However, if no amendments have been made then there will be no report stage.

Third reading: The House will vote on the final version of the bill which, if approved, will be passed on to the Lords for consideration.

If the Lords make amendments then it will be passed back to the Commons for further consideration. The Commons may accept the amendments or restore the bill to its original form.

The Parliament Acts of 1911 and 1949

Under the Parliament Act 1911, provided the Commons passed the same bill in three consecutive sessions, and the Lords rejected it, it could be presented for **Royal Assent** and become law in spite of the objections of the Lords. The Parliament Act 1949 amended the Parliament Act 1911: now the Commons need only pass the bill on two consecutive sessions. The Speaker of the Commons must issue a certificate to state that the above requirements have been met.

The Parliament Acts were used in relation to the:

* War Crimes Act 1991
* European Parliamentary Elections Act 1999
* Sexual Offences (Amendment) Act 2000
* Hunting Act 2004.

. . . .

R (on the application of Jackson) v Attorney General [2005] EWCA Civ 126

Litigants challenged the Commons' ability to pass legislation, ie the Hunting Act 2004. They argued that the Parliament Act 1911 was passed by the Lords and could only be lawfully amended with their actual consent. The Parliament Act 1949 was unlawful because it substantially amended the process accepted by the Lords in the Parliament Act 1911. Therefore, if the process under the Parliament Act 1949 was unlawful then it followed that the Hunting Act 2004 had been enacted unlawfully. The House of Lords held that the Hunting Act 2004 had been enacted lawfully and was valid; the Parliament Act 1949 did not fundamentally change the relationship between the Commons and the Lords. A bill could be enacted without the consent of the Lords.

. . . .

Role of the monarch in the legislative process

When a bill has been passed by Parliament, it is presented for **Royal Assent**. The Queen will indicate her approval to the enactment. Once received the bill becomes a valid law per Royal Assent Act 1967. It has not been refused since 1704, when Queen Anne refused to give approval to the Scottish Militia Bill.

Even after Royal Assent, an Act may not come into force straight away. The Easter Act 1928 has still not been brought into force even though it received the Royal Assent 70 years ago. Some Acts require a commencement order before they take effect, eg the Bees Act 1980. An Act will usually come into force at midnight after it receives Royal Assent per s 4 Interpretation Act 1978 unless there is a contrary provision per *Tomlinson v Bullock* (1879). An Act may require a commencement order, before the Act or sections of it take effect. Although a bill will normally take weeks or even months to become an Act, it is possible for the legislative process to be accelerated in cases of perceived urgency, eg the Prevention of Terrorism (Additional Powers) Act 1996 which was introduced into Parliament on the 2 April 1996 and received the Royal Assent the next day.

Courts cannot challenge the validity of legislation

Up to the time of the Glorious Revolution of 1688 it was thought that the courts could invalidate Acts of Parliament. In *Dr Bonham's Case* (1610) Coke CJ stated: **'When an Act of Parliament is against common right or reason, or repugnant or impossible to be performed, the common law will control it, and adjudge such Act to be void.'** However, today it is thought that the courts cannot question the validity of primary legislation. It was confirmed in *British Railways Board v Pickin* [1974] that the courts cannot declare a statute invalid and therefore unenforceable. Lord Morris stated:

> When an enactment is passed there is finality unless and until it is amended or repealed by Parliament. In the courts there may be argument as to the correct interpretation of the enactment; there must be none as to whether it should be on the statute book at all.

In *Cheney v Conn* [1968] Ungoed-Thomas J stated: 'What the statute itself enacts cannot be unlawful, because what the statute says is itself the law, and the highest form of law, and it is not for the court to say that a parliamentary enactment, the highest law in this country, is illegal.'

Revision Tip

When revising this area ensure that you have a good depth of knowledge of the legislative process, various stages including the various law reform sources, eg official law reform agencies. Ensure that you are aware of the importance of the Parliament Acts and can support their application with relevant case law where an Act, which has been created by this process, has had its validity challenged.

e interpretation of legislation

The process of **statutory interpretation** bestows considerable power on the courts, which can fundamentally limit the effectiveness of legislation. The law expressed in statutes should be clear but this is not always achieved. There are many reasons for this:

* a drafting error
* a broad term has been used and the courts must determine its scope
* the meaning of a word changes over time
* legislation may be applied in situations not envisaged by the original legislators.

Judges faced with a statutory provision which is unclear have a number of instruments available such as:

* rules/approaches to interpretation
* presumptions
* rules of language
* extrinsic aids
* intrinsic aids
* Interpretation Act 1978.

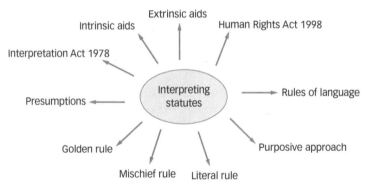

Figure 2.2

Rules of interpretation

There are three rules or approaches to the interpretation of statutes:

* the literal rule
* the golden rule
* the mischief rule.

Although there appears to be a hierarchy of rules of interpretation, a particular judge can choose which rule he wants to utilize. Despite the logical progression between the various approaches, eg the golden rule being used when the literal rule leads to absurdity, judges do not methodically apply these rules and in fact the rules can produce different results. There is also choice in the relative weighting given to internal and external aids and rules of language by any judge. The rules could lead to three different meanings of words and phrases used within an Act. Once an interpretation has been established it will form a binding precedent for future courts to follow.

Literal rule

The literal rule highlights the traditional view of the role of the judge, to apply the law and not to make it. The rule states that the intention of Parliament must be found in the plain, ordinary, natural meaning of the words used within the actual statute, even if this leads to an absurdity and appears to defeat the true intentions of Parliament. In *R v Judge of the City of London Court* [1892] Lord Esher stated:

> If the words of an Act are clear then you must follow them even though they lead to a manifest absurdity. The court has nothing to do with the question whether the legislature has committed an absurdity.

The rule respects parliamentary supremacy and the right of Parliament to make any laws it might wish, no matter how absurd. It fails, however, to recognize that the English language is sometimes ambiguous, words may have different meanings in different contexts, and it does sometimes lead to absurdities and loopholes that can be exploited by litigants. As a result Parliament may subsequently amend legislation to ensure that its true intentions are reflected in the law.

....

London & North Eastern Railway v Berriman [1946] AC 278 [1946] 1 All ER 255

A rail engineer, Berriman, was killed by a train whilst undertaking maintenance work on a rail line, oiling signalling apparatus. His widow tried to claim compensation for breach of statutory duty because there had not been a lookout man provided by the railway company in accordance with statutory regulations under the Fatal Accidents Act. This was required for the purposes of relaying or repairing the track. Compensation was only payable under the Act if employees were killed whilst engaging in 'relaying or repairing' tracks. However, the widow's actions failed. The court, the House of Lords, took the literal meaning of the words relaying and repairing and said this did not cover the dead man's activities at the relevant time. The victim's actions, doing routine maintenance, oiling the points, was merely maintaining the rail line and not 'repairing or relaying' and therefore, did not fall within the provisions of the statute and therefore compensation was not payable. The section did not cover the dead man's activities at the time even though the regulations were intended to improve safety for those working on railway lines.

....

The interpretation of legislation

✳✳✳✳✳✳✳✳✳✳

In *Magor and St Mellons RDC v Newport Corporation* [1950] in relation to the the Newport Extension Act 1934 and the issue of statutory interpretation, Lord Scarman within the House of Lords stated:

> If Parliament says one thing but means another, it is not, under the historic principles of the common law, for the courts to correct it. The general principle must surely be acceptable in our society. We are to be governed not by Parliament's intentions but by Parliament's enactments.

Also see *Whitley v Chappell* (1868) in the key cases section.

Golden rule

Baron Parke stated in *Grey v Pearson* (1857):

> the grammatical and ordinary sense of the words is to be adhered to, unless that would lead to some absurdity, …repugnance or inconsistency with the rest of the instrument. In which case the grammatical and ordinary sense of the words may be modified, …to avoid absurdity and inconsistency, but no further.

There are two forms of the golden rule and it leaves room for judicial law-making. The first states that if the literal rule produces an absurdity, the court should look for another meaning of the words that avoids the absurd result.

. . . .

Re Sigsworth [1935] Ch 89

A mother was murdered by her son. The mother had not made a will and so normally her estate would have been inherited by her next of kin according to the rules set out in the Administration of Justice Act 1925. The statutory provisions were clear but the court was not prepared to let her murderer benefit from his crime, so it was held that the literal rule should not apply, the golden rule would be used to prevent the repugnant situation of the son actually inheriting the mother's estate.

Also see *R v Registrar General ex p Smith* [1991].

. . . .

The second form states that if there are two or more meanings of a word or phrase then courts can substitute a reasonable interpretation. In *Jones v DPP* [1962] Lord Reid stated:

> it is a cardinal principle applicable to all kinds of statutes that you may not for any reason attach to a statutory provision a meaning which the words of that provision cannot reasonably bear. If they are capable of more than one meaning, then you can choose between those meanings, but beyond this you cannot go.

Mischief rule

The literal rule and golden rule are concerned with finding out what Parliament has said. The mischief rule requires the court to take into account the gap in the law that the statute was intended to fill, and interpret it to 'suppress the mischief' Parliament intended to remedy. The mischief rule is regarded as giving effect to the true intention of Parliament. In determining Parliament's supposed intention there is a risk of judicial law-making.

Four questions must be considered per *Heydon's case* (1584):

1. What was the common law before the making of the Act?
2. What was the mischief or defect which the common law did not provide for and which the statute is trying to cover?
3. What remedy has Parliament resolved in the Act?
4. What is the true reason of the remedy?

The office of all judges is always to make such construction as shall suppress the mischief and advance the remedy.

Under this rule the court looks to see what the law was before the Act was passed in order to discover what gap or mischief the Act was intended to cover. Then the court will interpret the word or phrase in the Act in such a way that the gap is covered.

....

Smith v Hughes [1960] 2 All ER 859

Six prostitutes were charged with soliciting 'in a street or public place' contrary to s 1(1) Street Offences Act 1959. One had been on a balcony; others had been sitting behind open or closed windows. The women were tapping on the window. Upholding their convictions, the court did not use the plain, ordinary grammatical meaning of the words 'in the street or public place'. The judges chose to look to see what the mischief the Act was designed to remedy and give effect to that remedy.

Also see cases such as *Elliott v Grey* [1959] and *Royal College of Nursing v DHSS* [1981].

....

The purposive approach

A new approach is gaining favour, the purposive approach. It involves the courts attempting to decide what they believe Parliament meant to achieve by the legislation in addition to merely identifying the gaps within the old law and remedying those. Lord Denning stated in *Bulmer (HP) Ltd v J Bollinger SA* [1974]:

No longer must they [the courts] examine the words in meticulous detail. No longer...argue...the precise grammatical sense. They must look to the purpose or intent...they must deduce from the wording and the spirit of the [the Act]...and gain inspiration from it. If they find a gap, they must fill it as best they can. They must do what framers of the instrument would have done if they had thought about it. So we must do the same.

The interpretation of legislation

✳✳✳✳✳✳✳✳✳

Presumptions

The courts have developed certain presumptions, which the judge can assume to have been intended by Parliament when passing a statute unless a contrary intention is apparent, eg:

- that the pre-existing common law will apply

....

Leach v R [1912] AC 305

A court was required to determine whether a wife could be compelled to give evidence against her husband under s 4(1) Criminal Evidence Act 1898. The House of Lords stated that as the Act did not expressly say otherwise the pre-existing common law rule that a wife could not be compelled to give evidence still applied.

....

- that *mens rea* is required for all criminal offences

....

Sweet v Parsley [1969] 1 All ER 347

A schoolteacher was convicted under s 5(b) Dangerous Drugs Act 1965 with being concerned in the management of premises used for drug taking. The House of Lords quashed her conviction. Lord Reid stated: 'When it comes to acts of a truly criminal character, and the statute is silent as to mens rea, there is a presumption based on many centuries' common law practice that to give effect to Parliament's wishes the courts should read in words appropriate to require mens rea unless the relevant circumstances clearly indicate otherwise.'

....

- that Parliament has not changed the law retrospectively – the statute does not make something illegal that was legal at the time it was done. (Parliament can displace this by express wording: see s 2(1) War Crimes Act 1991)
- that words are given the meaning they had at the time the Act was passed
- that the Crown is not bound by the statute. (In *Lord Advocate v Dumbarton DC* [1990], the House of Lords stated: 'the Crown is not bound by any statute except by express words or necessary implication')
- that Acts of Parliament, unless they say otherwise, are to have effect only within the United Kingdom. Some Acts *do* contain sufficiently clear express words. Section 4(1) Suppression of Terrorism Act 1978 states:

  If a person, whether a citizen of the United Kingdom...or not, does in a convention country [ie a country party to the 1977 European Convention on Terrorism] an act which if he had done it in...the UK would have made him guilty of [murder, manslaughter, or various other listed crimes]...he shall be guilty of the offence [and...

- against the statute depriving individuals of property
- against the statute infringing international law. (The courts presume that Parliament intends to honour its international obligations, particularly when the legislation is clearly meant to give effect to a convention or treaty)

- against deprivation of liberty
- that judges must read all primary and secondary legislation in a way that is compatible with the European Convention on Human Rights per s 3 Human Rights Act 1998. (According to s 4, if a provision is incompatible with a Convention right, the court may make a declaration of incompatibility. This does not invalidate the legislation – it merely draws Parliament's attention to the fact that the statute is incompatible and remedial action may be needed. A special procedure exists by which a minister of the government can change the domestic legislation if it feels obliged to do this)
- that Parliament does not intend to exclude the jurisdiction of the courts. (This is a very strong presumption)

Anisminic v Foreign Compensation Commission [1969] 1 All ER 208

An attempt was made to oust the jurisdiction of the courts in relation to the operation of the Foreign Compensation Act 1950. The House of Lords held that judicial review by the courts was available, and quashed the defendants' decision.

- that legal words and phrases are to be given their accepted legal meaning, if this is appropriate in the purposive context of the statute.

Interpretation Act 1978

The Interpretation Act 1978 contains numerous principles in relation to the construction of statutes:

- Words importing the masculine gender include the feminine.
- Words in the singular include the plural.
- The expression 'a person' includes a body corporate.
- Expressions referring to writing are construed as including printing, lithography, photography, and other modes of representing or reproducing words in a visible form.

Rules of language

Ejusdem generis rule: Where general words follow specific words, the general words must be construed as applying to the persons or things of the same class.

Powell v Kempton Racecourse [1899] AC 143

The defendant was charged with keeping a 'house, office, room or other place for betting'. He had been operating betting outdoors. The House of Lords decided that the general words 'other place' referred to indoor places since the words in the list were indoor places, and so the defendant was found not guilty.

The interpretation of legislation

✳✳✳✳✳✳✳✳✳✳

Expressio unius est exclusio alterius: that where specific words are used in a statute and are not followed by general words, the statute only applies to those things mentioned.

Tempest v Kilner (1846) 3 CB 249

The court had to consider whether the Statute of Frauds 1677, which required a contract for the sale of 'goods, wares and merchandise' of more than £10 to be 'evidenced in writing', applied to a contract for the sale of stocks and shares. The list of 'goods, wares and merchandise' was not followed by any general words, so the court held that only contracts for those three types of things were affected by the Statute of Frauds 1677, because stocks and shares were not specifically mentioned within the section, and were therefore not caught by the statute.

Nocistur a sociis: Ambiguous words may be determined by reference to those words appearing in association with them, within the same section or other sections of the Act.

Bromley London Borough Council v Greater London Council [1982] 1 All ER 129

At issue was whether the Greater London Council could operate a cheap-fare scheme on its transport systems, where the amounts being charged meant that the transport system would operate at a loss. The decision in the case revolved around the meaning of the word 'economy' in the Transport (London) Act 1969. The House of Lords looked at the whole Act and in particular at another section which imposed a duty to make up any deficit as far as possible. It decided that 'economy' meant running the transport system on business lines and running the transport system at a loss was not running it on business lines.

Extrinsic aids

External or **extrinsic aids** are those found in other material outside the statute which requires interpretation. They include:

- *Dictionaries*: The ordinary meaning of the words used in the statute (and alternative meanings if necessary) may be found from standard and/or specialist dictionaries per *Vaughan v Vaughan* [1973].

- *Explanatory Notes*: Acts of Parliament passed since the beginning of 1999 are provided with explanatory notes. These are published at the same time as the Act. They highlight the scope of the provisions and their basic operation. In *Westminster CC v National Asylum Support Service* [2002] UKHL 38, Lord Steyn stated 'that the Explanatory Notes often set out the context of the statute and the mischief at which it is aimed, and are thus admissible aids to the construction of the statute'.

- *White Papers*: Within these the Government details its firm proposals for new law following consultations via a Green Paper.

- *Official law reform agency reports*: These may be considered as evidence of the pre-existing state of the law and the mischief that the legislation was intended to deal with.

In *Black-Clawson International Ltd v Papierwerke Waldhof-Aschaffenburg AG* [1975] the House of Lords stated: 'Where there is an ambiguity in a statute, the court may have regard to a report which resulted in the passing of the Act in order to ascertain the mischief the Act was intended to remedy.'

- *Any previous Acts covering the same topic*: Definitions of words and phrases from one statute may be applied to another where the context allows, but only with great care: a word can easily mean different things in different Acts. See *R v Wheatley* [1979] in the key cases section.

- *Hansard*: This is the official record of Parliamentary debates when a bill is within the legislative process. The best guide to the intention of Parliament is probably Hansard, which records everything that was said while the bill was being debated. For over a century, the judiciary held that Hansard could not be consulted for the purpose of statutory interpretation but that rule has now changed. In *Davis v Johnson* [1979] the House of Lords maintained the hundred-year-old rule against using Hansard. The rule was set aside by the House of Lords in the following case.

....

Pepper v Hart [1993] 1 All ER 42

A dispute arose between the tax inspector and a public schoolteacher as to the value to be put on cut-price education for the teacher's children. The teacher's view was supported by a statement made by the minister when the relevant legislation was enacted, and he sought to use this as evidence to show the intention of Parliament. The House of Lords stated that whilst statute law consists of the words Parliament has enacted, a judge may use Hansard as an aid to the construction of legislation which is ambiguous or obscure, or the literal meaning of which leads to an absurdity, but only where the record discloses the mischief aimed at or the legislative intention behind the obscure or ambiguous words.

....

Limitations have been placed on the use of Hansard. The House of Lords in *Wilson v Secretary of State for Trade and Industry* [2003] stated only statements made by a minister or other promoter of the bill could be examined. Also, it could only be used to interpret the meaning of words in legislation; it could not be used to discover the reasons for the legislation. Using Hansard to discover the reasoning of Parliament, where there was no ambiguity, would go against the sovereignty of Parliament.

Intrinsic aids

Internal or **intrinsic aids** are those, which can be found in the statute itself:

- the long title sets out the purpose of the statute
- the Preamble establishing its legislative background
- an interpretation section explaining particular words or phrases in the context of the Act. (Section 34 Theft Act 1968 contains a definition of the word 'goods' used within

the statute. Section 189 Consumer Credit Act 1974 contains definitions of words and phrases used within the Act, eg 'hire purchase', 'credit sale', and 'conditional sale'. In s 5(2) Animal Boarding Establishments Act 1963, the word 'animal' is defined as meaning 'any dog or cat')

- Schedules within the Act itself.

Revision tip

When revising this area ensure that you highlight the various devices and aids, influences that can have an impact on a judge interpreting legislation. For a stronger examination answer these should be supported where applicable with relevant case law, judicial comment, and statutory provisions.

 *Looking for extra marks?*

A good discussion of how the judges actually interpret legislation and academic comment on this role can be found in F Quinn et al, *English Legal System*, 11th edn (Pearson Publishing, 2010), Chapter 3, pp 53–74. Remember that how the members of the judiciary themselves actually perceive their role within the English legal system can influence the choice of approach and devices used in relation to statutory interpretation. The facts and decisions of the extra cases highlighted within the key cases boxes can also be found in the above textbook.

Delegated legislation

The word 'delegate' merely means to pass something to another. Here Parliament is delegating law-making power to other individuals or organizations. Laws are then created with the authority of Parliament. The transfer of law-making power is undertaken via an Enabling Act (Parent Act). It lays down the scope of the delegated legislation and any special procedures, which must be complied with. Each type of delegated legislation will have a different Enabling Act. Parliament has also delegated law-making power to foreign organizations per the European Communities Act 1972.

There are three main types or forms of delegated legislation:

- statutory instruments (aka regulations)
- by-laws (aka bye laws)
- Orders in Council.

Statutory instruments

Ministers and government departments create 3,000 to 4,000 pieces of delegated legislation each year. By comparison, Parliament only creates between 40 and 60 statutes each Parliamentary session. There has been a significant increase in delegated legislation over the past hundred years. Delegated legislation created in this way is known as a statutory

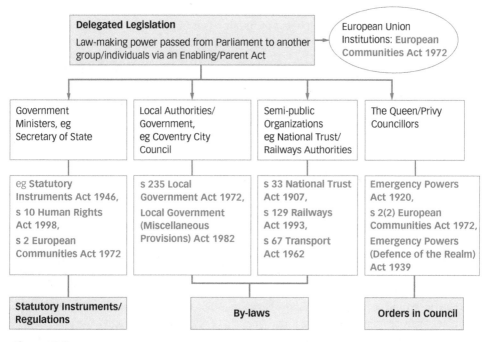

Figure 2.3

instrument or regulation, eg Greenhouse Gas Emissions Trading Scheme (Amendment) Regulations SI 2004/3390. A common form of statutory instrument is the commencement order, which can bring Acts of Parliament into force in stages; the Constitutional Reform Act 2005 has been the subject of nine such commencement orders. The procedure for creating delegated legislation in this form is usually laid down in the Enabling Act and within the Statutory Instruments Act 1946. For example there is a general requirement in relation to statutory instruments that they be published in order that they can be said to have been brought to the attention of the public per s 3(2) Statutory Instruments Act 1946.

There are many examples of statutes passing law-making powers to ministers of the Government:

- s 10 Human Rights Act 1998 gives ministers the power to amend le   ~here legislation is incompatible with the European Convention on Human R

- s 17(1) of the Road Traffic Act 1988 permits the 'Secretary of regulations prescribing (by reference to shape, construction or any o of helmet recommended as affording protection to persons on or in n injury in the event of accident'

Delegated legislation

✳✳✳✳✳✳✳✳✳✳

- s 2(2) European Communities Act 1972 was used to bring into English law Directive 93/13/EEC which dealt with issues on unfair terms in consumer contracts. In response, the Unfair Terms in Consumer Contracts Regulations SI 1994/3159 was created.

An Act which gives the executive wide powers to make delegated legislation is the Legislative and Regulatory Reform Act 2006. Under s 1 a Government minister is allowed to make 'any provision which he considers would [remove or reduce] any burden…resulting directly or indirectly for any person from any legislation'.

Orders in Council

Orders in Council are initially drafted by a minister of a Government department but need to be given formal approval by the Queen and Privy Council. Privy Councillors advise the Queen on the relevant issues and she will then give her formal approval. Orders in Council can be used to implement the provisions of the European Community under s 2(2) European Communities Act 1972. An example of an Order in Council implemented in this way was the Consumer Protection Act 1987 (Product Liability) (Modification) Order 2000. This Order in Council broadened the scope of consumer protection law to comply with a European directive.

The Queen and her Privy Councillors have the authority to make Orders in Council in times of emergency as stipulated by the Emergency Powers Act 1920 but such powers can only be used when Parliament is not sitting. Orders in Council were created by the monarch during the Second World War under s 1(1) Emergency Powers (Defence of the Realm) Act 1939, which stated that: 'His Majesty may by Order in Council make such Regulations as appear to him to be necessary or expedient for securing the…the defence of the realm,…maintenance of public order and the efficient prosecution of the war…'.

By-laws

By-laws are created by local authorities and other organizations for matters within their jurisdiction and area which involve the public. Law-making powers have been passed to local authorities via the Local Government Act 1972. Coventry City Council has created by-laws covering such matters as the fouling of footpaths by dogs and made it an offence to consume alcohol in a designated place via s 235 Local Government Act 1972. Section 235 states that '[A District Council] may make bye-laws for the good rule and government of the whole or any part of the District…and for the prevention of nuisances therein.' Under s 15(7) Local Government (Miscellaneous Provisions) Act 1982 Coventry City Council has created delegated legislation to regulate such activities such as tattooing and body piercing.

Where the power to create legislation is delegated to bodies other than ministers, the Enabling Act usually makes ministerial approval an essential part of the by-law creating process. This process is designed to ensure *inter alia* that:

- the organization has not acted ultra vires – that it had the power to make the delegated legislation in question
- a process of consultation was undertaken
- there is no conflict with existing legislation
- the by-law does not deal with a national issue – it deals with a specific, genuine local problem.

Once consideration of the delegated legislation has been undertaken, the minister is answerable to Parliament for his decision in relation to the by-law.

The National Trust was given the power under s 33 National Trust Act 1907 to make by-laws in relation to Trust property. Rail operators were given the power to make by-laws under s 129 Railways Act 1993 to regulate conduct of individuals on the rail network.

Once created, they can be enforced by the courts where they are breached by members of the public.

Boddington v British Transport Police [1998] 2 All ER 203

British Rail (before privatization) made a by-law under s 67(C) Transport Act 1962, which prohibited smoking where 'no smoking' notices were displayed. Post privatization, an independent train-operating company, Network South Central Rail, introduced a complete no-smoking ban on trains and displayed notices informing members of the public of this and the potential effect of failing to abide by such signs. A smoker, B, ignored the signs, was caught smoking, and was prosecuted. B sought to defend himself from a charge of illegally smoking on a railway carriage on the grounds that the posting of no smoking notices was ultra vires on the part of Network Rail. He was subsequently convicted and fined by the stipendiary magistrate but appealed against conviction. On appeal the House of Lords upheld his conviction.

Advantages of delegated legislation

- It saves Parliamentary time.
- Law can be passed to fulfil EU obligations.
- Expertise beyond that of Members of Parliament can be obtained.
- Greater detailed laws can be passed.
- Law can be passed quickly in times of emergency.
- It also allows local councils to make laws more appropriate to their local areas/local issues.

Delegated legislation

****

Disadvantages of delegated legislation

- There is limited scrutiny/mechanisms of control.
- There is lack of publicity.
- It is a less democratic method of law creation.
- There is a large volume of delegated legislation created.
- It raises issues of sub-delegation.
- It can give rise to the use of Henry VIII clauses (ie clauses that allow Government ministers to amend primary legislation).
- It may amount to an infringement of separation of powers.

Control by Parliament

Parliament can revoke or amend the Enabling Act and take the law-making power back from the person or group who abused the power given to them.

- Parliament can set the parameters within which the delegated legislation is to be made. Under the common law there is no duty for ministers to consult with outsiders before making regulations, but such a duty is often imposed by the Enabling Act and consultation is often common practice anyway. Those who make delegated legislation often consult experts within the relevant field and those bodies which are likely to be affected by it. See *Agricultural Training Board v Aylesbury Mushrooms* [1972] in the key cases section.
- A minister may also face direct questions by other Members of Parliament.
- Some statutory instruments are subject to an affirmative resolution procedure stipulated within the Enabling Act – the statutory instrument will not become law unless approved by Parliament within 40 days; eg the Secretary of State is given the power to make regulations under s 166(6) Criminal Justice and Public Order Act 1994 but under s 172(5) this can only be undertaken if 'a draft order has been laid before, and approved by a resolution of each House of Parliament'. Under the negative resolution process it is placed before Parliament for 40 days and automatically becomes law unless rejected within the stipulated time.
- A Delegated Powers Scrutiny Committee in the Lords was given the power to consider whether any provisions within bills delegated legislative powers inappropriately.
- A Joint Select Committee, the Scrutiny Committee, reviews statutory instruments and where necessary draws the attention of both Houses of Parliament. The Committee can only report back its findings to Parliament. It does not possess the power to amend any piece of delegated legislation. The Joint Committee reports to each House on any order or regulation which it feels deserves special attention because *inter alia*:
  - it is made under an Act, which precludes challenge in the courts

- it appears to make some unusual or unexpected use of the powers conferred by the statute or there appears to be doubt as to whether or not it is intra vires
- it purports to have retrospective effect
- it imposes a charge on public revenue or imposes or prescribes charges for any licence or consent for any services from a public authority
- the drafting is defective
- there appears to have been an unjustifiable delay in publication or laying before Parliament
- it calls for further elucidation.
- Prior to sending the report to Parliament the Committee will invite the minister, who drafted the delegated legislation, to respond to its criticisms and/or provide further clarification.

Control by the courts

The validity of a statute cannot generally be challenged by the courts as illustrated by comments made in *Cheney v Conn* [1968] and *British Railways Board v Pickin* [1974]. However, this general principle does not apply to delegated legislation such as statutory instruments and by-laws. The Queen's Bench Division of the High Court through **judicial review** can control delegated legislation. It can:

- declare it valid and enforceable, or
- invalid or partially valid, and in addition
- award any damages for loss caused.

Delegated legislation can be challenged if it is or is subject to:

- *Procedural ultra vires*: where it has been created without following the correct procedure as stipulated in the Enabling Act. (*Agricultural Training Board v Aylesbury Mushrooms* [1972] illustrates not only the control of delegated legislation by the High Court through judicial review but the issue of procedural ultra vires. The minister failed to consult with organizations as stipulated by the Enabling Act. The court rendered the instrument partially valid against those who were consulted)
- *Substantive ultra vires*: where the measures created are not within the powers granted in the Enabling Act
- *Unreasonable*: where it has been made in bad faith or is so perverse that no reasonable official could have made them.

See *Strickland v Hayes Borough Council* [1896] and *Agricultural Training Board v Aylesbury Mushrooms* [1972] in the key cases section.

Key cases

****

Revision tip

When revising this ensure that you are able to define what is meant by delegated legislation, the organizations that can create it, and the forms that delegated legislation can take. Highlight the various perceived advantages and disadvantages of this form of law as for instance compared with legislation. Ensure that you are aware of the various forms of controlling delegated legislation both via Parliament and via the courts. Support all the issues that you raise with relevant case law particularly in relation to the process and powers of the Queen's Bench Division. Provide a wide range of examples of Enabling Acts/Parent Acts highlighting the scope of such transfer of law-making powers and provide examples of actual delegated legislation created.

✅ Looking for extra marks?

An examination question on this area will usually be a critical analysis of delegated legislation. This would involve explaining how this area operates and how the form of law is created and then highlighting the various problems and benefits associated with this source of law, eg use of experts, lack of control mechanisms, etc. Most English legal system textbooks contain a stand-alone chapter which covers this form of law. A good analysis of delegated legislation can be found in the following texts, including a broad discussion of advantages and disadvantages of this form of law: T Ingman, *The English Legal Process*, 13th edn (Oxford University Press, 2010), pp 161–2; F Quinn et al, *English Legal System*, 11th edn (Pearson Publishing, 2010), pp 81–6.

(✳) Key cases

Case	Facts	Ratio/Held
Agricultural Training Board v Aylesbury Mushrooms [1972] 1 All ER 280	An Enabling Act required the Minister of Labour to consult 'any organisation or relevant body...appearing to him to be representative of substantial numbers of employers engaging in the activity concerned' prior to creating orders. However he failed to consult the Mushroom Growers Association, who were considered to be a 'relevant body' for the purposes of the Act in question, through a clerical error. It represented approximately 85 per cent of all mushroom growers in the UK. The court ruled that the consultation requirement was mandatory and that its breach made the order invalid as far as mushroom growers, who were members of the Mushroom Growers Association, were concerned.	The order was declared invalid because the requirement to consult with interested parties before making it had not been properly complied with. However the order was valid in relation to others affected by the order, such as farmers who were members of the National Farmers Union. The minister had consulted with the National Farmers Union, which represented such individuals.

Case	Facts	Ratio/Held
Anisminic v Foreign Compensation Commission [1969] 1 All ER 208	The defendants had under the Foreign Compensation Act 1950 a duty to determine the compensation payable to those whose property had been lost when in 1956 the Suez Canal was nationalized by the Egyptian Government. Section 4(4) Foreign Compensation Act 1950 stated no determination of the Commission was to be called into question in any court of law. The plaintiff's claim was rejected by the Commission, and he sought judicial review.	The House of Lords held that judicial review by the courts was available, and quashed the defendants' decision. The defendants had erred in law and acted ultra vires; their purported determination of the issue at hand was no true determination at all.
British Railways v Pickin [1974] 1 All ER 609	Pickin owned property next to a disused railway and claimed that he was entitled to the land no longer required for running the railway. He argued that Parliament had been deceived when enacting the British Railways Act 1968 through the private bill procedure.	The House of Lords held that the legal challenge be struck out as disclosing no cause of action.
Bromley London Borough Council v Greater London Council [1982] 1 All ER 129	At issue was whether the Greater London Council could operate a cheap fare scheme on its transport systems, where the amounts being charged meant that the transport system would operate at a loss. The decision in the case revolved around the meaning of the word 'economy' in the Transport (London) Act 1969.	The House of Lords looked at the whole Act and in particular at another section which imposed a duty to make up any deficit as far as possible. It decided that 'economy' meant running the transport system on business lines and ruled that the cheap fares policy was not legal since it involved deliberately running the transport system at a loss and this was not running it on business lines.
Leach v R [1912] AC 305	A man was charged with incest and his wife was called, against her will, by the prosecution, as a witness. The court was required to determine whether a wife could be compelled to give evidence against her husband under s 4(1) Criminal Evidence Act 1898.	The House of Lords, allowing the appeal against the husband's conviction, stated that as the Act did not expressly say that this would happen; the pre-existing common law rule that a wife could not be compelled to give evidence still applied.

Key cases

✳✳✳✳✳✳✳✳✳✳

Case	Facts	Ratio/Held
London and North Eastern Railway v Berriman [1946] 1 All ER 255	A rail engineer was killed by a train whilst undertaking maintenance work, oiling signalling apparatus. His widow tried to claim compensation for breach of statutory duty because there had not been a lookout man provided by the railway company in accordance with statutory regulations. The relevant section stated that a lookout should be posted for men working on or near the rail line for the purposes of 'relaying or repairing the track'.	The widow's actions failed. The court took the words relaying and repairing in their literal meaning and that the victim's actions, oiling the points, was merely maintaining the rail line and not repairing or relaying, and therefore did not fall within the provisions of the statute. The section did not cover the dead man's activities at the time.
Powell v Kempton Racecourse [1899] AC 143	The defendant was charged with keeping a 'house, office, room or other place for betting'. He had been operating betting at what is known as Tattersall's Ring, which is outdoors.	The House of Lords decided that the general words 'other place' had to refer to indoor places since all the words in the list were indoor places, and so the defendant was found not guilty.
R v Wheatley [1979] 1 All ER 954	A man W was found in possession of a metal pipe filled with sodium chlorate and sugar, and was charged with possessing an explosive substance contrary to s 4 Explosive Substances Act 1883. He argued that its effects would be pyrotechnic rather than explosive.	The Court of Appeal referred to the Explosives Act 1875, in which 'explosive' was defined as including 'pyrotechnic'. Since the long title of the 1883 Act referred expressly to the 1875 Act, the definition from the earlier statute could be imported into the latter. The defendant's conviction was therefore upheld.
Re Sigsworth [1935] Ch 89	A mother was murdered by her son. The mother had not made a will and so normally her estate would have been inherited by her next of kin according to the rules set out in the Administration of Justice Act 1925. This meant that her son would have inherited as her next of kin.	The statutory provisions were clear and there was no actual ambiguity in the words used within the Administration of Justice Act 1925, but the court was not prepared to let her murderer benefit from his crime; the golden rule would be used to prevent the repugnant situation of the son actually inheriting the mother's estate.

Case	Facts	Ratio/Held
Smith v Hughes [1960] 2 All ER 859	In this case six prostitutes were charged with soliciting 'in a street or public place' contrary to s 1(1) Street Offences Act 1959. One had been on a balcony above the street, and others had been sitting behind open or closed windows at first-floor level. In each case the women were attracting the attention of men by calling to them or by tapping on the window.	Upholding their convictions, the court did not use the plain, ordinary grammatical meaning of the words 'in the street or public place'. The judges chose to look to see what mischief the Act was designed to remedy and give effect to that remedy.
Strickland v Hayes Borough Council [1896] 1 QB 290	Under the Local Government Act 1888, Worcestershire County Council made it an offence to sing or recite any profane or obscene song or ballad, or to use any profane or obscene language generally 'in any street or public place or on land adjacent thereto'. S was prosecuted and convicted after speaking on a public footpath surrounded by many other people.	The Divisional Court quashed S's conviction. It stated the by-law was unreasonable and ultra vires and was consequently invalid. It went beyond the scope of the Parent Act (which was concerned with the prevention of annoyance to others) and it was too widely drawn in that it covered acts in private and in public and was consequently invalid.
Tempest v Kilner (1846) 3 CB 249	The court had to consider whether the Statute of Frauds 1677, which required a contract for the sale of 'goods, wares and merchandise' of more than £10 to be 'evidenced in writing', applied to a contract for the sale of stocks and shares.	The list of 'goods, wares and merchandise' was not followed by any general words, so the court held that only contracts for those three types of things were affected by the Statute of Frauds 1677. Stocks and shares were not specifically mentioned within the section, therefore they were not caught by the statute.
Whiteley v Chapell (1868) LR 4 QBD 147	A statute aimed at preventing electoral malpractice made it an offence to impersonate 'any person entitled to vote' at an election. A man, C, cast a vote in the name of a dead elector and was charged with 'impersonating a person entitled to vote'. C had pretended to be a person whose name was on the voters' list, but who had died.	The court said penal statutes were to be construed strictly, in favour of the defendant, and since the dead man would not have been entitled to vote, the offence was not made out. C was not guilty since a dead person is not, in the literal meaning of the words, 'entitled to vote'. A literal interpretation was used, even though it meant C was acquitted.

Exam questions

Essay question 1

Explain what is meant by the phrase 'delegated legislation' and how this form of law can be controlled both by the courts and by Parliament.

An outline answer can be found at the end of this book.

Essay question 2

Highlight the process by which Parliament creates legislation, the power by which the House of Commons can depart from this process, and the impact of European Union law.

An outline answer is available online at <http://www.oxfordtextbooks.co.uk/orc/concentrate/>.

#3
Sources of law III: Traditional sources of law

Key facts

- Custom is the oldest source of law. Many of its principles were incorporated into and provided the impetus for the early development of the common law (judge-made law). New customs can be recognized today provided they meet numerous stringent criteria stipulated by the courts. Once recognized, such customs can be enforced by the courts via the common law.

- Common law is now developed by the judiciary on the basis of previous case decisions, known as precedent.

- In order for a system of precedent to work, a system of law reporting and a settled court hierarchy are needed. The senior members of the judiciary in the higher courts have the greatest scope to develop the common law, and to depart from previous case decisions. Lower-court judges have little scope to do so unless they can avoid a previous case decision by distinguishing, for example.

- Equity is a source of law based on natural justice and fairness; it was originally developed to mitigate the harshness of the common law and the operation of the common law courts.

- Equitable principles can be used today – provided a litigant meets the equitable maxims, the principles on which equity is based. New equitable remedies can be developed to meet new situations. Equitable interests, remedies, and principles underpin the development of commerce, for instance the creation of mortgages and trusts.

- Books of authority can be a minor source of law. They are by judicial tradition books of antiquity, created prior to 1765 when law reporting was in its infancy. Such works were *inter alia* created by former senior members of the judiciary. Modern textbooks and journals are not seen as a source of law though they can have persuasive authority in relation to the development of the common law.

The common law

The historical basis of the **common law** is highlighted in a later section on custom law. In this section the operation/development of the common law in modern times will be examined. The common law is essentially created and developed by the judiciary following the principles of the doctrine of judicial precedent. Acts of Parliament do not cover all areas of the law and it is the responsibility of the judiciary to develop the law to cover such areas. It is well recognized that judges do use precedent to create new law and to extend old principles. There are many areas of the law which owe their initial existence to decisions made by the judiciary, such as the law of contract, the tort of negligence, and the criminal law. Judges clearly have a role to play in relation to law creation although traditionally they have seen themselves as declaring, rather than creating, the law, which is the prerogative of Parliament. Parliament has attempted to encompass some areas of the common law within statute but much of these legal areas is still regulated by judicial decisions and principles. The doctrine of precedent applies to the interpretation of statutes as well as to common law: if a higher court has given an interpretation of a particular word or phrase in a particular section of a particular statute, a lower court is bound to follow.

Judicial precedent

The principle that underpins precedent is that of *stare decisis*, which is Latin for 'let the decision stand or stand by what has been already decided'. Once a court has determined a legal issue then this legal reasoning will be followed in later cases with similar facts in order to promote certainty and to preclude a decision based on the whim of any particular judge. Basically, a judge must follow decisions made in courts which are higher up the hierarchy than his own. As well as being bound by the decisions of courts above them, some courts must also follow their own previous decisions. Some courts can depart from this general principle by way of exceptions and others by using the principle of distinguishing. Given the rule of *stare decisis*, the common law can still, however, be further developed:

- by amendments via legislation
- by cases raising novel points to be decided for the first time – so-called *original precedent*
- by the power of any judge to distinguish a case on its facts
- by superior courts utilizing special powers to depart from their own previous case decisions, eg the **Practice Statement** [1966]
- by the power of an appellate court to reverse or overrule a precedent set by a lower court.

The explanation of the legal principles on which the judgment is made is called the *ratio decidendi*. This is the part of the judgment, which must be followed. The parts of the judgment that do not form part of the *ratio decidendi* are called **obiter dicta** statements, ie 'things said by the way'. *Obiter dicta* statements usually deal with hypothetical situations. The *obiter dicta* statements do not have to be followed, though judges may be influenced by them. They are therefore, a form of persuasive precedent.

R v Seymour [1983] 2 All ER 1058

D had an argument with his mistress V as to who was to reverse, so the other could drive past in a narrow lane. D got into his lorry and drove forward to push V's car out of the way; V was trapped between the two vehicles and died of her injuries. The House of Lords upheld D's conviction for manslaughter, and Lord Roskill added *obiter* that the *Caldwell/Lawrence* definition of reckless-ness should apply to all offences involving recklessness except where Parliament had ordained otherwise.

R v Spratt [1991] 2 All ER 210

A young man D was firing his air gun from the window of his flat towards the dustbins outside; one shot struck a six-year-old girl whom D had not seen. The Court of Appeal quashed his con-viction for assault causing actual bodily harm. They declined to follow Lord Roskill's *dictum* in *Seymour* [1983], and said the recklessness required for offences under the Offences Against the Person Act 1861 was subjective recklessness as defined in *Cunningham* [1957] and earlier cases.

The division of judgments into two distinct parts is theoretical. Judges do not actually sepa-rate their judgments into the two clearly defined categories and it is for the person reading the case to determine what the actual *ratio decidendi* is. This process is made more difficult in appellate cases where each member of the judiciary presiding may deliver their own lengthy judgment. A judge very rarely says explicitly what part of his decision is the *ratio decidendi*, though there are isolated exceptions.

Re J [1992] 4 All ER 614

A child, J, of 16 months was severely disabled in several ways; his life expectancy was short, and his doctors took the view that he should not be resuscitated if his breathing were to fail. J's mother sought an order compelling the doctors to give 'all available treatment' to preserve his life, but the Court of Appeal refused to make such an order. Lord Donaldson MR said it would be an abuse of power for the court to order a doctor to carry out treatment which he believed contrary to his duty to his patient. The judge below had treated Lord Donaldson's views in *Re J* [1990] and again in *Re R* [1991] as *obiter dicta*; his Lordship therefore repeated them now and said expressly that they were part of the *ratio* of his present decision.

The common law

✳✳✳✳✳✳✳✳✳✳

Distinguishing

A judge can avoid applying the legal reasoning of a previous case, even of a higher court, if he determines that the facts of the present case before the courts are significantly different from those of the earlier case. This process is known as **distinguishing** and is a device available to all members of the judiciary irrespective of the position of the court in which they sit within the court hierarchy. The process of distinguishing can be illustrated in the following sets of cases:

Pepper v Webb [1969] 1 WLR 514

The plaintiff was a gardener. There was a history of complaints of insolence and inefficiency. The culminating incident occurred one Saturday when the employer challenged the employee about some unfinished work. The employee responded, 'I couldn't care less about your bloody greenhouse or your sodding garden,' and walked away. The court held this was a fundamental breach by the employee of the terms of the employment contract and so the dismissal was lawful. The employee had a duty to follow lawful and reasonable orders connected with his employment.

Wilson v Racher [1974] ICR 428

The plaintiff was employed as head gardener by the defendant. On a Sunday the defendant called over the plaintiff and wrongly and aggressively accused the plaintiff of various failings in his duties. The employer accused the employee of leaving work early. In fact the employee had stopped trimming the hedge because it was raining heavily, and so to continue would risk electrocution. An argument developed and the employee was provoked into saying, 'If you remember it was pissing with rain on Friday. Do you expect me to get f**king wet?' The employer sacked the employee. The Court of Appeal held that the employee's contract of employment had been wrongfully terminated. They distinguished the decision in the earlier case of *Pepper v Webb*. Clearly, the court was influenced by the fact that there was a risk to the health and safety of the employee if he followed the employer's orders.

Original and persuasive precedent

Where a judge is required to determine a legal issue that has never been raised within the courts, then whatever the judge decides in the present case, his *ratio* will form a new precedent for the future, known as an **original precedent**.

· Persuasive precedent is a previous decision/reasoning of a court etc, which does not have to be followed by a judge but can have influence and be adopted. Persuasive precedent comes from a number of sources, eg:

- decisions of courts in other legal jurisdictions based on common law principles, eg Canada, USA, Australia, New Zealand, etc
- decisions of lower courts

- decisions of the Judicial Committee of the Privy Council
- *obiter dicta* statements.

. . . .

Caparo v Dickman [1990] 1 All ER 568

The claimant bought shares in a company with a view to taking it over, and bought more after seeing the company's auditors' report. The shares then fell in value, and the claimant sued the auditors (Dickman) for their negligence in preparing the report. Giving judgment for the defendants, the House of Lords cited with approval the *dicta* expressed by Brennan J in the High Court of Australia in *Sutherland Shire Council v Heyman* (1985), that the law should: 'preferably develop novel categories of negligence incrementally and by analogy with established categories, rather than by a massive extension of a prima facie duty of care restrained only by indefinable considerations which ought to negative or limit the scope of the duty or the class of person to whom it is owed'. As a result of this decision, changes were made to the criteria for establishing a duty of care under negligence. It also limited the availability of damages for economic loss.

. . . .

Revision tip

When revising this area of the English legal system ensure that you learn the relevant terminology in relation to the operation of judicial precedent and development of the common law, eg *ratio decidendi, obiter dicta*, distinguishing, original precedent, persuasive precedent, etc. Ensure that you can explain what the phrases mean and can support these principles with relevant case law and judicial comment as highlighted above within this chapter.

✅ Looking for extra marks?

An excellent discussion of the operation of judicial precedent within the court system and relevant terminology can be found within the following text – A Gillespie, *The English Legal System,* 2nd edn (Oxford University Press, 2009), pp 69–86. The author supports his points with a wide range of case law which can be used in addition to those cases highlighted above and below within an answer on the operation of judicial precedent and the development of the common law. Better answers will be saturated with legal authority. Also see the following text for a general discussion on judicial precedent within the court system: T Ingman, *The English Legal Process,* 13th edn (Oxford University Press, 2010), pp 221–80.

What is needed for a system of precedent to operate?

If a system of judicial precedent is to operate effectively within any legal system then two basic elements must be present:

- an accurate system of law reporting
- a settled court hierarchy.

In order for judges to be bound by previous case decisions there must be in existence a reliable system of law reporting where they can find out what actually occurred in the previous

The common law

case and the legal reasoning. Written law reports have existed since the thirteenth century but were then brief and inaccurate. From the sixteenth century individuals who made a business out of selling reports to lawyers reported cases. However, the detail, quality, and accuracy of these reports varied. In 1865 the Incorporated Council of Law Reporting produced the most verbatim reports known as the Law Reports. These reports are revised by the judge within the case before publication.

The judgments of courts such as the Supreme Court (the former House of Lords), Court of Appeal are reported on the internet; eg see <http://www.supremecourt.gov.uk/decided-cases/index.html>. Other reports include the All England Law Reports and the Weekly Law Reports. Reports can also be located via legal databases, eg Westlaw. Newspapers and law journals also publish some case reports. Many forms of law reports are published by profit-making companies. Traditionally only barristers reported cases; since they were the only branch of the legal profession that could litigate in the superior courts it was believed only they could fully understand the complexity of proceedings and issues raised. This monopoly enjoyed by the Bar was removed by s 115 Courts and Legal Services Act 1990. Now a reporter, regardless of profession, must be fully qualified, ie have the right to conduct litigation within the courts which he reports.

In order for the doctrine of judicial precedent to operate effectively there must be a settled court hierarchy. A judge must be able to determine his place in the court system, which decisions in the court system he is bound by, and the scope for departing from decisions of his own court. The Judicature Acts 1873 to 1875 primarily established a settled court hierarchy.

The Supreme Court (the former House of Lords)

The Constitutional Reform Act 2005 established the new Supreme Court. It now undertakes the work of the Appellate Committee of the House of Lords. The final appeal case heard by the former House of Lords was *R (on the application of Purdy) v Director of Public Prosecutions* [2009]. The Supreme Court is now the highest court in the English legal system. The same judges who formerly sat in the House of the Lords, the 12 so-called Lords of Appeal in Ordinary, now sit in the new Supreme Court as Justices of the Supreme Court. The powers and procedures of the new Supreme Court are virtually identical to those of the former House of Lords especially in relation to the development of the common law. The court was due to start operations in April 2009 but this did not happen. The court finally came fully into operation in October 2009. The Supreme Court now sits in the Middlesex Guildhall building on the western side of Parliament Square separate from its previous location in the Palace of Westminster. The rationale for the existence of the Supreme Court is the desire for there to be a clear separation of powers in respect of the judiciary, legislature, and executive. As a result, under s 137 Constitutional Reform Act 2005 a judge may not sit

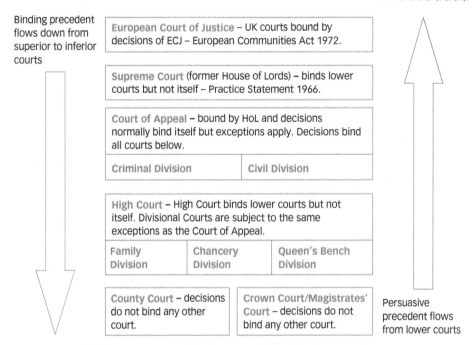

Figure 3.1 Judicial precedent within the court hierarchy

within the House of Lords in its legislative capacity during their employment, although he is free to sit when they have retired.

Until 1898 the House of Lords (now the Supreme Court) were not bound by its previous case decisions; this may have been due to the lack of quality and reliability in relation to the early law reports. However, in order to promote consistency and to bring an end to litigation, the House decided in *London Tramways Co Ltd v London County Council* [1898] that it would be bound by its own previous case decisions. Once the House of Lords laid down a legal principle it could only be changed by Parliament. This approach proved restrictive as it prevented development in the common law.

The then Lord Chancellor issued a Practice Statement [1966] designed to promote flexibility within the common law. It stated:

> the use of precedent...provides certainty. Their Lordships...recognise that...adherence to precedent may lead to injustice in a particular case and also unduly restrict the proper development of the law. They propose to modify...present practice and,...depart from a previous decision when it appears right to do so...

The common law

✳✳✳✳✳✳✳✳✳✳

The House of Lords rarely overrules one of its earlier decisions, as it is conscious to avoid any reduction in the degree of certainty required in the law. Lord Reid in *Knuller Ltd v DPP* [1973] stated:

> our change of practice in no longer regarding previous decisions of this House as absolutely binding does not mean that whenever we think a previous precedent was wrong we should reverse it. In the general interest of certainty in the law we must be sure that there is some very good reason before we so act.

Lord Cross stated in *Miliangos v George Frank (Textiles) Ltd* [1975]:

> [The *Practice Statement* of 1966] does not mean that whenever . . . a previous decision was wrong we should reverse it.

There are, however, a range of cases where the House of Lords (now the Supreme Court) has been prepared to apply the Practice Statement both within criminal and civil cases:

- In *Conway v Rimmer* [1968], the House of Lords overruled its decision in *Duncan v Cammell Laird & Co* [1942]. In *Duncan*, the House of Lords held that an affidavit sworn by a relevant government minister was sufficient for the Crown to claim public interest immunity, to prevent certain government documents from being disclosed to a court. In *Conway*, the House decided that it is up to the court to decide whether to order disclosure of such documents, balancing the possible prejudice to the state and the potential injustice to the individual litigant.

- In *Miliangos v George Frank (Textiles) Ltd* [1975], the House of Lords overruled its decision in *Re United Railways of Havana & Regla Warehouses Ltd* [1960]. In *United Railways*, it had been held that in English civil cases damages could only be awarded in sterling. In *Miliangos* it held that damages can be awarded in the currency of any foreign country specified within the contract.

- In *Arthur J S Hall v Simons* [2000], the House overruled the decision in *Rondel v Worsley* [1969]. In *Rondel v Worsley* the House of Lords stated that barristers had immunity against claims for negligence in relation to advocacy. In *Arthur JS Hall & Co v Simons* [2000] it refused to follow this earlier decision on the basis of professional liability in negligence generally.

- In *R v Howe* [1987], the House overruled its earlier decision in *Director of Public Prosecutions for Northern Ireland v Lynch* [1975]. In *Lynch*, it was stated that the defence of duress was available to a defendant who had participated in murder as an aider and abettor. In *Howe* it was held that the defence was not available to a person charged with murder as a principal or a secondary party.

Revision tip

When revising the operation of judicial precedent and development of the common law ensure that you are aware that the House of Lords in its judicial capacity has been replaced by the →

→ new Supreme Court; that the powers of this new court are identical to those of the House of Lords in relation to the development of precedent; and that the Constitutional Reform Act 2005 has not removed the House of Lords in relation to the English legal system. It still exists in relation to the legislative process where its composition is different from the former House of Lords in relation to its judicial capacity.

The Court of Appeal

The Court of Appeal is bound by decisions of the Supreme Court (the former House of Lords). It is normally bound by its own previous decisions and its decisions are binding on the inferior courts in the hierarchy. The Court of Appeal is split into two divisions.

The Civil Division is usually bound by its own previous decisions, but it will not be bound if one of the principles laid down in the case of *Young v Bristol Aeroplane Co Ltd* [1944] applies:

- *where two previous decisions of the Court of Appeal conflict with each other. (In such a case the Court of Appeal can decide which decision to follow and which to ignore.* In *Tiverton Estates Ltd v Wearwell* [1974] the court chose to follow older precedents rather than follow its decision in *Law v Jones* [1974].)

- *where the Supreme Court (the former House of Lords) has overruled a previous decision of the Court of Appeal expressly or impliedly. (In Family Housing Association v Jones* [1990] the court believed its earlier decisions had been impliedly overruled by the decision of the House of Lords in *AG Securities Ltd v Vaughan* [1988] and *Street v Mountford* [1985].)

- *where a previous decision of the Court of Appeal has been made* per incuriam – *in ignorance of a relevant law, part of a statute or a binding precedent that would have led to a different conclusion. (In Rickards v Rickards* [1989] the Court found its decision in *Podberry v Peak* [1981] had been made *per incuriam* as the Court had misunderstood and misapplied principles of law laid down by the House of Lords' decision in *Laine v Eskdale* [1891].)

The Criminal Division may depart from its own previous decisions if it is satisfied that the law was misapplied or misunderstood and potential loss of liberty is at stake. Lord Goddard in *R v Taylor* [1950] stated that:

> This court, however, has to deal with questions involving the liberty of the subject, and if it finds, on reconsideration that, in the opinion of a full court assembled for that purpose, the law has been either misapplied or misunderstood in a decision which it has previously given, and that, on the strength of that decision, an accused person has been sentenced and imprisoned it is the bounden duty of the court to reconsider the earlier decision with a view to seeing whether that person had been properly convicted.

The Divisional Courts and the High Court

The High Court is divided between the Divisional Courts and the ordinary High Court. The Divisional Courts are the Queen's Bench Division, the Chancery Division, and the Family Division. The Divisional Courts of the High Court are bound by decisions of the Supreme Court (the former House of Lords) and the Court of Appeal. Decisions of the Divisional Courts are binding on inferior courts.

....

R v Home Secretary ex p Anderson and Taylor (2001) The Times, 27 February

Two convicted murderers sought judicial review of the Home Secretary's decision to increase their 'tariff' sentences beyond those recommended by the trial judge. Their argument was that under the Human Rights Act 1998 their sentences should be set by an independent judge, not by a politician. The High Court reluctantly dismissed their application, saying that tariff-setting for mandatory life prisoners was not the same as sentencing in all other cases. Had the matter been free of authority, they would have said the 1998 Act clearly applied, but they were bound by the decisions of the House of Lords in *ex p Doody* [1994] and of the European Court of Human Rights in *Wynne v UK* [1994].

....

The two civil Divisional Courts, the Chancery Division and the Family Division, which both deal with civil appeals, are normally bound by their own previous decisions, unless one of the exceptions in the case of *Young v Bristol Aeroplane Co Ltd* [1944] applies. There is also a greater degree of flexibility in relation to appeals in criminal cases determined by the Queen's Bench Division of the Divisional Court for similar reasons to those pertaining in the Criminal Division of the Court of Appeal per *R v Greater Manchester Coroner ex p Tal* [1984] where the court refused to follow its earlier decision in *R v Surrey Coroner ex p Campbell* [1982]. It can refuse to follow its own earlier decision if the court is convinced that the earlier decision is wrong.

The Divisional Courts bind the ordinary High Court. Decisions of the High Court are binding on courts which are inferior to it in the hierarchy. The High Court does not regard itself as bound by its own previous decisions, but they are of strong persuasive value.

The Crown Court

All the courts above it bind the Crown Court. Its decisions do not form binding precedents, though High Court judges' judgments form persuasive precedents which must be given serious consideration in successive cases. When a circuit district judge is sitting, no precedents are formed. Since the Crown Court cannot form binding precedents, it is not bound by its own decisions.

County courts and magistrates' courts

Their own decisions are not binding on any courts and they are not bound by their own decisions. They are bound by decisions made by courts higher up the court hierarchy.

Revision tip

When highlighting the operation of precedent, explain what requirements must be met before such a doctrine can operate effectively, eg settled court hierarchy etc. Ensure that you can explain how precedent operates within the various courts of the English legal system highlighting any special mechanisms by which a court can depart from its previous case decisions, eg the Practice Statement, the rule in *Bristol Aeroplane*, etc. Again, provide a range of case examples illustrating how precedent and the devices can operate within the court system.

Precedent and the European dimension

Under s 3 European Communities Act 1972, English courts have been bound by decisions of the European Court of Justice (ECJ) in relation to EU law. The ECJ usually follows its own previous decisions but can overrule its own decisions if necessary. There are still areas of English law which are unaffected by EU law and for these the Supreme Court (the former House of Lords) is the final appeal court.

....

R v Secretary of State for Transport ex p Factortame [1990] 2 AC 85

The EU fishing policy limited fishing within 12 miles of Member States' shores to boats from their own country. To preserve fish stocks, each state was allocated a quota of fish. Soon after the rules were in place, the UK became concerned that Spanish fishing boats were registering as British vessels, so that their catches counted against the British quota rather than the Spanish and as a result genuine British fishermen were getting a smaller share. The Merchant Shipping Act 1988 was passed and prevented Spanish trawlers taking advantage of the British quota. Spanish boat owners challenged the Act, claiming that it was in conflict with EU law on the freedom to set up business anywhere in the Community and the House of Lords (now the Supreme Court) agreed. They stated that s 2(4) European Communities Act 1972 has:

> precisely the same effect as if a section were incorporated in the 1988 Act [saying] that the provisions with respect to registration of British fishing vessels were to be without prejudice to the directly enforceable Community rights of nationals of any member state…it has always been the duty of a United Kingdom court, when delivering judgement, to override any rule of national law found to be in conflict with any directly enforceable rule of Community law.

....

The European Court of Human Rights is an international court, which hears cases that involve alleged breaches of the European Convention on Human Rights. Under s 2 Human Rights Act 1998 an inferior court can avoid – overrule – the decision of a superior court if the court feels the decision was incompatible with a decision of the European Court of Human Rights. An English court is required to take account of cases that are decided by this court per **s 2 Human Rights Act 1998**. The House of Lords (now the Supreme Court) stated **in** *R (on the application of Alconbury Developments Ltd) v Secretary of State for the Environment* [2001] that:

> in the absence of some special circumstances it seems to me that the court should follow any clear and constant jurisprudence of the European Court of Human Rights. If it does not do so there is at least a possibility the case will go to that court which is likely to follow its own…jurisprudence.

Where a lower national court is faced with conflicting decisions between the highest national court and that of the European Court of Human Rights, the lower courts should follow the decision of the highest national court but be granted permission to appeal per *Lambeth London Borough Council v Kay* [2004]. See also *Leeds CC v Price* [2006].

Revision tip

When revising precedent, ensure that you cover the potential impact and implications of precedent in relation to European Union law, eg decisions of the European Court of Justice under the European Communities Act 1972. Also highlight the decisions of the European Court of Human Rights in relation to the Convention on Human Rights and Fundamental Freedoms and powers of the domestic courts under the Human Rights Act 1998. Ensure that you support your answer with relevant cases and judicial comment.

The advantages and disadvantages of judicial precedent

Advantages

- *Certainty, consistency, and fairness*: Cases will be treated alike, rather than judges making random decisions. It is seen as just and fair that similar cases should be decided in a similar way. The law must be consistent if it is to be credible. This helps people plan their affairs. It allows lawyers to advise clients on the outcome of potential legal action.

- *Time saving*: Where a principle of law has been established, cases with similar facts are unlikely to go through the lengthy process of litigation.

- *Flexibility*: Law needs to be flexible to meet the needs of a changing society. There is scope for the law to change as the Supreme Court (the former House of Lords) can use the Practice Statement to overrule cases and the Court of Appeal can use various exceptions to avoid its previous decisions. In addition, all courts have the ability to distinguish cases, which gives the courts the ability to avoid past decisions and develop the law.

Disadvantages

- *Complexity and volume*: Since there are half a million reported cases it is not easy to find the relevant case law. Even with computerized databases it can be time-consuming.

The judgments are often very long with judges making no attempt at readability, with no clear distinction between *ratio decidendi* statements and *obita dicta* statements, making it difficult to actually identify and extract the ratio to be followed.

- *Rigidity*: The rules of judicial precedent mean that judges should follow a binding precedent. This means that bad judicial decisions are perpetuated before they come before a higher court with the power to overrule them. Changes in the law will only take place if parties have the time, persistence, and money to appeal to the highest courts.

- *Illogical distinctions*: As binding precedents must be followed, it can lead to judges making minute distinctions between the facts of a previous case and the case before them in order to avoid the previous precedent, known as *distinguishing*. This can lead to a mass of cases all establishing different precedents in very similar circumstances, and cause complexity.

- *Lack of research*: Judges are not concerned with the social and economic implications of their decisions, and cannot commission research or consult experts as Parliament can when changing the law. When making case law the judges are only presented with the facts of the case and the legal arguments, and their task is to decide on the outcome of that particular dispute.

- *Retrospective effect*: Changes made by case law apply to events which happened before the case came to court, unlike legislation, which usually only applies to events after it comes into force. This may be considered unfair, since if a case changes the law, the parties concerned in that case could not have known what the law was before they acted.

- *Undemocratic*: The judge is not answerable to the people. Precedent can actually give judges a good deal of discretion, and allow them to decide cases on grounds of political and social policy. This raises the question of whether judges, who are unelected, should have such freedom.

- *Slowness of growth and piecemeal development*: Members of the judiciary in the senior courts may well be aware that some areas of the law need reforming, however they cannot make the decision unless there is a case before the courts to be decided. There may be a long wait for a suitable case to be appealed as far as the Supreme Court.

Law reform and judicial precedent

The common law can bring about some reform.

. . . .

R v R (Rape: Marital Exemption) [1991] 4 All ER 481

The House of Lords (now the Supreme Court) declared that a husband who has sexual intercourse with his wife without her consent may be guilty of rape. Before this decision, the law on rape within marriage was based on statements made by state lawyer Sir Matthew Hale from the eighteenth century that 'by marrying a man, a woman consents to sexual intercourse with him and may not

The common law

✳✳✳✳✳✳✳✳✳

retract that consent'. The judiciary had attempted to circumvent the rule if certain circumstances existed. However, Parliament had failed to debate and remove the rule when considering a new Sexual Offences Bill in 1976. An appeal was made to the House of Lords (now the Supreme Court). Lord Keith felt that Hale's statement 'reflected the social times in which it was written, but that this no longer reflected the status of women and the marriage relationship in modern times. The modern view was that husband and wife were equal partners and this therefore meant that the wife could no longer be considered to have given irrevocable consent to sex with her husband', and that the common law should evolve to reflect such changes in society.

However, major reforms in the law are rarely undertaken by the courts for many reasons:

- The courts can only deal with such points as they arise in the cases before them, and this depends on the parties involved having sufficient finance, determination, and interest to take their case up through the courts. Therefore law reform proceeds not on the basis of which areas of law need changing but on a haphazard presentation of cases.

- Judges have to decide cases on the basis of the way issues are presented to them by the parties. They cannot commission research or consult with interested bodies to find out the possible effects of a decision on individuals and organizations other than those in the case before them – yet their decision will apply to future cases.

- Judges have to recognize the doctrine of precedent and for much of the time, unless a case reaches the Supreme Court, this limits judicial creativity and radical reforms.

- Many judges feel that, as they are not elected, they should not make decisions that radically change the law in areas of great moral or social controversy. They will often impose limits on their ability to make major changes and declare that it is Parliament that must undertake such reforms.

- Law reforms made by Parliament come into force on a specified date in the future; judicial decisions, however, are retrospective.

In *C (A Minor) v DPP* [1996] the House of Lords (now the Supreme Court) stated that judges should be cautious in relation to law creation, and a number of factors must be borne in mind by the judiciary in such circumstances:

- Where the solution to a dilemma was doubtful, judges should be wary of imposing their own answer.

- Judges should be cautious about addressing areas where Parliament had rejected opportunities of resolving a known difficulty, or had passed legislation without doing so.

- Areas of social policy over which there was dispute were least likely to be suitable for judicial law-making.

- Fundamental legal doctrines should not be lightly set aside.

- Judges should not change the law unless they can be sure that doing so is likely to achieve finality and certainty on the issue.

Revision tip

When revising this area, ensure that you explain how members of the judiciary can reform the law through precedent and provide cases where the courts have specifically considered the issue of law reform, such as *R v R (Rape: Marital Exemption)* [1991] and *C (A Minor) v DPP* [1995] and highlight any potential limitations that have been expressed by senior members of the judiciary.

 *Looking for extra marks?*

When tackling an examination question on the development of the common law, comment on the issue as to whether the judiciary do and should create the law. A good discussion of these issues is highlighted within Elliott and Quinn's textbook on the *English Legal System*, 11th edn (Longman, 2010), Chapter 1, pp 24–33. Opinion on this issue is divided and you would gain credit for highlighting viewpoints expressed by both academics and members of the judiciary.

Equity

Equity is a source of law based on principles of fairness and natural justice. Historically, equity developed as a result of the defects in the common law and its system of administration. Cases in the common law courts were started on the basis of a writ. The writ laid down the grounds of a prospective case. The rules of procedure were strictly adhered to within the common law courts and if, for instance, the litigant had taken out the wrong writ then the claim would fail and the litigant would have to go through the time and expense of starting the case all over again. Writs were created to meet new situations until the Provisions of Oxford 1258 when the creation of new writs was restricted. As a result, from then on for a litigant to take a case to the courts, the grounds for the dispute had to meet a pre-existing writ. If no writ was suitable then a case could not be taken to the court. The judges attempted to use fictions so that circumstances of cases would meet previously created writs. In other words they would assume certain facts existed.

Another problem was the availability of adequate remedies. The only remedy available if a litigant successfully won their case at common law was damages. However, in many situations this remedy was simply not adequate.

In order to overcome some of these issues and enable individuals to achieve justice, dissatisfied litigants could petition the King directly. He would decide a course of action based on what *he* thought was right. Eventually, this role was handed over to the Keeper of the King's Conscience, the High Lord Chancellor, a senior member of the clergy, and an ecclesiastical lawyer. The Chancellor based his decisions on principles of natural justice and fairness. He was prepared to look beyond legal documentation, ordered parties to appear before him, and required them to explain their behaviour. New remedies were developed to meet novel cases that came before him. Equity was initially uncertain as each new Lord Chancellor applied their own idea of fairness and justice. A seventeenth-century jurist, John Seldon, observed 'equity varied with the length of the Chancellor's foot'.

Equity

✳✳✳✳✳✳✳✳✳✳

Eventually, the number of petitions that were received increased so dramatically that the Lord Chancellor set up a court to hear the influx of petitions. The court was known as the Court of Chancery. The court was free from strict common law procedures and was not bound by precedent. Decisions continued to be made on the basis of the merits of each case. The court continued to develop new remedies to meet novel situations. A number of problems were caused by the dual system of courts, one administering common law principles and the other equity:

- Firstly, tensions between the common law and equitable courts developed. The common law lawyers were angry that equity could be used to restrict their jurisdiction. Where the common law courts gave a litigant a right, the Court of Chancery could issue an injunction which prevented that party from exercising those rights, if it felt to do so would be unjust. The Court of Chancery proved popular with litigants, which increased friction with the common law lawyers.

....

Earl of Oxford's case (1615) 1 Rep Ch 1

The common law courts, headed by Chief Justice Coke, gave a judgment, which was alleged to have been obtained by fraud. The Chancellor, Lord Ellesmere, issued an injunction preventing the successful party from enforcing the judgment. The conflicting judgments of the common law courts and the Courts of Chancery were referred to the King, James I, for resolution of the issue. The King decided that where there was a conflict between the common law and equity, equity was to prevail.

....

- Secondly, if a litigant wanted to obtain a common law remedy and an equitable one, two court actions were needed. This caused additional expense and was considerably time-consuming in operation. This problem was partially resolved by the Chancery Amendment Act 1850 and the Common Law Procedure Acts 1852 to 1860. The Chancery Amendment Act 1850 allowed the Court of Chancery to grant common law remedies and the Common Law Procedure Acts 1852 to 1860 allowed the common law courts to grant equitable remedies. However, the courts remained separate until the Judicature Acts of 1873 to 1875 merged the common law courts and equitable courts into one coherent court structure and allowed a single judge to apply principles of common law and equity. Section 25 of the Judicature Acts of 1873–1875 reiterated the decision as made in the Earl of Oxford's case (1615): 'where there is any conflict or variance between the rules of equity and the common law, the rules of equity will prevail'.

The maxims of equity

As highlighted previously, the principles of equity were not implemented on the basis of precedent but at the discretion of the Chancellor/judge dealing with the case. There were initially few guidelines to follow and this made the system of equity unpredictable. Eventually, to provide some certainty in the operation of equity, guidelines were developed initially by various Lord Chancellors between 1673 and 1827, known as maxims. If an **equitable maxim** were not satisfied then equitable remedies would be denied. The Chancery Courts eventually began to follow their own past decisions. Such maxims include:

* He who comes to equity must come with clean hands.

D & C Builders v Rees [1966] 2 QB 617

A building firm undertook a small building project for a couple named Rees. The couple, knowing that the builders were in severe financial difficulties, refused to pay the full sum owed, £732, stating that the work was defective and merely offered a final payment of £300. The builders accepted this amount due to their financial situation. When the builders decided to sue for the outstanding amount the couple argued that the principle of equitable estoppel applied, which basically prevented the builders from suing for the outstanding sum. Lord Denning refused to allow the couple to use the doctrine on the grounds that they had not come to equity with clean hands as they had attempted to take unfair advantage of the builders' difficulties.

* Equity looks at intention not the form.
* He who seeks equity must do equity.

Chappell v Times Newspapers [1975] 1 WLR 482

Newspaper employees had been threatened by their employer that they would be sacked if they did not stop the strike action they were undertaking. The employees sought an injunction to prevent the employers from carrying out their threat. The court decided that the employees, to benefit from equitable remedies, such as an injunction, must act equitably themselves and return to work. The injunction was refused as they failed to return to work.

* Delay defeats equity.

Leaf v International Galleries [1950] 1 ALL ER 693

The court refused to grant the remedy of rescission as the delay of five years between the purchase and the discovery that a painting was not by the painter, Constable, was found to be excessive. Delay defeats equity.

* Equity will not suffer a wrong to be without a remedy.

Central London Property v High Trees Ltd [1947] KB 130

A block of flats was leased to a company for a period of 99 years, and the company then sublet the flats to individual tenants. During the Second World War many people moved away from London due to bombing raids conducted by the German Luftwaffe. As a result it was difficult for the company to sub-let the flats and many remained empty. The main landlord agreed that, whilst the war lasted, the company leasing the block of flats need only pay half of the annual rent. After the war the landlord tried to claim the full rent for the period of the war. Strictly speaking the original contract for the 99-year-old lease would have allowed the landlord to make such a claim.

The court held that the landlords would be estopped and prevented from claiming the unpaid rent.

One of the most important aspects of equity was that it created new remedies to supplement those available at common law. This maxim clearly postulates that new remedies can be developed by the courts to meet new situations. Two new expansions to the arsenal of equitable remedies include:

- *Anton Piller Order*: a court order which allows a party to search the other party's premises and take away documents or other material that may be relevant to the case. This prevents a party destroying or otherwise disposing of relevant documents: *Anton Piller KG v Manufacturing Process Ltd* [1976]
- *Mareva injunction*: a freezing injunction which allows the courts to order that third parties such as banks must freeze any assets under their control where there is a risk that one of the parties may remove their assets out of the UK. This order ensures that there are assets which can be made available to pay damages or costs that the court awards: *Mareva Compania Naviera SA v International Bulkcarriers SA* [1975]

However, these remedies are discretionary so that the court does not have to grant them, even if the claimant wins the case. This is in direct contrast to the common law remedy of damages, which are available as of right. An equitable remedy will only be granted if the court thinks it is fair in the circumstances. If a party ignores an equitable remedy ordered by the court then this will be considered a contempt of court. This may result in a fine or imprisonment being imposed. Section 37(1) Supreme Court Act 1981 stated that the High Court can grant an equitable remedy where 'it appears just and convenient to do so'.

The main equitable remedies are:

- *specific performance*: an order that compels a party to perform their contractual obligations

Beswick v Beswick [1967] 2 All ER 1197

The owner of a small business agreed to transfer the business to his nephew, in return for the nephew promising to pay a sum of money to him during his lifetime and an annuity to the man's widow after his death. After the uncle died the nephew refused to pay the annuity to the uncle's widow. The widow could not sue in her own right, because she was not privy to the contract (she was a third party in relation to the construction of the contract), so she sued as the executrix of her husband's estate. The House of Lords held that damages would not have been a satisfactory remedy, because the loss to the estate was negligible, so she was granted an order of specifc performance directing the nephew to perform his part of the contract.

- *rescission*: an order that returns as far as possible the parties to their original pre-contractual position

Redgrave v Hurd (1881) LR 20 ChD 1

A solicitor R advertised for a partner, giving an exaggerated account of the firm's profitability. H answered the advertisement and, post negotiations, agreed to join the firm as a partner, but retracted when he discovered the true position. R sued for specific performance. H defended and counter-claimed for rescission and damages. The Court of Appeal refused damages but said H was entitled to rescission of the contract, which had been entered into because of R's misrepresentations.

Also see *Leaf v International Galleries* [1950] in the key cases list below.

- *rectification*: where a legal document contains errors the court will alter it in order to reflect the true intentions of the parties

Re Posner [1953] 1 All ER 1123

A testator P left most of his property to 'my wife Rose Posner', though in fact the woman concerned, with whom P actually lived, was married to someone else and was not P's legal wife. In interlocutory proceedings the judge said that unless fraud could be proved the will could be amended and the words 'my wife' deleted so that P's true intentions could be carried out.

- *injunction*: an order of the court in the form of a decree compelling the defendant in a case to cease from doing certain acts. In *Kennaway v Thompson* [1980] an injunction was granted in order to prevent power boats being raced on a lake during certain specified times.

Lumley v Wagner [1843–60] All ER 814

W agreed to sing at L's theatre for a certain period, and during that time not to sing elsewhere. Subsequently W contracted to sing at another theatre and refused to perform her contract with L. The court held that an injunction should be granted to prevent W from singing elsewhere. The court would not, however, grant an order for specific performance to compel W to sing for L.

- Also see *Warner Bros v Nelson* [1936] where an injunction was issued to prevent the actress Bette Davis from being employed by another film company in breach of her contract of employment.

Revision tip

When dealing with a question that asks for a critical evaluation of the operation of *judicial precedent* it is important to highlight the operation of equity. Equity remedied the defects that were inherent in the early operation of the common law legal system, lack of available writs, and lack of remedies, etc. Explain how equity developed historically and its role today within the civil justice system, the importance of the equitable maxims, and highlight these issues with case law and examples.

Custom law

Custom is important in two ways within the English legal system:

- as the original catalyst for the development of the common law
- as a minor source of law.

Custom and the development of the common law

Prior to the Norman Conquest of 1066, the law varied throughout the country. It was based on the practices and customs brought by invaders, from the Continent, who settled in the various regions of England. These customs varied from region to region. In north and north-eastern England, Danelaw had been adopted. Mercian law governed central England, and Wessex law applied in southern and western England. These customs were enforced by the:

- shire court
- hundred court
- franchise courts.

At this time, England had no effective central government, and the King had little control over the country.

When the English throne was seized following the Battle of Hastings, King William was faced with a number of problems:

- no uniform set of laws applicable throughout England
- a lack of a central government.

As a result of these problems, he established his court, the Curia Regis, and a strong central government at Westminster. More importantly, he undertook the initial steps of providing uniformity in the law of England. Members of the King's Court, the Curia Regis, known as itinerant judges, were sent around the regions of England, to check the local administration and decide local disputes based on the local customs in the King's name.

When these judges returned to Westminster, they discussed the customs in operation. They were required by the monarch to sift the various customs they encountered, adopt those that were in common usage, reject the unreasonable ones, and adopt those that appeared to operate rationally. Subsequent monarchs continued this process until the reign of Henry II. As the various customs were recognized and adopted by the judiciary, eventually a single body of rules began to evolve. Legal principles established by the judiciary to meet novel situations were also adopted within this new body of rules. The result of this was that by 1250 a common law had been produced that applied throughout the land, irrespective of the local laws applied by communities in the various regions. Lord Justice Sir Edward Coke in his study of the whole of English Law within the *Institutes of the Laws of England* (1628–41) described customs as thus being 'one of the main triangles of the Laws of England'.

Custom as a minor source of law

Custom is a minor potential source of law today. Custom, in this context, is used where a person claims that he is entitled to some local right or practice, such as a right of way, or a right to use land for a particular purpose, because this is what has always happened locally for centuries. The onus of proof of a local custom rests on the person claiming that a custom actually exists and should be recognized. The courts are then asked to enforce these ancient rights/practices as subsequent landowners etc have challenged their validity.

A number of tests must be met before the courts today will recognize and enforce a custom:

- The custom must have existed since time immemorial. It must have existed from the commencement of legal memory, arbitrarily fixed at the year AD 1189, fixed under the Statute of Westminster 1275. It is difficult to trace a custom back that far; the courts allow it to be proved by calling the oldest inhabitant of the locality to testify that it has happened for as long as they can remember. If such evidence can be given the courts presume that the custom existed since AD 1189.

....

Simpson v Wells (1872) LR 7 QB 214

It was proved that a right to set up a refreshment stall on a public footpath had been given by statute in the fourteenth century. There was documentary evidence in the form of a statute that it had not in fact existed since the prescribed date of AD 1189 but had come into existence two centuries later.

....

....

Wyld v Silver [1963] 1 QB 169

Local residents claimed that they had a right to hold a fair on particular land, which, therefore, prevented the landowner from building on a particular piece of land. The landowner argued that the right to hold an annual fair had not actually been implemented in recent times. The court upheld the customary right and prevented the landowner building via an injunction. The court highlighted that the custom need not actually have been exercised continuously since 1189, merely that it should have been possible to exercise the customary right since that date.

Also see *Mercer v Denne* (1905) in the key cases list below.

....

- The custom must be reasonable.
- The custom must be certain and clear and capable of precise definition and relate to a specific locality. The custom must be applicable/relate to a particular geographical area – a district known to law, eg a parish, a manor, or shire. Custom is only ever a local source of law. Where a custom is recognized as granting a right, it grants that right only to those specified within that specific locality.

Books of authority (aka books of antiquity)

✱✱✱✱✱✱✱✱✱✱

- The custom must have been exercised peaceably, openly, and as of right. No one must have given permission for the customary right to be exercised (*nec precario*), eg via a licence/contractual arrangement etc. If a right is exercised by permission, then it cannot be claimed to be exercised as 'of right'. The custom must in addition have been carried out without using force, ie peaceably (*nec vim*), and must have been exercised openly and not in secret (*nec clam*). See *Mills v Colchester Corporation* (1866–7) in the key cases list below.
- The custom must be consistent with those already recognized.
- The custom must not conflict with statute law.

It is, therefore, the judiciary utilizing the tests above who decide which local customs will actually be recognized, and thus enforced.

It is unusual for a new custom to be considered by the courts today, however there are some recent examples. In *Egerton v Harding* [1974] the Court of Appeal upheld a customary duty to fence land against straying cattle on common land. In *New Windsor Corporation v Mellor* [1974] 2 All ER 510 a local authority was prevented from building on land because the local inhabitants proved there was a custom that they had the right to use the land for lawful sports.

Books of authority (aka books of antiquity)

By judicial tradition only books of antiquity can strictly be regarded as a source of law. These were written primarily by senior members of the judiciary when law reporting had barely begun. For example, the former Lord Chief Justice of England, Sir Edward Coke, in *Institutes of the Laws of England* (1628–41) laid down his definition of murder. Murder occurred:

> When a person of sound memory and of the age of discretion unlawfully killeth any reasonable creature in rerum natura under the King's peace. With malice aforethought, either expressed by the party or implied by law, so as the party wounded, etc. die of the wound or hurt etc, within a year and a day after the same.

This subsequently formed the basis of the *actus reus* and *mens rea* for the common law offence of murder. This definition has been refined by the judiciary through subsequent decisions over the past few centuries.

The following, *inter alia*, are accepted as books of authority:

- Glanvil – *Tractus de Legibus et Consuetudinibus Angliae* (1189)
- Bracton – *De Legibus et Consuetudinibus Angliae* (1250)
- Sir Edward Coke – *Institutes of the Laws of England* (1628–41)
- Sir Matthew Hale – *History of the Pleas of the Crown* (1736)
- Hawkins – *Pleas of the Crown* (1716)
- Sir Michael Foster – *Crown Law and Cases* (1762).

However:

- Many of these ancient texts were published post the author's death and therefore could not be corrected, amended, or clarified by the author prior to publication.

- In addition, these works generally reflect the operation of law and values of society/morality at the time that they were written. Therefore it could be argued that such books may be out of touch with the values and morality of today's modern society.

In *R v R (Rape: Marital Exemption)* [1991] the House of Lords declared that a husband who had sexual intercourse with his wife without her consent would be guilty of rape. Before this decision, the law on rape within marriage was based on an assertion by Sir Matthew Hale in *History of the Pleas of the Crown* (1736), that:

> by marrying a man, a woman consents to sexual intercourse with him, and may not retract that consent.

This position had been found offensive for many years, with many members of the judiciary attempting to limit the application of this rule. Parliament considered it during a debate on the Sexual Offences Bill in 1976 but decided not to make changes at that time. It was not until 1991 that the House of Lords held that rape within marriage should be considered an offence. Lord Keith stated that Hale's assertion reflected:

> the status of women within marriage in his time…[But since then the] Status of women and the marriage relationship had changed. The modern view of husband and wife as equal partners meant that a wife could no longer be considered to have given irrevocable consent to sex with her husband…the common law was capable of evolving to reflect such changes in society, and it was the duty of the court to help it do so.

By 1765 a system of reliable/accurate/accesible law reporting was established ensuring that no later book would be deemed by the judiciary to be an ancient text and therefore a source of law in its own right.

Academic writing

Academic writing via modern textbooks/journals is frequently referred to within the courts by counsel as part of their argument in a case. However, these texts only have persuasive authority in relation to the development of the common law. The court *may* accept the academic writer's view of what the law should be and develop the common law accordingly.

Megarry LJ in *Cordell v Second Clanfield Properties Ltd* [1968], stated:

> I would…give credit to the words of any reputable author in book or article as expressing tenable and arguable ideas, as fertilisers of thought and as conveniently expressing the fruits of research in print, often in apt and persuasive language. But I would do no more than that; and in particular I would expose those views to the testing and refining process of argument.

Key cases

****

In *R v Shivpuri* [1986] the House of Lords stated:

> [we] cannot conclude…without disclosing that [we] have had the advantage, since the conclusion of the arguments…of reading an article by Professor Glanville Williams entitled 'The Lords and Impossible Attempts, or *Quis Custodiet Ipsos Custodes*?' [1986] CLJ 33…it would be foolish,…not to recognise the force of the criticism and…the assistance…derived from it.

Revision tip

Custom law and books of authority as topic areas for revision purposes would be relevant where you are asked a question generally about the sources of law within the English legal system or where you are asked a question on the development of the common law. Ensure that you are aware not only of how custom law operates and is recognized within the courts today, but also of the relationship with the early development of the common law dating back to the Norman Conquest. In addition ensure that you are aware of the difference between a book of antiquity and modern academic writing and the problems associated with such texts and the influence and impact of these sources in relation to the common law. Again, ensure that you support information with relevant case law and any academic/judicial comment where applicable to support points made.

 Key cases

Case	Facts	Ratio/Held
Caparo v Dickman [1990] 1 All ER 568	The claimant bought shares in a company with a view to taking it over, and bought more after seeing the company's auditors' report. The shares then fell in value, and the claimant sued the auditors (Dickman) for their negligence in preparing the report.	The court demonstrated the use of persuasive precedent. Giving judgment for the defendants, the House of Lords cited with approval the *dicta* expressed by Brennan J in the High Court of Australia in *Sutherland Shire Council v Heyman* (1985).
Central London Property v High Trees Ltd [1947] KB 130	Concerning a landlord who during the Second World War agreed that, whilst the war lasted, the company leasing his block of flats need only pay half of the annual rent. After the war the landlord tried to claim the full rent for the period of the war. Strictly speaking the original contract for a 99-year lease would have allowed the landlord to make such a claim.	The court held that the landlord would be estopped, ie prevented, from claiming the unpaid rent.

Case	Facts	Ratio/Held
Chappell v Times Newspapers [1975] 1 WLR 482	Newspaper employees had been threatened by their employer that they would be sacked if they did not stop the strike action they were undertaking. The employees sought an injunction to prevent the employers from carrying out their threat.	The court decided that the employees, to benefit from equitable remedies, such as an injunction, must act equitably themselves and return to work. The injunction was refused as they failed to return to work.
D & C Builders v Rees [1966] 2 QB 617	A building firm undertook a small building project for a couple named Rees. The couple, knowing that the builders were in severe financial difficulties, refused to pay the full sum owed, £732, stating that the work was defective and merely offered a final payment of £300. The builders accepted this amount due to their financial situation. When the builders decided to sue for the outstanding amount the couple argued that the principle of equitable estoppel applied, which basically prevented the builders from suing for the outstanding sum.	Lord Denning refused to allow the couple to use the doctrine on the grounds that they had not come to equity with clean hands as they had attempted to take unfair advantage of the builders' difficulties.
Earl of Oxford's case (1615) 1 Rep Ch 1	The common law courts, headed by Chief Justice Coke, gave a judgment, which was alleged to have been obtained by fraud. The Chancellor, Lord Ellesmere, issued an injunction preventing the successful party from enforcing the judgment. The conflicting judgments of the common law courts and the Courts of Chancery were referred to the King, James I, for resolution of the issue.	The King decided that where there was a conflict between the common law and equity, then equity was to prevail.
Leaf v International Galleries [1950] 1 ALL ER 693	A painting was sold which was mistakenly believed to be by the painter Constable. In fact it was not. Five years had passed since the purchaser realized that the painting was not in fact a genuine Constable. The purchaser attempted to rescind the contract.	The court refused to grant rescission as the delay of five years between the purchase and the discovery that the painter was not Constable had been excessive. The claimant had contravened the principle that delay defeats equity.
Mercer v Denne [1905] 2 Ch 538	The defendant owned part of a beach and wanted to erect houses on it. Local fishermen sought to stop this by claiming that they had a local customary right to dry their nets on this beach. Witnesses proved that the custom dated back for 70 years at least and reputedly earlier, raising the presumption of antiquity.	The court upheld the customary right and restrained the defendant from building houses on the land.

Key cases

✱✱✱✱✱✱✱✱✱✱

Case	Facts	Ratio/Held
Mills v Colchester Corporation (1866–7) LR 2 CP 476	Local fishermen claimed a customary right to fish for oysters from a particular piece of land. However, the opposing party were able to show that fishing in this area could only be exercised following a successful application for a licence from the landowner.	This meant that the customary practice could only be carried on with permission, and was not available as of right, and on this basis the court refused to enforce this custom.
R v Home Secretary ex p Anderson and Taylor (2001) *The Times*, 27 February	Two convicted murderers sought judicial review of the Home Secretary's decision to increase their 'tariff' sentences beyond those recommended by the trial judge. Their argument was that under the Human Rights Act 1998 their sentences should be set by an independent judge, not by a politician.	The High Court reluctantly dismissed their application, saying that tariff-setting for mandatory life prisoners was not the same as sentencing in all other cases. Had the matter been free of authority, they would have said the 1998 Act applied, but they were bound by the decisions of the House of Lords in *ex p Doody* and of the European Court of Human Rights in *Wynne v UK*.
R v R (Rape: Marital Exemption) [1991] 4 All ER 481	The law on rape within marriage prior to 1991 was based on statements made by state lawyer Sir Matthew Hale from the eighteenth century that 'by marrying a man, a woman consents to sexual intercourse with him and may not retract that consent'. An appeal was made to the House of Lords.	The House of Lords declared that a husband who has sexual intercourse with his wife without her consent may be guilty of rape. Lord Keith felt that Hale's statement 'reflected the social times in which it was written, but that this no longer reflected the status of women and the marriage relationship in modern times' and that the common law should evolve to reflect such changes in society.
R v Secretary of State for Transport ex p Factortame [1990] 2 AC 85	Following the introduction of an EU policy allocating fishing quotas to Member States, the UK became concerned that Spanish fishing boats were registering as British, so that their catches counted against the British quota. The Merchant Shipping Act 1988 was passed, which prevented Spanish trawlers taking such an advantage. Spanish boat owners challenged the Act as in conflict with EU law on the freedom to set up business anywhere in the Community.	The House of Lords agreed. They stated that since s 2(4) European Communities Act 1972 it has 'always been the duty of a United Kingdom court, when delivering judgement, to override any rule of national law found to be in conflict with any directly enforceable rule of Community law'.

Case	Facts	Ratio/Held
Re J [1992] 4 All ER 614	A child, J, of 16 months was severely disabled in several ways; his life expectancy was short, and his doctors took the view that he should not be resuscitated if his breathing were to fail. J's mother sought an order compelling the doctors to give 'all available treatment' to preserve his life.	The Court of Appeal refused to make such an order. Lord Donaldson MR said it would be an abuse of power for the court to order a doctor to carry out treatment which he believed contrary to his duty to his patient. The judge below had treated Lord Donaldson's views in *Re J* [1990] 3 All ER 930 and again in *Re R* [1991] 4 All ER 177 as *obiter dicta*; his Lordship therefore repeated them now and said expressly that they were part of the *ratio* of his present decision.
Warner Bros v Nelson [1936] 3 All ER 160	Nelson, the actress Bette Davis, agreed to give her services exclusively for a certain period to Warner Bros. In addition she agreed that during the period of the agreement she would not give her services to any other person. During that time, however, N contracted to act for another film company.	The court held that an injunction could be issued to prevent the actress from being employed by another film company in breach of her contract of employment with Warner Bros.
Wyld v Silver [1963] 1 QB 169	Local residents claimed that they had a right to hold a fair on particular land, which, therefore, prevented the landowner from building on a particular piece of land. The landowner argued that the right to hold an annual fair had not actually been implemented in recent times.	The court upheld the customary right and prevented the landowner building via an injunction. The court highlighted that the custom need not actually have been exercised continuously since 1189, merely that it should have been possible to exercise the customary right since that date.

Exam questions

Essay question 1

There is no scope within the doctrine of judicial precedent for the judiciary to depart from previous case decisions and create the law.

Assess the validity of this assertion.

An outline answer is available at the end of the book.

Essay question 2

There is no relationship between equity, custom and the common law today. [Anonymous]

Critically evaluate this viewpoint detailing the historical and modern relationship between the above sources of law.

An outline answer is available online at <http://www.oxfordtextbooks.co.uk/orc/concentrate/>.

#4

Civil justice process

- Ninety-seven per cent of all civil cases are settled without a hearing.
- Following the Woolf reforms:
  - most cases have to be commenced in the county court;
  - in the county court, a case is placed on a 'track' usually according to its value:
    - < £5,000 – small claims
    - £5,000–£25,000 – fast track
    - > £25,000 – multi-track
  - parties in civil cases are expected to use ADR (alternative dispute resolution):
    - negotiation
    - mediation
    - conciliation.
- Tribunals are being reformed in accordance with Sir Andrew Leggatt's Report *Tribunals for Users: One System, One Service.*

Introduction

Civil justice involves the settlement of non-criminal disputes often through the courts, although many civil disputes fall to be resolved in **tribunals** or by alternative dispute resolution (ADR). It should be remembered that the majority of cases are of low value (most damage awards in county courts are under £3,000) although some cases in the High Court may concern millions of pounds. Whilst the courts, tribunals, and ADR are separate methods of civil dispute resolution, there is a significant overlap. This is exemplified in the courts' encouragement of ADR even for cases before them. However, many statutes specify that some cases (usually between the individual and the state) have to be heard before a tribunal rather than before the 'normal courts', although there may be an appeal route from the tribunal to the courts. Thus, the various civil dispute resolution mechanisms are both separate and interlinked as shown in Figure 4.1.

This chapter will look at the civil dispute resolution methods through civil litigation, ADR, and finally tribunals.

 ✅ Looking for extra marks?

A good answer will emphasize that ADR offers methods of dispute resolution outside the court system, but the two systems are not wholly isolated from each other. A failed attempt at ADR does not prevent use of the court system; and the courts will enforce arbitration awards.

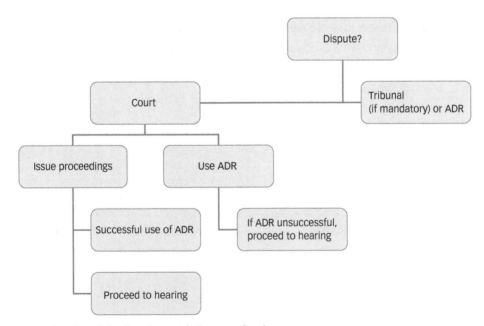

Figure 4.1 Possible dispute resolution mechanisms

Civil litigation – criticisms

Access to justice is accepted as a constitutional right (see *R v Lord Chancellor ex p Witham* [1998]), and in the last decade, civil litigation has undergone a fundamental review that has readdressed both its objectives and the process of litigation. In 1994, Lord Woolf was asked to conduct an inquiry into the civil justice system and make proposals for its modernization. In so doing, he identified civil litigation as being:

- *Costly*: Litigation **costs** could exceed the amount in dispute and so eat into (or eat up) the award. This is particularly so in small cases, eg in 33 per cent of cases costs exceeded amount in dispute – Zander, *The Guardian Gazette*, 25 June 1975. The fear of prohibitive costs (eg after a payment into court) may induce the claimant to accept a low offer.

- *Lengthy*: In many instances, the length of the process may be as a result of matters which may be external to the courts' and parties' control such as:
  - awaiting a medical condition settling
  - problems over evidence and awaiting trial date

  but there was evidence, in some cases, of delay and the lack of promptness by parties as a tactic of intimidation to pressure parties to settle.

- *Complex*: There remains a variation in practices between the **county court** and **High Court**.

- *Uncertainty of outcome*: There is evidence that where a party is unrepresented, or the service is of poor quality, the compensation is usually inadequate.

Access to Justice and the Woolf reforms

Lord Woolf's Final Report *Access to Justice* argued that these factors – cost, length, complexity, and uncertainty – were interrelated and arose from the lawyers' control of litigation. It recommended a number of key reforms (including the overriding objective that the courts deal with cases 'justly' through judicial case management) many of which are implemented by the Civil Procedure Rules (CPR), Practice Directions, Pre-Action Protocols, the Civil Procedure Act 1997, and the Access to Justice Act 1999. CPR 1.1(1) states an objective is that the court deals with cases 'justly', which under CPR 1.2 is to ensure the parties are on equal footing; saving expense; dealing with the case in a manner proportionate to value, importance, complexity, and financial position of each party, fairly and expeditiously; and applying an appropriate share of court's resources.

Revision tip

The Woolf reforms are relevant to discussions about various aspects of the civil litigation process including funding. The reforms regularly feature in English legal system questions.

Introduction
✳✳✳✳✳✳✳✳✳✳

Active case management

One principle was that litigation 'should not be too easy an option'. CPR 1.4 states the objective is to 'actively' manage cases, including encouraging parties to cooperate, early identification of issues, prompt investigation of issues, ordering of resolution of issues, encouraging ADR if appropriate, assisting **settlement**, controlling case progression, value for money evaluations, dealing with matters *in absentia*, using technology, and giving directions for quick and efficient trial.

Lord Woolf's specific key recommendations included:

- the limit for small claims jurisdiction progressively increased to £5,000
- rules to allow cases to be dealt with through different procedures according to the amount of money involved and their complexity
- straightforward cases not exceeding £10,000 (subsequently increased to £25,000) to be put on a fast-track procedure for trial in a short but reasonable time
- a new multi-track for cases above £10,000 (subsequently increased to £25,000) spanning both High Court and county court cases
- empowering the courts to impose and enforce strict timetables (for the completion of the different stages of litigation)
- judicial active management of cases, including case management conferences and pre-trial review
- unified and simpler rules for the county court and High Court
- reduced reliance on adversarial techniques and oral arguments
- fixed and limited costs in some types of cases
- development and application of information technology to manage and track cases
- ensuring that the most complex and important cases are heard only by High Court
- appointment of a senior judge to head the civil justice system.

Other reforms

The Woolf reforms included several other proposals:

- *Costs*: There has been only very limited success in the implementation of rules on fixed and limited costs. There is a regime of fixed costs for pre-trial minor road accidents.
- *Allocation of cases*: The rules allow greater judicial flexibility in moving cases between the tiers of the court.
- *Case management*: Active case management empowers the judiciary to control the litigation. In most cases there will be a judicial case management conference to review the progress of the case and make further orders, eg giving permission for oral evidence or limiting each side to one expert witness. It is also intended to encourage settlement or ADR.
- *IT*: Greater use of information technology for recording and tracking case progression.

One trend is that litigation is often commenced only as a protective step (to satisfy the **limitation periods**) and also to facilitate settlement by negotiation. An evident consequence of the recommendations has been to redistribute cases so that the overwhelming majority of civil cases are now commenced in the county court and the courts are empowered to direct the manner in which the litigation is conducted.

Legal language

To help individuals understand the legal process and to make the system user-friendly, Lord Woolf suggested that archaic language be replaced by plain English, eg:

'Plaintiff' has become 'Claimant'

'Guardian *ad litem*' has become 'Litigation Friend'

'Writ' has become 'Claim Form'

'Leave' has become 'Permission'

'Pleadings' has become 'Statement of Case'

'Interlocutory Relief' has become 'Interim Remedies'

'*Ex parte*' has become 'Without Notice'.

It is unclear whether the simple step of changing the vocabulary has helped non-lawyers to understand the underlying litigation process and concepts.

The civil litigation process

Parties used to have the choice of court (usually the county court or the High Court) in which the case was to be held; but the Woolf reforms removed this choice and most cases are now heard in the county courts. The High Court is now for personal injury cases over £50,000 and other cases where the value of the claim exceeds £25,000. Below these limits, cases are normally started in the county court where they are allocated to one of three tracks (based on the completion of a questionnaire):

Small claims

Jurisdiction:

* for claims up to £5,000 (CPR 26.6)
* for tenant's claims against landlords in relation to defective premises where the cost of repairs do not exceed £1,000 (CPR 26.6).

Procedure:

* relatively informal and simplified
* can be conducted on paper if both parties agree
* **hearing** based on arbitration

Introduction

✳✳✳✳✳✳✳✳✳✳

- no costs order normally made
- disclosure of evidence is limited
- no expert evidence without leave of court
- limited grounds for appeal.

Fast track

Jurisdiction:

- for claims between £5,000 and £25,000 (CPR 26.6(4)).

Procedure:

- pre-trial check-list (CPR 28.5)
- use of standard directions intended to facilitate a swifter and less costly procedure for claims of this size (CPR 28.6)
- time limits:
  - trial date set down within 30 weeks
  - county court hearing normally lasts for one day
  - fixed times for serving defence, disclosing evidence, and enforceable by costs orders
  - limited judicial discretion to extend time limits.
- expert evidence limited to one or two experts per party (CPR 26.6(5))
- a case subsequently found to be of greater value can be reallocated to the multi-track (CPR 26.10).

Multi-track

Jurisdiction:

- all cases over £25,000
- cases of less than £25,000 where the case is too complex or too important to be dealt with on the other two tracks.

Principles of procedure:

- this track will involve more intensive case management
- greater scope for the judicial intervention and imposition of directions as appropriate for fair and efficient disposal of the case
- the procedural judge (which in cases of greater importance and complexity can be a Circuit Judge or a High Court Judge) will:
  - effect scrutiny of all cases in order to allocate them to the appropriate management track

- conduct the case management conference, unless it is more appropriate that the trial judge does so
- monitor the case's progress and take action on parties' failure to comply with timetables or directions
- alert parties to ADR where appropriate and desirable.

Revision tip

Merely reciting all the reforms will not suffice. Questions may ask you to address a specific aspect of the reforms, so be careful to include only what is relevant.

The claim

The injured party (or his solicitor or another person authorized under s 40 Access to Justice Act 1999) starts proceedings by issuing a claim form (CPR Pt 7), with a Statement of Case/Particulars of Claim and a Statement of Truth. These proceedings have to be issued within the relevant limitation period (eg three years for personal injury actions) and served on the defendant within the relevant time limit for service. The CPR require strict observance of time limits for service (as well as issue) although CPR 7.6 does allow the court to grant an extension if service is not possible and the party has promptly asked for an extension. In *Vinos v Marks & Spencer Plc* [2001], the court refused to allow an extension and also refused to exercise its powers under CPR 3.10 to remedy a procedural error. The deemed day of service prevails over actual day of service (CPR 6.7(1)).

....

Godwin v Swindon Borough Council [2001] EWCA Civ 1478

Godwin had to serve a claim by Friday 8 September 2001 and sent it by first-class post on 7 September 2001. The documents were received the following day (Friday) but the CPR 6.7(1) stated that postal service deemed delivery the second day after posting.

The date of service had to be beyond challenge and CPR 6.7(1) was a fiction, but was not rebuttable.

....

Procedural steps

Upon receipt of the proceedings, the defendant may:

- do nothing – the claimant can get summary judgment after 14 days from the service of the particulars of claim
- file an acknowledgement of service
- admit the claim by serving an admission
- admit part of the claim and defend part of the claim
- make an offer

- make a payment into court (at any time: CPR 36.4) – see below for costs rules
- defend the claim by serving a defence
- with or without a defence, assert a counterclaim.

Upon receipt of the defence, the claimant issues a reply addressing all the points raised in the defence. The procedural judge will then allocate proceedings to the appropriate track. Witness statements are then exchanged, and under CPR 31.6, relevant documents are disclosed and may be inspected. Standard disclosure covers the documents that support his case and also those which adversely affect his case or the other party's case.

The importance of costs rules

When the defendant makes a payment into court, the claimant has to decide whether to accept or not. The importance lies in the costs rules.

The usual rule is that a successful party is entitled to have his costs paid by the unsuccessful party but where funds are paid into court this rule is amended:

- if claimant accepts the payment, the action is discontinued and claimant is entitled to costs to date of payment
- if claimant does not accept the payment, the action continues and
    - the claimant is entitled to costs provided amount recovered exceeds payment into court but
    - the defendant is entitled to costs from date of payment into court if amount recovered does not exceed amount paid into court.

This principle confuses the separate issues of liability and **quantum**.

 Looking for extra marks?

Understanding the costs rules will also be relevant to conditional fee agreements (see Chapter 8) and in the discussion of ADR and the courts.

The hearing

Usually the claimant presents the case, with evidence and witnesses whom the defendant has an opportunity to cross-examine. Then the defendant will present the defence (also with evidence and witnesses) together with that for any counterclaim. In each case, the length of the speeches is limited. The burden of proof is upon the claimant and the onus of proof is on the balance of probabilities.

Usually a successful party is entitled to have his costs paid by the unsuccessful party, although this rule may be amended where there has been a payment into court or an unreasonable refusal to attempt ADR (see below).

In January 2010 Lord Jackson published a controversial report critical of the current rules on costs which, for some types of litigation, he found to be 'excessive or disproportionate' and criticized the 'the present system for achieving costs protection for claimants [as] the most bizarre and expensive system that it is possible to devise'. His proposed reforms include:

- retaining CFAs but the success fees becoming capped at 25 per cent and payable by the client

- allowing US style contingency fees (whereby lawyers receive a percentage of no more than 25 per cent of the awarded damages)

- fixed costs on fast-track cases

- ensuring that, though the defendant will continue to be liable for the successful claimant's costs, unsuccessful claimants will not liable for the defendant's costs.

Have the Woolf reforms been effective to give 'access to justice' and deal with cases 'justly'?

The answer depends upon the objective against which it is to be measured, but overall it is unclear. When the Woolf reforms were announced, Professor Zander questioned the cost-effectiveness of the measures, which, he argued, would front-load costs as parties would have to incur more cost before the case came to court. Other criticisms were that judicial time spent reading papers prior to trial can be saved only if the case comes to trial: that time is wasted if the case is settled. Moreover, a saving will be achieved only if the reading judge is the trial judge. As 97 per cent of cases were settled before trial, the savings in those cases coming to trial would be outweighed by the increased costs in the cases settled before trial.

As different cases have different needs they will also progress at different speeds, and may need some delay to allow time to negotiate a settlement. Fenn, Gray, and Rickman (*The Impact of Sources of Finance on Personal Injury Litigation* (2002), available at <http://www.dca.gov.uk/research/2002/7-02es.htm>) suggested that reduced costs could increase delays and management of judicial teams would become more difficult, and it has been observed that there has been inconsistency between judges in their approach to the new rules. It is unclear whether the courts have become more user-friendly as fewer cases have been instituted in the High Court and ADR (mediation) is increasingly used successfully. The Woolf reforms now tend to keep cases out of courts and encourage use of ADR, but this is counterbalanced by the increased number of unrepresented litigants (because of lack of legal aid), and the increased staff and judicial time required to assist them to present cases. It is noted that 'front-loading' of expenses has increased costs but more cases are being settled earlier; and there has been some under-resourcing of information technology. Lord Jackson's report aims to shift the emphasis from costs to the merits of the case.

Limitations on rights of appeal

To reduce the workload of the higher courts, the appeal process was reformed by Access to Justice Act 1999 (following the Bowman Report 1996) which removed the automatic right to appeal to the Court of Appeal and imposed the requirement of permission to appeal to the Court of Appeal. Now two judges may hear the case in the Court of Appeal and there is a requirement of written skeleton arguments prior to the hearing date.

Key issues in civil litigation

The fundamental question is 'what are the functions of the system?' which reflects a nervous tension between the concept of 'access to justice' and the damaging nature of litigation. The civil litigation process involves the consideration and balancing of some of the most fundamental legal issues:

- The need to provide a workable civil justice system whilst discouraging claims in the courts, ie should civil litigation only be a last resort?
- A reduction in the barriers to 'access to justice' could increase the number of contested cases.
- Should litigation be a private or public process, ie should the state provide the facilities (court, judge, etc) free of charge at point of delivery but restrict the resources to be allocated to it or should it be self-funded and responsive to demand?
  - Many civil cases are private in nature and have a limited impact with the outcome of placing parties in the position they occupied before the cause of action. Where cases are against the Government, then they have a public quality and can involve 'punitive' measures, so clear categorization is difficult.
  - Given that it is the parties who decide to initiate proceedings, should it not be the parties who decide the speed and manner of those proceedings? The effective management of cases through the imposition of time limits against the wishes of both sides indicates the public character of the civil litigation process.
- During the 1990s, court fees were increased to make the courts self-funding, but the allocation of restricted resources or fees for access to the courts may be at odds with Lord Woolf's principle of dealing with cases 'justly'.
- A single litigation process may not be appropriate:
  - The litigation process has to fulfil a number of different functions: simple debt collection cases need to be quickly resolved whereas more time needs to be available for the more complex cases.
  - In cases that are more complex, speed may inhibit the effective preparation and presentation of cases and thereby damage the litigation process.
- Litigants are being encouraged to use ADR, but where settlement cannot be achieved then there needs to be a litigation system that is cheap and efficient.
- Whilst making litigation expensive can encourage parties to resolve the dispute out of court, expensive litigation creates the risk that, through fear of cost, a weak party

may be pressured into accepting an out-of-court settlement considerably below the real value of the claim.

• The indications are that the main reason for not taking action is a lack of funding (ie legal aid) and the main group not taking action is those who had low education and incomes.

Revision Tip

Questions on the civil litigation process will usually invite you to consider a wide variety of issues, legal, social, moral, and even philosophical.

ADR and tribunals

Not all disputes are resolved by the courts. In many cases, the disputing parties can try to settle the dispute by other means – ADR (typically negotiation, mediation, conciliation, and arbitration). A dispute between an individual and the state may often be heard by a tribunal.

Alternative dispute resolution

ADR is the voluntary resolution of a dispute without recourse to the courts and so avoiding adversarial hearings. Its attraction lies in its difference from resolution of disputes through the ordinary court system. ADR aims to save time and to avoid much of the costs and stress of normal court proceedings, and can be particularly advantageous if the case involves highly technical points. It is seen as being cheaper and does not necessarily require lawyers. In contrast to the courts' adversarial process, the tribunal process is usually inquisitorial and may be in private, thereby being particularly attractive to businesses. Furthermore, ADR can provide a proportionate response, ie a flexible, tailor-made solution.

In ADR, an impartial third party assists in achieving a resolution of the problem by negotiation, mediation, conciliation, or arbitration as shown below. In *Halsey v Milton Keynes General NHS Trust* [2004], the court confirmed that it could encourage, but *not require*, litigants to use ADR. See key cases.

Negotiation

This is the process of trying to resolve the dispute by negotiation (ie a dialogue between the parties, either personally or through lawyers). Negotiation has the advantage of privacy and frequently continues even after proceedings have been issued – as evidenced by the high number of proceedings settled before hearing (although sometimes only on the day of the hearing).

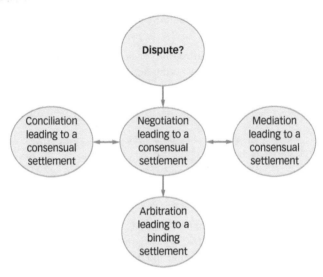

Figure 4.2

Mediation

In mediation, a third party attempts to help the disputing parties to reach a settlement, eg by acting as a go-between, clarifying the parties' views. The mediator initially sees both parties jointly to explore common ground and then moves between the parties in separate rooms. However, the mediator is not an active participant: he will not offer an opinion on the merits of the respective parties' cases. In contrast to the adversarial process, mediation is consensual, and, consequently, any outcome is consensual. As parties to mediation are open to resolving the dispute, the dispute is more likely to be resolved. The outcomes are non-binding and may be more an application of commercial sense rather than strictly in accordance with law; but, in practice, parties who have agreed outcomes will willingly implement them.

Where the dispute is not resolved, the mediation can clarify issues for the subsequent court hearing. The Centre for Effective Dispute Resolution in London claims an 80 per cent success rate for mediation.

Conciliation

Conciliation is similar to mediation in that any outcome is consensual, and where the dispute is not resolved, it may clarify issues for the court hearing. However, it differs from mediation in that the third party actively intervenes to help parties reach a settlement, eg by suggesting steps forward/options and the possible basis of a settlement. As parties to conciliation are open to resolving the dispute, the dispute is more likely to be resolved.

A less common variation of conciliation is a formal settlement conference – in effect a mini-trial before representatives of each party and a neutral third party.

Arbitration

Arbitration can result from a clause incorporated into a contract, the terms of a standard form contract, a trade association arbitration scheme (eg ABTA), or by subsequent agreement of the parties, eg after the dispute has arisen. The parties choose the arbitrator or have a procedure for appointment in the event of a dispute, and submit to the arbitrator brief written submissions unless there is a full hearing with legal representatives, evidence, and witnesses. In *Northern Regional Health Authority v Derek Crouch Construction Ltd* [1984], Sir John Donaldson described arbitration as 'litigation in the private sector'. Arbitration is useful in commercial disputes, particularly as the dispute resolution is in private, but has proved less popular in small private disputes. Its advantages include:

- flexibility
- parties' consensus
- privacy
- lower costs
- enforceable award (in contrast to mediation and conciliation outcomes)
- the parties' right to choose:
    - their own arbitrator (and ensure that the arbitrator has appropriate technical knowledge)
    - the time and location of any hearing; flexibility and suitability of the procedure (subject to the protection of the Human Rights Act 1998 and Article 6 European Convention on Human Rights).

However, arbitration does have disadvantages: the risk of an error of law by an arbitrator who is not legally qualified; cost of a professionally qualified arbitrator; costs of a formal hearing with witnesses; and delay in arranging hearing days. Moreover, under the Arbitration Act 1996, the rights of appeal and challenges are very limited (usually only on serious irregularity or point of law).

ADR in the courts

ADR has always enjoyed judicial support and the courts will uphold a contractual clause requiring ADR to be attempted. In *Scott v Avery* (1856), the court stayed an action in contract to uphold a clause requiring disputes under the contract to be referred to arbitration; see also *Cable & Wireless plc v IBM* [2002]. In addition, the courts and tribunals use ADR. Mandatory arbitration is commonly used in the small claims court, where it has proved successful although the court has no power to award costs in favour of the successful claimant (which can disadvantage the individual against large well-funded organizations). In addition, claims filed with the Employment Tribunal are referred to the Advisory, Conciliation and Arbitration Service in an attempt to use ADR to achieve a settlement of the claim before the tribunal hearing. The Woolf reforms encouraged the use of ADR as an alternative to 'normal' litigation, and case management includes encouraging parties to use ADR through costs sanctions – *Halsey v Milton Keynes General NHS Trust* [2004].

ADR should be attempted even where one party is a public authority – *R (Cowl) v Plymouth City Council* [2001] – and even before the issuing of proceedings – *Burchell v Ballard* [2005]. See key cases.

....

Dunnett v Railtrack plc [2002] EWCA Civ 303

Railtrack resisted a claim by Dunnett and asked for costs. In the earlier proceedings the judge had advised Dunnett to use ADR but Railtrack had rejected the suggestion.

The Court of Appeal denied the successful party its costs because of its unreasonable refusal to agree to ADR.

....

Evaluation of ADR

ADR may be a statutory or procedural requirement, but compulsory mediation in divorce has been postponed in view of the need for professional representation. Its principal advantages include informality and avoidance of the problems and delays of the civil courts. Ironically, its disadvantages include a lack of a system of precedent, and difficulty of enforcement – which are found in the courts. However, as in the courts, an imbalance of power can still undermine a fair outcome allowing a well-funded litigant to pay for professional representation against the unrepresented claimant who may thus be intimidated into settling a case.

Revision tip

Be careful to distinguish conciliation from mediation and note that they are not usually binding whereas arbitration is binding.

Tribunals

Administrative tribunals are an alternative to the courts and mandatory for certain disputes. Tribunals are established by Act of Parliament to provide a cheaper, faster, and less formal process for determining statutory rights and challenging official decisions taken by administrators or others, eg on entitlement to welfare benefits, tax, and discrimination, without increasing the volume of cases in the courts. Therefore, applicants cannot use the courts – they must use the tribunal specified. In effect, tribunals constitute an administrative justice system (ie for administrative law) concurrently with, but not – at least as yet – as a wholly integrated part of, the courts' system. In 1979, the Benson Commission on Legal Services reported that tribunals heard six times more cases than courts, but this masks an imbalance: eg the Special Commissioners for Income Tax heard about a hundred cases annually in contrast to 84,000 heard by the Immigration Adjudicators.

Proliferation

Tribunals have proliferated greatly since the Second World War and have now become very important and extensive, eg covering asylum and immigration matters that can determine whether an individual be returned to their state of origin. Prior to the implementation of the Tribunals, Courts and Enforcement Act 2007, there is no single model for tribunals and they vary widely. Under that Act tribunals usually comprise a first tier (dealing with most cases at first instance) and an appellate upper tier; and they comprise a legally trained chairman and two non-legal members with relevant specialist knowledge.

Tribunals exercise a great variety of jurisdiction reflecting in part the complexities of the modern relationship of citizen and state. Sir Andrew Leggatt's report *Tribunals for Users* (upon which the 2007 Act is based) was predicated upon the principle of lay self-representation. Thus the tribunal rules encourage parties to represent themselves, without professional legal representation, but the lack of professional representation effectively displaces the adversarial system and necessitates an inquisitorial approach. Applicants are encouraged to present their own cases in their own words. Both parties are given a chance to put their case, and tribunals have procedures and rules that are more flexible than those in the courts (so, members of a tribunal will often ask questions of the parties), all of which allow applicants to feel that they have had a 'fair hearing'. Legal aid is not usually available.

Advantages and disadvantages

Tribunals are seen to have several significant advantages, although those advantages can also be disadvantages. They are acknowledged as being cost-effective. The lack of legal aid encourages applicants to represent themselves, ie without professional legal representation, and tribunals rarely make an order for costs. The consequence is that an applicant does not risk incurring expenses if unsuccessful. However, an unrepresented applicant is less likely to be successful in either winning a case or in securing higher payments (Hazel Genn and Yvette Genn, *The Effectiveness of Representation at Tribunals* (HMSO, 1989)).

Originally, tribunals were seen as offering swifter decision-making, but many tribunals became burdened with delays due to the combination of the increased volume of cases and the use of part-time lay members. Moreover until fairly recently, tribunals used simple procedures without formal rules of evidence and held hearings in private which created a lack of coherence between tribunals, an apparently unstructured approach, and confusion for unrepresented applicants: these factors combined with the complexity of the subject matter did not make tribunals user-friendly. Moreover, although most hearings came to be heard in public and most tribunals started to give consistent decisions, there was no proper system of precedent except in Employment Tribunals. Under s 10 Tribunals and Inquiries Act 1992 reasons had to be given, but usually only if requested. Tribunal chairmen were expected to assist an unrepresented applicant to present his case by adopting an inquisitorial approach, but this is not universally done (J Baldwin, N Wikeley, and R Young, *Judging Social Security* (Oxford University Press, 1992)).

ADR and tribunals

Until recently, the structure of the tribunal system was fragmented and inconsistent. At one time, tribunal chairmen were often appointed by the sponsoring department, which gave rise to the criticism of a lack of impartiality. Following the recommendations of the Franks Committee in 1957, the Council on Tribunals recommended potential chairmen. In some tribunals, there were lay members with specialist knowledge in fields other than legal and awareness of the legislative policy relevant to the cases before them; but other tribunals have specialist members. Nevertheless, the flexibility, cost, and speed produced inconsistent, hurried decisions.

Controlling tribunals

The courts exercised control in the appeals system in two ways. First, the Act of Parliament establishing each tribunal did not always allow for an appeal, but the Tribunals and Inquiries Act 1992 provided for an appeal on points of law from most tribunals. In some cases the appeal was initially to the High Court (eg the Special Commissioners of Income Tax), and in other cases to an appeal tribunal (eg the Employment Appeal Tribunal); and, in both cases, thereafter, with permission, to the Court of Appeal. This ensured some consistency through the application of judicial precedent.

Secondly, tribunals were inferior to the courts (see *Peach Grey & Co v Sommers* [1995] in the key cases) and were subject to **judicial review** whereby the courts exercised supervisory jurisdiction over tribunals to ensure the proper conduct of hearings, eg a breach of natural justice such as bias. This differs from an appeal as the court (the Queen's Bench Division) could not substitute its own decision for that of the tribunal: normally it would quash the tribunal's decision and order a rehearing.

In addition, the Council on Tribunals established by the Tribunals and Inquiries Act 1958 supervised and reviewed the work of tribunals. Its members were appointed by the Minister for Constitutional Affairs. It issued an annual report of its work (as recommended by the Franks Report) commenting on the operation of the tribunals (against the Franks criteria of openness, fairness, impartiality, accessibility, cost-effectiveness, user-focus, organization and resourcing, and responsiveness to the needs of all sections of society. However, it had no powers of enforcement.

The Leggatt Report 2001

Sir Andrew Leggatt was tasked with producing a report to provide a more coherent development of tribunals and to reflect the Human Rights Act 1998 and the need to ensure compliance with the ECHR, eg independent and impartial. The result was *Tribunals for Users: One System, One Service*.

In 2003, some of the most important tribunals (eg the Mental Health Review Tribunal and the Tax Tribunals) were brought together within the Tribunals Service with other tribunals joining later.

The Leggatt Report had noted that some tribunals were becoming less user-friendly – individuals appearing before a tribunal found the experience daunting. So it sought to redress this through greater accessibility and making tribunals more accessible to users by encouraging individuals to present a case without professional representation; better provision of information to users; and a change in culture to prioritize informality, simplicity, efficiency, and proportionality.

To avoid a conflict of interest and evidence and to allow independence from the sponsoring departments (ie those responsible for the policies and decisions under challenge), the 2007 Act established a Unified Tribunals Service administered by the Department for Constitutional Affairs (Ministry of Justice) so as to be independent of the relevant government departments, and headed by a Senior President (a High Court judge). The advantages of such a structure include: efficiency, coherence, independence from departments, improved procedure (including case management), and simpler appeals system to an appellate tribunal (and then onwards to Court of Appeal), all of which will facilitate user participation.

Within that single Tribunal Service, cognate tribunals have been allocated to a Division, thereby minimizing duplication of efforts and facilitating common processes and standards, eg exchange of evidence prior to the hearing. In addition, there is a single set of procedural rules and a route of appeal, with permission, on point of law, to the appellate (second) tier, and therefrom, again with permission, to the Court of Appeal.

Leggatt also recommended that lay (ie not legally qualified) members should sit on a panel only if they fulfilled a specific function. Other provisions include an Administrative Justice Council to replace the Council on Tribunals, and a Tribunals Board to advise the Department for Constitutional Affairs on qualifications, supervise the appointment procedures, and train chairmen and panel members to ensure that the panel members are independent of the relevant departments.

Domestic tribunals

Some private bodies and professional associations also have domestic tribunals, eg to determine whether there has been a breach of the rules. These tribunals fall outside the 2007 Act but do have to apply natural justice, and are subject to judicial review. In some cases there may be an appeal to the Judicial Committee of the Privy Council (eg from the Disciplinary Committee of the General Medical Council).

 Key cases

Case	Facts	Ratio/Held
Burchell v Ballard [2005] EWCA Civ 358	The complexity of this case escalated and in the final judgment, there was no clear 'winner'. The householder was ordered to pay the builder's costs of the claim and the builder to pay the householder's costs of the counterclaim.	ADR was ideal for small building disputes and the householder had behaved unreasonably by refusing ADR, which would have cost less than court proceedings. However, the court would not impose a costs sanction for unreasonable failure to use ADR as this had occurred before the *Halsey* case.
Cable & Wireless plc v IBM [2002] EWHC 2059	The contractual terms permitted ADR without preventing court proceedings but Cable & Wireless argued that this was unenforceable for lack of certainty.	The court found that the parties had agreed in the contract to an enforceable obligation to participate in ADR procedures. Thus, the dispute should be referred to ADR and court proceedings should not be commenced.
Dunnett v Railtrack plc [2002] EWCA Civ 303	Railtrack resisted a claim by Dunnett and asked for costs. In the earlier proceedings the judge had advised Dunnett to use ADR but Railtrack had rejected the suggestion.	If a party rejected ADR when a court had suggested it, that party would suffer consequences in awarding costs.
Halsey v Milton Keynes General NHS Trust [2004] EWCA 576	Halsey had unsuccessfully claimed against the hospital for negligent treatment of her husband whilst in hospital. The hospital had refused Halsey's wish to take part in ADR.	The hospital had been reasonable to refuse ADR as the costs of mediation would have been disproportionately high compared with the claim's value and mediation had not been shown to have a reasonable prospect of success.
Peach Grey & Co v Sommers [1995] 2 All ER 513	An application was made to the High Court to prevent Sommers from interfering with a witness in an Industrial (now Employment) Tribunal claim.	Sommers was guilty of a contempt of court and the High Court had jurisdiction because the tribunal was an inferior court.
R (Cowl) v Plymouth City Council [2001] EWCA 1935	Cowl sought to quash the council's decision to close his residential home and order the council to follow government guidelines before a decision was made.	This was not a dispute that was amenable to judicial review but the parties should have used ADR and not made an application to the courts.

Case	Facts	Ratio/Held
Vinos v Marks & Spencer Plc [2001] 3 All ER 784	Claimant's solicitors had issued a claim form in the county court within the limitation period and stated that full particulars of claim would be soon filed.	CPR 7.6(3) allowed extensions of time only in specific circumstances and so there was no general discretion to allow an extension on any other basis.

Exam questions

Essay question 1

Critically evaluate the role of ADR in the litigation process.

An outline answer is available at the end of the book.

Essay question 2

Does the civil justice system provide access to justice?

An outline answer is available online at <www.oxfordtextbooks.co.uk/orc/concentrate/>.

#5
The criminal justice system

- Herbert Packer identified two opposing models for criminal justice systems: due process and crime control. Each model had different objectives, one designed to protect the innocent from wrongful conviction, the other to maximize convictions even at the potential expense of convicting the innocent. He believed criminal justice systems in the world fell somewhere between these two.

- The police are primarily responsible for detecting and investigating crime within England and Wales. Other agencies can investigate crime, eg the Serious Organised Crime Agency, etc.

- The police have a range of powers regulated primarily by the Police and Criminal Evidence Act 1984 such as stop and search, arrest, detention, and interrogation. Safeguards are contained within the Act and within the Codes of Practice created under the Act, eg reasonable suspicion, etc.

- The decision to prosecute, following investigation of a crime, was originally undertaken by the police, who would hire lawyers to take cases to the court system on their behalf. However, because of the high number of cases being discontinued by the courts, due to lack of evidence, etc, a new agency was created, the Crown Prosecution Service (CPS). The agency would independently review the decision to prosecute by the police.

- The CPS is now responsible for undertaking the initial decision to prosecute, and actually prosecutes cases, within the criminal court system, through its teams of Associated

Prosecutors, Crown Prosecutors, and Higher Court Advocates. The service uses two tests to determine whether a prosecution should take place: evidential and public interest tests. A prosecution can be discontinued at any time if the tests are no longer satisfied.

- The location of any trial is determined on the basis of the seriousness of the offence that is alleged to have been committed by the defendant. Summary offences are minor criminal offences and can only be tried in the magistrates' court. Hybrid offences can be tried in either the magistrates' court or the Crown Court; at present, the defendant has a choice of venue. Indictable offences are the most serious form of criminal offence and can only be tried in the Crown Court before judge and jury.

- The basic process within the courts, irrespective of location, is that the charges will be read out and the defendant will be asked to plead. The prosecution will then present their case, providing their witnesses to the court, whom they will question – a process known as examination in chief. These witnesses are cross-examined by the defence. Once the prosecution have made their case, the defence can ask the court to discontinue the case on the basis that there is no case to answer.

- If the court denies the request of no case to answer, the defence then present their witnesses and question them – a process known as examination in chief. These witnesses can be cross-examined by the prosecution.

- Each side will summarize the main points of the case and then, in the case of the Crown Court, the judge will summarize the evidence and points of law for the jury, who will retire and reach a verdict. Once a verdict is reached, if guilty, the jury is dismissed and the judge will determine sentence. In the magistrates' court, the magistrates will retire at this stage to reach a verdict; if they find the defendant guilty they will proceed to sentencing.

Investigation and detection

Herbert Packer identified two opposing models for criminal justice systems (*The Limits of the Criminal Sanction* (Stanford University Press, 1968)):

- *Due process*: This gives priority to fairness of procedure and to protecting the innocent from wrongful conviction. Such a system would accept that a high level of protection for suspects makes it more difficult to convict the guilty and that some guilty people will go free.
- *Crime control*: This gives priority to convicting the guilty with minimal or non-existent measures/safeguards to protect the innocent from wrongful conviction.

Criminal justice systems need to strike a balance between punishing the guilty and protecting the innocent. Any system needs safeguards, which prevent the innocent being found guilty, but those safeguards must not make it impossible to convict those who are guilty. The police have claimed that the balance has tipped too far in favour of suspects' rights at the expense of convicting the guilty. Civil liberties groups argue that the system has not learned from past miscarriages of justice such as the Guildford Four and the Birmingham Six, and that protections for suspects are inadequate.

The aims of the criminal justice system are to:

- detect and convict
- avoid convicting the innocent
- regulate the process without impeding it
- maintain public confidence in the system
- achieve a balance between justice and efficiency.

Revision tip

It is essential that you support the information you give in a problem scenario or essay-based question with legal authority, eg cases and statutory provisions. If, for instance, you are writing an answer on police powers, you can abbreviate statutes in order to save excessive repetition and wasting time writing the full name of a statute. For instance, at the start of your essay write the name of the statute out in full, eg Police and Criminal Evidence Act 1984, then in brackets next to the full name write the chosen abbreviation for the Act, eg PACE. You can then refer to the Act using the abbreviation.

Police organization

Rather than having one national police force, the UK has 43 police forces. These are independent locally run police forces, designed to forge links between the police and local communities.

Working alongside police officers are Community Support Officers (CSOs), civilians employed by police authorities per the Police Reform Act 2002. Their powers include the ability to:

- issue fixed penalty notices for anti-social behaviour
- carry out searches and road checks
- stop and detain school truants
- deprive an individual of their liberty for up to 30 minutes until a police officer arrives, where the suspect fails to provide his name and address or it is reasonably suspected that the details provided are inaccurate.

The Serious Organised Crime and Police Act 2005 created a national investigation agency, the Serious Organised Crime Agency, to tackle the heads of organized crime who undertake illegal enterprises such as drug trafficking, paedophile rings, and people-smuggling. A specialist team of prosecutors helps the organization secure convictions. It has a national team of investigators who have more powers than ordinary police officers.

The main agency responsible for the detection and investigation of crime is the police, whose powers are primarily regulated by the Police and Criminal Evidence Act 1984 (PACE). The **Royal Commission** on Criminal Procedure (Phillips Commission) (Cmnd 8092, London: HMSO) was set up by the Labour Government following a series of miscarriages of justice. These highlighted the need to examine police procedures. The Commission concluded in 1981 that a balance needed to be struck between the:

> interests of the community in bringing offenders to justice and the rights and liberties of persons suspected of crime.

It recommended the creation of a single statute to regulate police powers and to replace a confusing mixture of common law, legislation, and local by-laws. The resulting Act covered such powers as:

- stop
- search
- arrest
- detention and interrogation.

The Act stipulated safeguards for suspects in relation to the operation of police powers. The Act has been extended/modified by subsequent legislation such as the Criminal Justice and Public Order Act 1994.

Codes of Practice are drawn up by the Home Office under s 66 PACE. These do not form part of the law but provide details on procedural requirements. Breach of the Codes can give rise to disciplinary procedures and may result in evidence obtained being excluded at trial.

In an exam always ensure that when you are looking at police powers you provide the correct section for the police power that you are highlighting. If discussing the issue of stop and search (see below) be sure to define how a concept such as reasonable suspicion applies.

Informal questioning and stop and search

Officers can ask members of the public questions in order to prevent and detect crime, but members of the public can refuse to answer such questions. However, there is a fine line between refusing to answer questions and the offence of obstructing an officer in the execution of their duty.

....

Ricketts v Cox (1982) 74 Cr App R 298

Two officers were looking for youths responsible for a serious assault. They approached the defendant in the early hours of the morning. The defendant was said to have been abusive, uncooperative, and used obscene language designed to provoke and antagonize the officers. The magistrates found that the police acted in a proper manner and were entitled to put questions to the defendant, and his behaviour and attitude amounted to an obstruction of the police officers in the execution of their duty. Appeal dismissed.

....

Section 1 PACE states an officer may search a person or vehicles in public for stolen or prohibited articles, eg offensive weapons, tools used in connection with burglary, articles intended to cause criminal damage, etc. Under s 1(3), the power can only be used where the officer has 'reasonable grounds for suspecting that they will find stolen or prohibited articles', a safeguard to protect the public from random searches:

- Officers must identify themselves and the station where they are based and the grounds for the search per s 2(3).
- Clothing cannot be removed in public, except for an outer coat, jacket or gloves per s 2(9).
- The officer must make a written record of the search. A copy must be given to the person searched. The record will state why the person was stopped and the outcome.

Any stolen or prohibited articles found can be seized per s 1(6). Reasonable force may be used under s 117 to undertake the search.

There must be actual suspicion on the part of the officer and there must be objectively reasonable grounds for that suspicion. It was stated in *Castonia v Chief Constable of Surrey* (1988) that this amounted to 'honest belief founded upon reasonable suspicion leading an ordinary cautious man to suspect that the person arrested was guilty of an offence'. **Code of Practice A** states in relation to stop and search:

that powers of stop and search must be used…with respect for people being searched and without unlawful discrimination…on the grounds of race, colour, ethnic origin, nationality or national origins.

Code of Practice A states 'reasonable suspicion':

> depends on the circumstances in each case. There must be an objective basis for that suspicion based on facts, information, and/or intelligence which are relevant to the likelihood of finding an article of a certain kind…and can never be supported on the basis of personal factors…race, age, appearance, previous convictions cannot be used…as the reason for searching that person. [It] cannot be based on generalisations or stereotypical images of certain groups or categories of people and can [stem] from the behaviour of a person an officer encounters on the street at night who is trying to hide something.

Further police powers of stop and/or search can be found in, *inter alia*:

- s 23 Misuse of Drugs Act 1971
- s 60 Criminal Justice and Public Order Act 1994
- s 65 Criminal Justice and Public Order Act 1994
- s 71 Criminal Justice and Public Order Act 1994
- s 44 Anti Terrorism, Crime and Security Act 2001.

✅ Looking for extra marks?

If you are asked to criticize the issue of police powers, remember that there are some statutes which provide the police with powers of stop and search which can be authorized in certain situations where the normal safeguards such as reasonable suspicion on the part of a police officer are not necessary. You may want to comment on the problems that this may cause, for instance damage to police relationship with community and certain ethnic groups.

Arrest

In *Spicer v Holt* (1977) Lord Dilhorne stated:

> whether or not a person has been arrested depends not upon the legality of the arrest, but on whether or not he has been deprived of his liberty to go where he pleases.

An arrest can be made with or without a warrant. Under s 1 Magistrates Court Act 1980 the police can apply for an arrest warrant to be issued by the magistrates' court. Such a request is made in writing, with oral statements made by the police officer, under oath. Reasonable force can be used to make an arrest per s 117 PACE and an officer can enter any premises to make the arrest.

Under s 24 an officer can arrest a person without a warrant, to detain a person against their will, if they reasonably suspect that a person has committed, is committing, or is about to commit an offence and have reasonable grounds for believing that it is necessary to arrest that person:

- to prevent the person disappearing

- to allow the prompt and effective investigation of the offence or of the conduct of the person in question
- to protect a child or vulnerable person
- to prevent the person from causing physical injury to himself or another, causing loss or damage to property, committing an offence against public decency, or obstructing the highway
- because they will not give their name and address, or the officer reasonably suspects that the name or address given is false.

At the time of the arrest the officer must inform the person arrested that they are under arrest and the grounds for the arrest per s 28. They may conduct a search under s 32 if there are reasonable grounds for believing that the suspect is in possession of evidence or anything that may assist their escape or present a danger.

Under s 24A PACE members of the public have a power of arrest provided that they have a reasonable belief that the individual arrested has committed an indictable offence and where 'it is not reasonably practicable for a police officer' to make an arrest. This is more commonly known as a citizen's arrest.

Police detention and questioning

An arrested person must be taken to a designated police station, one with detention facilities, after the arrest per s 30. They should be taken to the **custody officer** who decides whether sufficient evidence exists to charge the person. If on arrest there is already sufficient evidence to charge the suspect, they must be charged and then released on bail unless there are reasons why this is not appropriate per s 38(1). A person who has been charged and is being held in custody must be brought before the magistrates' court as soon as practicable, and not later than the first sitting after being charged per s 46. The custody officer, in relation to the suspect in their care, must complete a custody record. The suspect should be provided with a copy of the Codes of Practice and informed of their rights whilst in police custody:

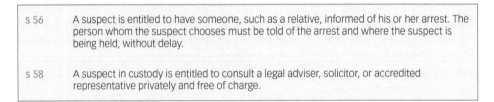

s 56	A suspect is entitled to have someone, such as a relative, informed of his or her arrest. The person whom the suspect chooses must be told of the arrest and where the suspect is being held, without delay.
s 58	A suspect in custody is entitled to consult a legal adviser, solicitor, or accredited representative privately and free of charge.

These rights may be suspended for up to 36 hours if detention is in connection with an indictable offence, and the authorizing officer reasonably believes that this would lead to:

- interference with, or harm to, evidence connected with a serious arrestable offence

* alerting of other suspects

* interference with or injury to others

* hindrance in recovering any property or profits gained as a result of a serious arrestable offence or in drug trafficking offences.

If there is insufficient evidence to charge the suspect, then the person can be detained for questioning per s 37. The usual reason for detaining a suspect is so that the police can question them in the hope of obtaining a confession. Confessions are seen by judges and juries as reliable evidence of guilt. Many miscarriages of justice have centred on the obtaining of confession evidence. A custody officer should assess whether there are grounds for continued detention after the first six hours and then at intervals of not more than nine hours per s 40. The police can detain a person for up to 36 hours from the time of arrival at the police station after which they must charge or release the suspect per s 41. Detention can be extended for a further 12 hours if the detention is necessary to secure or preserve evidence and the offence is an indictable offence. Detention up to 96 hours is possible but approval must be sought from the magistrates' court.

Under the Codes of Practice interview rooms must be adequately lit, heated, and ventilated, and suspects must be allowed to sit during questioning and given adequate breaks for refreshments and sleep. A person must be cautioned on arrest and before questioning in relation to any involvement in an offence:

> You do not have to say anything, but it may harm your defence if you do not mention when questioned anything which you later rely on in court. Anything that you do say may be given in evidence.

The caution takes into account changes made by the Criminal Justice and Public Order Act 1994. It provides the following situations in which, if the suspect chooses not to speak, at trial the court will be entitled to draw inferences from that silence:

s 34	When questioned under caution or charge fails to mention facts which they later rely on as part of their defence and which it is reasonable to expect them to have mentioned.
s 35	Are silent during the trial, including choosing not to give evidence or to answer any question without good cause.
s 36	Following arrest fail to account for objects, substances, or marks on clothing when requested to do so.
s 37	Following arrest, fail to account for their presence at a particular place when requested to do so.

In order to detect oppressive treatment, threats being used during interviews and the fabrication of confessions, s 60 states that interviews must be tape-recorded. After the interview the officers must make a record of it, which is kept on file.

Search at the police station

s 54	This provides the police with the power to search arrested persons on arrival at the designated police station and to seize anything which they reasonably suspect might be used to injure anyone, make an escape from custody, or be evidence of an offence, or have been obtained as a result of an offence.
s 55	This provides the police with the power to conduct intimate searches of suspects' bodily orifices. The search must be authorized by a superintendent, who must have reasonable grounds for believing that a weapon or drug is concealed and must be carried out by a registered medical practitioner.
ss 27 and 61	This allows the police to take fingerprints from a suspect.
s 62	This permits the police to take intimate samples from the suspect, *inter alia* blood, saliva, semen.
s 63	This permits the police to take non-intimate samples, *inter alia* hair, nail clippings.

Exclusion of evidence

A confession must not be obtained by oppression. Section 76(8) defines oppression as torture, inhuman or degrading treatment, or the use or threat of violence. Where a confession has been improperly obtained the courts may refuse to admit evidence per s 76. Section 78 provides that the court can refuse to hear evidence if it appears to the court that the admission of such evidence would have such an adverse effect on the fairness of the proceedings that the court ought not to admit it. These provisions have been utilized to render evidence **inadmissible** where the police have breached PACE and/or its Codes of Practice. To consider whether evidence is admissible a **voir dire** hearing will be held by the court.

Police disposal options

Section 37 PACE states that where someone is being investigated by the police after arrest they may take one of four actions:

1. release the suspect without charge and on bail for the purpose of enabling the CPS to decide whether to prosecute
2. release the suspect on bail but not for the purpose of enabling the CPS to decide whether to prosecute, ie to permit further investigations to be made
3. release without charge and without bail
4. charge.

The custody sergeant has the sole responsibility in deciding which option to take per s 37(7A) PACE. Previous practice had been for the police to decide whether to charge a defendant and then send the file to the CPS to proceed with the prosecution. Section 28 Criminal Justice Act 2003 has moved the decision to charge from the police to the CPS. The police only retain the right to charge for certain minor offences.

Revision tip

Use various methods to review the material in this section; key cards, wall charts, etc. Remember that when preparing revision aids you are still in fact revising the material. You have to read the material, determine what is relevant, and then actually write the revision aids. Though this may appear a time-consuming process this is still time well spent in the long run.

Decision to prosecute and charge

Not every criminal offence committed leads to a prosecution. Many crimes are never reported to the police. Even where detection and investigation have identified a criminal perpetrator the offender may be cautioned rather than be the subject of a prosecution. There is substantial discretion involved within the prosecution process. The **Attorney General**, Hartley Shawcross, stated (*House of Commons Debates*, vol 483, col 681, 29 January 1951):

It has never been the rule in this country and I hope it never will be, that suspected criminal offences must automatically be the subject of prosecution.

The agency responsible for prosecuting 80 per cent of crimes is the **Crown Prosecution Service** (CPS). According to the Code for Crown Prosecutors paragraph 1.1, 'The…CPS is the *principal* prosecution service for England and Wales.' Since January 2010 the Revenue and Customs Prosecution Office has merged with the CPS. However, criminal offences can also be prosecuted by, eg:

- Health and Safety Executive
- Pollution Inspectorate
- local authorities.

Many of these agencies will only initiate a prosecution as a matter of last resort. They will usually seek to use other administrative mechanisms in order to avoid a prosecution.

Private prosecutions

English law is founded on the basis that private citizens may launch a prosecution – a private prosecution. In *Gouriet v Union of Post Office Workers* [1978] Lord Diplock argued that the private prosecution was an important constitutional safeguard 'against capricious corrupt or biased failure or refusal of those authorities to prosecute offenders'.

✳✳✳✳✳✳✳✳✳

Section 6(1) Prosecution of Offences Act 1985 (POCA 1985) preserves private prosecutions. The DPP has the right to take over prosecutions per s 6(2):

- to prosecute the offender rather than require the private individual to do so
- to discontinue a prosecution per s 23.

....

Hayter v L [1998] 1 WLR 854

Two boys assaulted another boy and caused him actual bodily harm. After investigations the police cautioned the defendants but decided not to prosecute. The victim's father brought a private prosecution, but the magistrates dismissed the case as an abuse of process. The High Court allowed the appeal by way of case stated and remitted the case for rehearing by a new Bench. Thus, the right of private prosecution was preserved by the POCA 1985, and subject to the procedural limitations in the Act the court should not impose further constraints.

....

Before 1986, the police would act as both the investigators and prosecutors of crime. The police as private citizens brought prosecutions. Although the police employed solicitors to undertake advocacy and case preparation, their relationship was a normal client relationship and the police were not obliged to act on the solicitor's advice. In many cases the court, due to insufficient evidence, acquitted defendants. This wasted court time, taxpayers' money, and placed victims and defendants under undue distress. The police were concerned with winning or losing a case; the aim of the prosecutions should be the discovery of the truth.

 **Looking for extra marks?**

When dealing with examination questions remember that in relation to the cases that you use you usually do not have to remember the full citation for the case; the names of the parties would be enough, while adding the case year would be advisable. Always remember to provide case facts and the decision of the court and clearly outline the legal principle which the case is designed to illustrate. If you cannot remember both parties when in the exam, highlight the name of the party you do remember. Remember that it is essential that you support your points with relevant legal authority whether that is case law or statute law etc. Failure to do so will mean that you are merely providing a **layperson's** view of the law and are unlikely to pass no matter how sophisticatedly and intelligently you have argued your viewpoint.

Historical background

In 1970, **JUSTICE** (a law reform pressure group) criticized the role of the police, that it was not in the interests of justice for the same body to be responsible for the two functions of investigation and prosecution. It prevented the prosecution from being independent and impartial (*The Prosecution Process in England and Wales* (1970)). The 1981 Royal Commission on Criminal Justice highlighted:

* a lack of uniformity in prosecution decisions nationally, with differing procedures and standards on such matters as whether to prosecute or caution
* inefficient and inadequate preparation of cases.

It recommended that a central prosecuting authority be established so that the investigation and prosecution of crimes could be undertaken by separate agencies. A national prosecution service was established, providing separate local services for each police force area.

The Government followed the main recommendations but rejected the establishment of separate local services. POCA 1985 created the CPS. The **Director of Public Prosecutions (DPP)** is the head of the CPS per s 1(1)(a) POCA 1985. (The DPP, since February 2010, also has responsibilities as the head of the Revenue and Customs Prosecutions Office per s 39 Commissioners for Revenue and Customs Act 2005.) The premise of the CPS was that it independently examines the actions of the police and decides whether the full engagement of the law is required. The prosecution of offences became separated from the detection and investigation of crime, undertaken by the police. The police retained the power to determine what charges were brought, with the CPS merely reviewing that decision to prosecute. In 1986 the CPS was organized into 31 areas but the number of areas was subsequently reduced to just 13 areas covering the 43 police forces.

The CPS ran into problems from its inception, subsequently confirmed by Sir Ian Glidewell in his 1998 report *The Review of the Crown Prosecution Service* (London: HMSO, 1998). The Home Office had underestimated the cost of the new service:

* Salaries offered were low, which made it impossible to attract the services of lawyers, and many lawyers who initially worked for the CPS left to work in private practice or for corporations where salaries were more attractive.
* The number of staff required was double that originally envisaged, costing twice as much as the previous prosecution arrangements.
* Relations between the police and the CPS were not good. The police resented both the demands for a higher standard of case preparation and the high number of discontinued cases. The CPS saw a high rate of discontinued cases as a success.
* There was insufficient correlation between the CPS and police areas.
* The agency was overly bureaucratic and did not properly represent a professional prosecuting agency.
* It had not achieved the goals set out upon its creation.
* The CPS was too centralized and focused on administration.

Investigation and detection

✳✳✳✳✳✳✳✳✳

The Glidewell Report concluded that:

- The enlargement of CPS areas into 13 areas nationally had been a mistake as it made the organization too centralized and excessively bureaucratic.
- There was a problem with judge-ordered acquittals where cases were deemed to be too weak to be left to a jury, due to poor case preparation.
- There was drafting of inadequate, erroneous indictments by non-qualified staff without adequate supervision.

The report recommended:

- devolution of powers to the CPS areas, with the London headquarters playing a more limited role
- replacing the 13 CPS areas with 42 areas corresponding to actual police force areas
- that teams of CPS lawyers, police, and administrative caseworkers known as the Criminal Justice Unit should be established to prepare and deal with many straightforward cases in their entirety – case preparation and court advocacy
- that the Central Casework section, which deals with serious cases, should be provided with more staff, increased training, and closer monitoring
- that CPS lawyers should be allowed to concentrate more on court work rather than paperwork
- that the DPP should play less of a role in the administration of the CPS.

The CPS today

The modern CPS is less centralized now with 42 areas. Each area corresponds to the area covered by a police force. The two police forces in London are covered by one CPS area. Each CPS area is headed by a **Chief Crown Prosecutor** (CCP). Each of the CCPs is a mini DPP, holding delegated authority from the DPP and is responsible for making decisions for their area. Delegating authority allows the DPP to concentrate most of his effort on his legal responsibilities. Each CPS area has its own area business manager who acts as a local chief executive, ie assisting the CCP with administrative responsibilities.

 ✅ Looking for extra marks?

When dealing with a general essay-based question on the CPS, for instance, ensure that you provide information on the problems associated with the decision to prosecute before the service was set up and problems associated with the service when it was initially set up. Provide criticism and recommendations for change, for instance made by the Glidewell Report. In addition, highlight changes that have been made to the service since the report. This critical approach will add weight to your answer.

Diversion

The CPS may decide to divert a person away from the criminal justice system by sending the case back to the police for them to administer a diversionary measure such as a **caution**. Section 37B PACE sets out the responsibilities of the CPS when a case is referred to it. If there is sufficient evidence and it is in the public interest for formal action to be taken, then the prosecutor must consider whether to charge the person with a particular offence or whether the matter could be dealt with by a caution per s 37B(3) PACE. As highlighted by paragraphs 7.1 and 7.6 of the Code for Crown Prosecutors, prosecutors can consider alternatives to prosecution. These 'out of court disposals' such as cautions and conditional cautions can only be utilized when they are deemed to be a 'proportionate response to the seriousness and consequences of the offending'. If such 'offers' are 'refused' or the suspect 'does not make the required admission of guilt' then a prosecution 'must follow' per paragraph 7.4.

Decision to charge

Originally, the police had the power to determine if and what charges were brought. However, the charging system was inconsistent. Policies and practices differed over different types of offences and this all led to a position whereby it was thought that the CPS was being called upon to review prosecutions that were too weak even at the investigation stage, let alone the prosecutorial stage. The decision whether to charge rested with the custody officer who would be influenced by the arresting officer in charge of the case, especially where that person was senior in rank.

The situation today

This has now been resolved under a statutory charging scheme per s 28 Criminal Justice Act 2003. The CPS and not the police has the responsibility to decide whether an offender should be charged. Having investigated a crime and collected the necessary evidence, the police turn over the file to the CPS. The CPS now has the discretion as to whether a prosecution is brought and on what charge/s. The police now only have the power to charge in relation to minor offences and administer diversionary measures such as cautions.

A duty prosecutor will be available within the designated police stations during normal working hours. Investigating officers can have immediate discussions with a prosecution lawyer as to the strength of the case and the most appropriate charges. Lord Justice Auld in his *Review of the Criminal Courts of England and Wales* (London: HMSO, 2001) (<http://www.criminal-courts-review.org.uk>) hoped this would improve the relationship between the CPS and the police so that they work efficiently together in the preparation of cases for trial. Outside of working hours the officers can make use of CPS Direct, a system of on-call prosecutors who work outside of normal office hours and provide advice from home.

A common criticism of the CPS in the past was the issue of downgrading; the police would opt for one charge but the CPS would either reduce the charge to a lesser offence or accept a plea of guilty to a lesser charge. Glidewell concluded that there was no evidence to suggest

Investigation and detection

downgrading although he believed it took place (I Glidewell, *The Review of the Crown Prosecution Service* (London: HMSO, 1998), p 84). Her Majesty's Inspectorate found that the police were systematically over-charging offenders and critical of the CPS for not taking prompt action to remedy this (HM Crown Prosecution Service Inspectorate (2004), 96). Far from systematically downgrading charges inappropriately it was merely the correction of the initial mistake by the police.

The Code for Crown Prosecutors (the Code) is issued by the DPP under s 10 Prosecution of Offences Act 1985. It provides two tests that must be satisfied before any prosecution may be started. The Code gives guidance 'on the general principles to be applied when making decisions about prosecutions' per paragraph 1.1. A new Code, the sixth edition, was issued in February 2010.

Assuming that the relevant prosecution tests have been satisfied, the next step is to decide what a person should be charged with. The Code in paragraph 6.1 states that the CPS should ensure that the charge:

1. reflects the seriousness and extent of the offending

2. gives the court adequate powers to sentence and impose appropriate post-conviction orders

3. enables the case to be presented in a clear and simple way.

According to paragraph 6.3, 'prosecutors should never go ahead with more charges than are necessary just to encourage a defendant to plead guilty to a few' or go ahead with a more serious charge just 'to encourage a defendant to plead guilty to a less serious one'.

When the CPS receives the file per paragraph 3.1, it reviews whether a prosecution should be brought on the basis of criteria set out by the Director of Public Prosecutions in the Code per s 10 POCA 1985. The Code per paragaph 1.1 is designed to ensure that 'fair and consistent prosecution decisions' are taken. CPS staff now work alongside officers in the Criminal Justice Units to prepare cases for court. As stated in paragraph 1.5, 'Although the prosecution service works closely with the police...it is independent of them...[This is] of fundamental constitutional importance.' *The decision to prosecute is a serious step and, as stated by* paragraph 2.1, *'fair and effective prosecution is essential to the main-tenance of law and order'*. The two tests which must be satisfied before any prosecution is initiated are:

- the evidential test

- the public interest test.

Each case 'must be considered on its own facts and merits' per paragraph 2.3. According to paragraph 2.4, prosecutors must not let any 'personal views' influence their decisions and not be 'affected by improper or undue pressure'. Per paragraph 3.2, 'prosecutors must ensure that they have all the information they need to make an informed decision'.

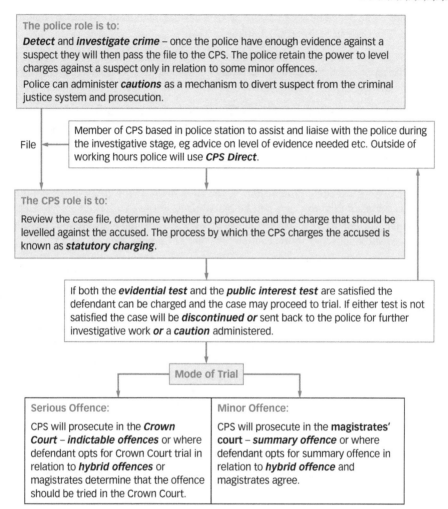

The police role is to:

Detect and **investigate crime** – once the police have enough evidence against a suspect they will then pass the file to the CPS. The police retain the power to level charges against a suspect only in relation to some minor offences.

Police can administer **cautions** as a mechanism to divert suspect from the criminal justice system and prosecution.

File ◄—— Member of CPS based in police station to assist and liaise with the police during the investigative stage, eg advice on level of evidence needed etc. Outside of working hours police will use **CPS Direct**.

The CPS role is to:

Review the case file, determine whether to prosecute and the charge that should be levelled against the accused. The process by which the CPS charges the accused is known as **statutory charging**.

If both the **evidential test** and the **public interest test** are satisfied the defendant can be charged and the case may proceed to trial. If either test is not satisfied the case will be **discontinued or** sent back to the police for further investigative work **or** a **caution** administered.

Mode of Trial

Serious Offence:

CPS will prosecute in the **Crown Court – indictable offences** or where defendant opts for Crown Court trial in relation to **hybrid offences** or magistrates determine that the offence should be tried in the Crown Court.

Minor Offence:

CPS will prosecute in the **magistrates' court – summary offence** or where defendant opts for summary offence in relation to **hybrid offence** and magistrates agree.

Figure 5.1 The role of the police and the Crown Prosecution process within the criminal justice system

The evidential test and the public interest test

Under the evidential test, prosecutors must be satisfied that there is sufficient admissible evidence to provide a 'realistic prospect of conviction', ie that a court is more likely to convict. If not, the CPS will discontinue the case (or return the file to the police for further investigation). The police have criticized the CPS in relation to its over-cautious application of this test. The Code in paragraph 4.5 states:

> Crown Prosecutors must be satisfied that there is enough evidence to provide a realistic prospect of conviction against each defendant on each charge. They must consider what the defence case may be, and how likely to affect the prosecution case.

CPS prosecutors must examine all the evidence and make judgements as to whether it is likely to be admissible and what weight is likely to be given to the evidence by a tribunal of fact and its reliability per Code paragraphs 4.5–4.7. This is an objective test per paragraph 4.6. If there is insufficient evidence then a person should not be charged or, if charged, then the prosecution should be halted per paragraphs 3.3 and 3.6. The matter should be kept under review throughout the history of the case and if at any stage the evidential test is no longer satisfied then the case will be halted per paragraphs 3.3 and 3.6. As indicated by paragraphs 12.1 and 12.2 a decision *not* to prosecute or to stop a prosecution can also be reconsidered and a subsequent prosecution take place or prosecution restarted.

....

R (Da Silva) v DPP [2006] EWHC 3204

An innocent man was shot and killed by police officers who mistook him for a terrorist. The victim's family sought to challenge the CPS's decision not to prosecute any individual police officer for murder or manslaughter, but their application failed. The court agreed that such a decision was in principle open to judicial review, but only where it was based on some unlawful policy, failed to comply with the Code, or was perverse. In the instant case, the CPS felt that it would be unable to prove to a jury that the officers had not acted in self-defence. The case therefore failed the evidential test and the DPP's decision not to prosecute was lawful and rational.

....

If the case passes the evidential test, the CPS must then consider whether the **public interest** requires a prosecution per paragraph 4.11. Just because someone has committed a crime does not necessarily mean that they should be prosecuted. The Code provides a list of factors that make it more or less likely that a prosecution will take place and the public interest requires prosecutors to take these into account. Under paragraph 4.16, factors in favour of a prosecution include:

- A conviction is likely to result in a significant sentence.
- A weapon was used or violence was threatened during the commission of the offence.
- The offence was committed against a person serving the public, eg traffic warden, police officer, nurse, prison officer.
- The defendant was in a position of authority or trust.
- Evidence shows that the defendant was a ringleader or an organizer of the offence.
- There is evidence that the offence was premeditated.

- There is evidence that the offence was carried out by a group.
- The offence was motivated by any form of discrimination.
- The offence is widespread in the area where it was committed.

Factors against a prosecution per paragraph 4.17 include:

- The court is likely to impose a nominal penalty.
- The offence was committed as a result of a genuine mistake or misunderstanding.
- There has been a long delay between the offence taking place and the date of trial.
- The defendant was elderly or was at the time of the offence suffering from significant mental or physical ill health.
- A prosecution is likely to have a bad effect on the victim's physical or mental health.
- Details may be made public that could harm sources of information, international relations, or national security.

Crown Prosecutors must balance factors for and against prosecution carefully per paragraph 4.12 and, per paragraph 4.13, 'decide the importance of each public interest factor in the circumstances of each case and make an overall assessment'. Per paragraph 4.12, a 'prosecution will usually take place unless there are public interest factors tending against prosecution which clearly outweigh those tending in favour'. Prosecutors 'should' when determining the public interest test take into account 'any views expressed by the victim' regarding the impact that the offence has had per paragraph 4.18.

At the end of this two-stage test, the CPS may decide to:

- go ahead with the prosecution
- send the case back to the police for a caution instead of a prosecution
- take no further action – discontinuance.

The Crown Prosecution Inspectorate in 2003 criticized the CPS for failing to eliminate differential treatment by not discontinuing weak cases against ethnic minorities. Acquittal rates for black and Asian defendants stood at 42 per cent, compared with 30 per cent for white defendants. In 1990, the Home Affairs Committee expressed concern that the large proportion of discontinued cases were not dropped until the court hearing. In 1993 the Royal Commission on Criminal Justice found that a third of discontinuances were dropped on public interest grounds. Of these, half were discontinued because the offences were trivial or the likely penalty was nominal. Only 5 per cent of cases were discontinued before any court appearance and, where cases were terminated at the court, the decision to discontinue was taken before the hearing but not communicated to the defendant in time to save a court appearance because the decision was taken too late.

To improve police and CPS relations, police and CPS staff work in integrated teams within police stations to prepare cases for court.

Investigation and detection

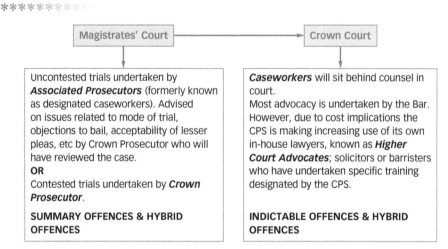

Figure 5.2 Crown Prosecution Service personnel within the courts

The CPS and the Crown Court

Originally, barristers had to be paid by the CPS to carry out the advocacy required for prosecutions in the Crown Court, because lawyers employed in the CPS did not have rights of audience in the Crown Court. The Access to Justice Act 1999 has allowed CPS lawyers to carry out this work themselves, known as Higher Court Advocates, with the aim of achieving greater efficiency whilst saving money. CPS employees are increasingly carrying out the advocacy themselves in the Crown Court and less work is being passed on to the Bar.

The CPS and the magistrates' court

Section 53 Crime and Disorder Act 1998 confers powers on employees of the CPS who are not qualified lawyers. Such employees, known as **Associated Prosecutors**, can be given the power to review files and present straightforward guilty-plea cases in the magistrates' courts. Section 55 Criminal Justice and Immigration Act 2008 has extended the range of hearings. **Crown Prosecutors**, however, will still undertake contested trials and be on hand to advise Associated Prosecutors.

DPP and Attorney General

The DPP produces an annual report detailing the performance of the CPS. This is given to the Attorney General who lays this before Parliament. The Attorney General can be asked questions on the operation of the CPS but not on individual cases. The DPP and Attorney General have certain powers to control the bringing of prosecutions; certain prosecutions can only be brought if the Attorney General or DPP has given his consent.

R (Pretty) v DPP [2002] 1 All ER 1

A woman, P, suffering from motor neurone disease sought an undertaking from the DPP that if her husband were to help her die, as she wished, he would not be prosecuted under s 2(4) Suicide Act 1961. When the DPP declined to give such an undertaking, P applied for judicial review. Rejecting her application, the Court of Appeal said the DPP had no power to give such an undertaking, which would be tantamount to a pardon for a crime not yet committed: his discretion to consent or refuse consent to a prosecution was to be exercised only after the crime had occurred. The House of Lords agreed that whilst the DPP might lawfully make general statements of policy, he could not lawfully grant immunity in respect of some future crime.

The Attorney General has the power to stop proceedings that would be brought before the Crown Court, known as granting a *nolle prosequi*.

Bail

Where a person is charged the police have the initial option of either releasing the person on **bail** or **remanding** the offender in custody until the next available meeting of the magistrates' court per s 47(3A) PACE. The custody officer makes this determination.

When the matter is brought before the magistrates' court then the court will decide the issue of bail. Where an offender has been denied police bail then the magistrates' court will be the first court that a suspect is brought before even when the matter is a serious case and one that will automatically be transferred to the Crown Court.

Section 4 Bail Act 1976 creates a presumption of unconditional bail. However, the court can deny bail if there are substantial grounds for believing that:

- the defendant would fail to surrender to custody
- the defendant would commit an offence whilst on bail
- the defendant would interfere with witnesses
- the defendant would obstruct the course of justice
- custody is necessary for the defendant's own protection.

The court should always consider **conditional bail** before remanding someone to custody per s 4 Bail Act 1976. It may be imposed per s 3(6) Bail Act 1976 to ensure:

- he surrenders to custody
- he does not commit an offence whilst on bail
- he does not interfere with witnesses or obstruct the course of justice
- he makes himself available for the purpose of enabling enquiries or a report to be made to assist the court in dealing with him for the offence
- he attends an interview with an authorized advocate
- the protection of the offender.

✱✱✱✱✱✱✱✱✱

The conditions a court can impose are wide and can include a direction to live at a particular location, the imposition of a curfew, a requirement to report to a police station, finding sureties, surrendering a passport, and avoiding certain places or people.

Under s 7 Bail Act 1976 a court can issue a warrant where an offender fails to surrender to the court at the date he was supposed to. If a warrant is backed by bail then the police should release once arrested. If the warrant is not backed by bail he should be kept in custody and brought before the appropriate magistrates' court the next day. Section 7 also provides the police with a power of arrest if they have reason to believe that bail conditions have been breached, or are likely to be breached per s 7(3) Bail Act 1976. Absconding whilst on bail is a criminal offence per s 6 Bail Act 1976.

Where the magistrates' court denies a suspect bail he can make an application to the Crown Court, which has the power to overturn the decision. Judicial review is possible but only where the decision of the magistrates was perverse.

The prosecution can appeal per s 18 Criminal Justice Act 2003 to the Crown Court by providing an immediate verbal indication at the conclusion of the hearing and by written confirmation within two hours per s 1(4) and s 1(5) Bail Amendment Act 1993. The defendant will be remanded in custody pending the appeal and this will be heard within 48 hours per s 1(8) Bail Amendment Act 1993.

Revision tip

When revising this area of your course, review your seminar questions as these will give you an idea of the type/forms of question that may appear in the ultimate examination. Questions that are commonly asked in this area are problem scenarios where you are asked to advise an individual on the process by which he will be tried in the court system, or on his interaction with the police who are utilizing their investigative powers. A topic area that is suited to an essay-based question is that of the decision to prosecute and the operation of the Crown Prosecution Service.

Trial process

Once a person has been charged, the next matter to be considered is how and where that accusation should be tried. Two first instance courts hear criminal matters:

* the magistrates' court
* the Crown Court.

Classification of offences

The seriousness of the offence will determine where the case will be tried.

* **Summary offences**: triable only summarily in the magistrates' court – minor criminal offences, eg common assault, criminal damage valued under £5,000, etc. The magistrates (or the District Judge) deal with the entire case themselves, deciding both the verdict and (if appropriate) the sentence.

- **Indictable offences**: triable only on indictment in the Crown Court – serious forms of criminal offence, eg murder, treason, piracy, etc. Generally, a judge will determine issues of law and the jury will determine guilt/innocence.

- **Hybrid offences**: aka **triable either way offences** – can potentially be tried in the magistrates' court or in the Crown Court – offences of varying degrees of seriousness, eg theft, assault occasioning actual bodily harm, etc.

Mode of trial

Summary offences

Where a person has been arrested by the police and charged, the charge sheet will be sent to the magistrates' court. Where the defendant is charged by the CPS then the prosecutor prepares a document listing the charges and this is laid before the magistrates' court. Once the information has been placed before the court a summons will be sent out and delivered to the defendant, stipulating the offence committed, the location of the court where he is required to appear, and the date when he must attend.

Indictable offences

Under s 51 Crime and Disorder Act 1998, where an offender is charged with an indictable offence the matter is sent directly to the Crown Court. Such defendants will appear once in the magistrates' court to determine issues such as funding from the **Legal Services Commission**, bail, and the use of statements and exhibits. The magistrates' court then provides defendants with a statement of the evidence against them as well as a notice setting out the offence(s) for which they are to be sent for trial and the place where they are to be tried.

Under paragraph 2, Schedule 3 Crime and Disorder Act 1998 a defendant can make an application to a Crown Court judge for the case against him to be dismissed for lack of evidence. This will be granted if the judge is of the opinion there is insufficient evidence for the jury to properly convict.

Hybrid offences

The defendant has the option to have his case dealt with in the Crown Court or the magistrates' court. The defendant will be required to make a plea before venue. If the defendant pleads guilty then the magistrates will adjourn the case for sentencing at a later date. If the defendant indicates that he will plead not guilty then the court needs to determine the ultimate location of the trial, taking into account the wishes of the defendant. Magistrates, when making their determination, will be provided with:

- the history of the offender
- details of the offence
- previous convictions

- allocation guidelines produced by the Sentencing Guidelines Council, eg must take into account limited powers of sentencing.

Under Schedule 3 Criminal Justice Act 2003, where the magistrates decline **jurisdiction** or where the defendant elects trial by jury the case is transferred direct to the Crown Court under s 51 Crime and Disorder Act 1998. A defendant can ask for an indication as to a likely sentence to be imposed if the magistrates are of the opinion that the matter should be tried in the magistrates' court under s 20(3) and s 20(4) Magistrates' Courts Act 1980.

Trial process – summary trials

Summary trial takes place before the magistrates' court and the primary individuals involved are:

- Bench or single **District Judge (Magistrates' Court)**
- **clerk to the justices**
- representative of the Crown Prosecution Service – Crown Prosecutor or Associated Prosecutor
- solicitor representing the defendant
- witnesses
- defendant.

The first stage of summary trial is where the defendant makes a plea on the basis of the information laid before the court. The clerk will read out the charges against the defendant. If the defendant pleads guilty then the court will determine the sentence. If the defendant pleads not guilty then the case will proceed to trial. The case will be adjourned to be tried on a fixed date a few weeks later.

The defendant can in relation to minor offences plead guilty by post per s 308 Criminal Justice Act 2003. The summons that is sent out will detail the procedure to follow per s 12 Magistrates' Courts Act 1980. The defendant has the right to make a written representation to the court including **mitigating circumstances** for the purposes of sentencing. The court will usually proceed to sentence the offender without the defendant being present but will require attendance if the court wishes to impose a custodial sentence.

The court also has discretion to try the defendant if he fails to attend court when required to do so per s 11 Magistrates' Courts Act 1980, provided they believe that the summons has properly been served on the defendant. If the court wishes to proceed then the plea that will be entered will be not guilty. Again, if the court wishes to pass a custodial sentence then the court will attempt to bring the defendant before the court. Section 54 Criminal Justice and Immigration Act 2008 creates a presumption that, if defendants fail to attend for trial without good cause, magistrates will use their powers to try them in their absence and sentence them if convicted.

Prosecution case and defence case

In any criminal trial, following the submission of a plea the prosecution must present their case to prove the charges against the defendant on the basis of evidence presented to the court, eg real evidence such as physical objects or evidence presented by witnesses. The defendant is innocent until proven guilty. The prosecution must discharge their burden of proof by proving their case beyond a reasonable doubt. If not, then the defendant is entitled to be acquitted.

....

Woolmington v DPP [1935] AC 462

D was charged with murdering his wife, and the trial judge directed the jury that once it was proved that D shot his wife, the onus was on him to show that it was an accident. The House of Lords quashed D's conviction. Lord Sankey LC said there was a golden thread running through English criminal law, that with very few exceptions the legal burden of proving any fact essential to a crime, including D's state of mind, lay upon the prosecution.

....

Where the prosecution call a witness, they can adduce evidence from that witness by questioning, known as examination in chief. The witness can then be asked questions by the defence, known as cross-examination. The prosecution, on the basis of any answers given, can re-examine the witness. The magistrates may also question the witness through the Chair of the **Bench**, or directly if a District Judge is presiding.

Not all witnesses must give evidence in person; a witness statement can be read to the court per s 9 Criminal Justice Act 2003. Where the defence objects, then the witness must attend court to be cross-examined.

If it is felt that a witness may not attend court when required to do so then the court per s 97 Magistrates' Courts Act 1980 can issue a summons. If the witness ignores this then the court can issue an arrest warrant. The court itself has the power to call a witness to the court per R v Haringey Justices ex p DPP [1996] if they feel the witness may have relevant testimony. The court must ensure that all relevant evidence has been adduced in order to assist in their final deliberations.

If the defence feel there is insufficient evidence against the defendant then they can ask the court to consider that there is no case to answer. The court will determine if it feels that it can convict on the basis of the evidence presented per Practice Note [1962]. If the court agrees with the defence then the defendant is acquitted. If the submission fails then the trial will continue with the defence having to present their case.

The defence might not call any witnesses or provide any evidence to the court as it is the prosecution who must prove that the defendant is guilty, not for the defendant to prove that he is innocent. The defence may wish to call the defendant first to give evidence. The defendant is competent to give evidence but cannot be compelled to do so. If the defendant does not give evidence then the court can draw inferences against him per s 35 Criminal

Trial process

✳✳✳✳✳✳✳✳✳

Justice and Public Order Act 1994. These cannot be the sole reason upon which to base a conviction per s 35(3) Criminal Justice and Public Order Act 1994.

Where the defence call a witness, it can adduce evidence by questioning known as **examination in chief**. The witness can then be asked questions by the prosecution known as **cross-examination**. The defence, on the basis of any answers given, can re-examine the witness. The magistrates may also question the witness through the Chair of the Bench or directly if a District Judge is presiding.

Youth offenders

The Youth Justice and Criminal Evidence Act 1999 contains a range of provisions which are designed to make it easier for children, individuals who are disabled, and vulnerable witnesses to give evidence within the courtroom. Witnesses may, for instance, be able to give evidence via a video link, pre-recorded evidence, behind screens, and proceedings may be less formal.

Young offenders are usually tried in **youth courts** within the magistrates' court building. Proceedings will take place only with those who have a direct interest in the trial. Access by members of the public and press is restricted. Parents or guardians of children under 16 must attend the court. Young persons can be tried in the Crown Court if the offence is sufficiently serious, eg murder, and where the co-defendant is an adult.

The courts have a range of measures which they can implement in order to ensure that the trial process is not intimidating to the young offender. What measures are implemented will depend on the age, maturity, and development of the young defendant on trial. Such measures include court familiarization visits, the court adapted so that everyone sits on the same level, and defendants should sit next to or close to relatives or appropriate adult and their lawyer. Wigs and gowns are not to be worn by legal professionals. The police should ensure that the defendant is not exposed at any time to intimidation or abuse.

The verdict and sentencing

At the end of the evidence, each side may summarize its case very briefly and present any arguments on points of law. If a Bench is presiding they will retire from the courtroom to reach their verdict. The magistrates will discuss the case in private in order to reach an agreement on the possible verdict. If, however, a District Judge is presiding he will usually not retire but will give his verdict immediately.

Once the **lay magistrates** have reached their verdict they will return to the court. The Chair of the **Bench** will then deliver the verdict in relation to all charges. If the defendant is found not guilty, ie the case has not been proved, the court must acquit him. Where the defendant has been found guilty, ie the case is proved, the case will go on to the next stage, that of **sentencing**.

If the defendant pleads guilty, or is found guilty after a trial, the magistrates must decide a sentence. Where the offence is a minor one the magistrates are likely to proceed immediately with sentencing. The magistrates may postpone sentencing to obtain social or medical reports, particularly if they are considering custody. The prosecutor will outline the facts of the case, if there was no trial, and list the defendant's previous convictions. The defence may offer a plea in mitigation, usually arguing for a light sentence.

Under s 154 Criminal Justice Act 2003 the maximum **custodial sentence** that can be imposed is 12 months or a fine up to level 5 on the standard scale, at present £5,000. They can impose **community penalties** and order the defendant to pay compensation and/or some or all of the prosecution's costs.

When a hybrid offence is tried, then after hearing all the evidence the magistrates may decide that their own sentencing powers are insufficient. In such a case they may commit the defendant to the Crown Court for sentencing per s 53 and Schedule 13 Criminal Justice and Immigration Act 2008 which amended Schedule 3 Criminal Justice Act 2003.

Trials on indictment

Trials on indictment take place before the Crown Court. Numerous individuals are involved, *inter alia*:

- judge
- jury
- prosecution lawyer, independent barrister, or Higher Court Advocate employed and paid by the CPS assisted by a caseworker
- defence lawyers, eg barrister etc
- court clerk
- defendant
- witnesses.

Preliminary issues and plea and case management hearings

The judge has the responsibility for the proceedings and sole responsibility for determining questions of law such as admissibility of evidence and sentencing upon a finding of guilt. Admissibility of evidence will be determined with the jury being removed following representations by counsel, eg s 76 and s 78 PACE in relation to the admissibility of confession evidence and other forms of evidence obtained by the police during investigations. The jury makes the determination of guilt in the Crown Court but there are certain situations where a judge may sit alone. There are numerous forms of judge who potentially can hear a case in the Crown Court:

- Judge of the High Court
- Circuit Judge or Deputy Circuit Judge
- Recorder (including District Judges (Magistrates' Court) who sit as Recorders per s 65 Courts Act 2003).

The seriousness and class of criminal offence will determine the form of judge.

Trial process

✳✳✳✳✳✳✳✳✳

At the Crown Court there is a plea and case management hearing before a judge alone per the Criminal Procedure Rules 2005 designed to encourage the early preparation of cases before trial. These hearings are held in open court with the defendants present. The prosecution and defence will have to identify the key issues, and provide any additional information required to organize the actual trial, such as which witnesses will have to attend, facts that are admitted by both sides, and issues of law that are likely to arise.

Part of this procedure is that of disclosure; the prosecution have a legal obligation to disclose all evidence prior to the beginning of the trial proper – not only evidence they are going to rely on but also unused evidence per s 3(1) Criminal Procedure and Investigations Act 1996 and must:

> disclose…any prosecution material which…might reasonably be considered capable of undermining the case for the prosecution against the accused or of assisting the case for the accused.

The defence have a duty of disclosure to the prosecution under s 33 Criminal Justice Act 2003. They have to identify any defences they intend to rely on and any points of law they intend to raise, give the prosecution the names and addresses of all witnesses, and the name of any expert witness.

The trial will begin at the **arraignment**. This is when the charges, listed on the indictment, are formally put to the defendant by the court clerk and the defendant will be asked to enter a plea. The indictment lists the particulars of each offence with which the defendant is charged and a brief summary of when the law was breached. In relation to a hybrid offence a defendant will already have indicated his plea of guilty or not guilty in the magistrates' court.

Where the plea is guilty then the matter will proceed to sentencing without the empanelment of a jury. Where the plea is not guilty then the matter will proceed to trial. The judge will give any necessary directions and set a date for the trial proper.

At the start of the trial, a jury is empanelled and sworn. The prosecution or defence can object to a particular juror for good cause and vetting can take place. When each juror is selected they will, dependent on religious conviction, either affirm or take an oath which basically stipulates that they will:

> try the defendant and give a true verdict according to the evidence.

Once all 12 jury members are sworn in the jury is complete and the trial can begin. We will return to the issues surrounding the jury within the chapter on lay participation.

Revision Tip

Revision does not have to be a solitary experience. Brainstorming sessions and quizzes can be used to assist revision. Get yourself into a revision group and decide on a topic to revise. The whole group will then revise the topic and prepare ten questions each on the topic area. When the group meets again each member of the team asks their questions.

Prosecution case and defence case

The prosecution have the burden of proving their case against the defendant so will present their case first. The prosecution will provide an opening speech to the jury where they will briefly outline their case against the defendant. They will then proceed to produce their evidence and witnesses to support their contentions.

Where the prosecution call a witness, they can adduce evidence from that witness by questioning in open court, known as examination in chief. The witness can then be asked questions by the defence, known as cross-examination. Where there is more than one defendant then each defendant has the right to cross-examine the witness. The prosecution on the basis of any answers given can re-examine the witness. The judge may also question the witness on his own behalf or on behalf of the jury.

Following the closing of the prosecution case the defence may submit that there is no case to answer if they feel that they have not adduced sufficient evidence to demonstrate that the defendant is guilty. If the judge agrees he will direct the jury that they acquit the defendant. The Court of Appeal in *R v Galbraith* [1981] stated:

> if the judge comes to the conclusion that the prosecution evidence…is such that a jury properly directed could not properly convict upon it, it is his duty to stop the case.

If the submission is unsuccessful then the defence will present their case. They will make an opening speech criticizing the prosecution evidence and identifying flaws in the evidence. The defence will support this by producing witnesses. If the defendant is to give evidence then he will give his evidence first followed by subsequent witnesses. If the defendant does not give evidence then inferences can be drawn against him per **s 35 Criminal Justice and Public Order Act 1994**. However, these inferences on their own cannot be the sole reason for a conviction per **s 35(3) Criminal Justice and Public Order Act 1994**. If there is more than one defendant they will present their evidence in turn.

Where the defence call a witness, they can adduce evidence from that witness by questioning, ie examination in chief. The witness can then be asked questions by the prosecution, ie cross-examination. Where there is more than one defendant then they have the right to cross-examine the other defendant's witnesses. The defence on the basis of any answers given can re-examine the witness. The judge may also question the witness on his own behalf or on behalf of the jury but must not adopt the role of an advocate.

. . . .

R v Gunning [1980] Crim LR 592

D was charged with theft. During the course of D's evidence in chief, the judge asked him 165 questions, compared with 172 asked by his own counsel. The Court of Appeal quashed D's conviction, saying the judge had deprived D of the opportunity of developing his defence. The judge is not an advocate, said Cumming-Bruce LJ. Under the English system of criminal trials he is much more like the umpire at a cricket match. He is certainly not the bowler, whose business is to get the batsman out.

Closing speeches, summing up, verdict, and sentence

Both the prosecution and the defence are entitled to produce a closing speech. The prosecution will go first. If there is more than one defendant they are all entitled to their own individual closing speech. The speeches can only comment upon information and evidence presented in court.

Once completed the judge will sum up the case for the jury, direct the jury in relation to the law and remind them of the evidence and facts presented. The determination of guilt/innocence is the jury's alone and the jury cannot be directed to convict per *R v Wang* [2005]. The jury will elect a foreman and retire to reach a verdict. During the deliberations the jury will be under the control of the Court Bailiff and must abide by s 8 Contempt of Court Act 1981.

A jury must strive initially to reach a unanimous verdict, where all jury members are agreed on the verdict. However, s 17 Juries Act 1974 allows the judge to accept a majority verdict after two hours and ten minutes of jury deliberations. If the jury fail to reach a verdict then the judge will implement a *Watson* direction and ask the jury foreman to state that the jury cannot reach a verdict. The jury will then be discharged and a retrial will be considered.

If a guilty verdict is reached then the trial will move on to sentencing issues, which will be determined by the judge alone. The case may be adjourned in order for the court to obtain all relevant information in relation to the potential sentencing options. During sentencing the prosecution and defence will highlight aggravating and mitigating factors to the court.

If the verdict reached is not guilty then the defendant is free to leave the courtroom theoretically with his character unblemished. If the defendant pleads guilty, or is convicted after trial, the judge decides a **sentence**; the jury play no part in this. The prosecutor per paragraph 11.1 of the Code for Crown Prosecutors outlines the facts (if there was no trial) and draws the court's attention to:

- any aggravating or mitigating factors disclosed by the prosecution case
- any victim personal impact statement
- appropriate evidence of the impact of the offending on the community
- any statutory provisions or sentencing guidelines which may assist
- any relevant statutory provisions relating to ancillary orders
- the defendant's previous convictions
- challenges of any assertion made by the defence in mitigation that is inaccurate, misleading, or derogatory.

The defence may offer a plea in mitigation, arguing for a light sentence. Under para-graph 11.5 of the Code, prosecutors should challenge any assertion 'made by the defence in mitigation that is inaccurate [and] misleading'. The judge may postpone sentence to obtain social or medical reports, particularly if he is considering custody. The maximum sentence that can be imposed is mandatory life imprisonment and an unlimited fine dependent on the nature of the offence.

Plea bargaining

Plea bargaining is the name given to the negotiations between the prosecution and defence lawyers over the outcome of a case. Following the Court of Appeal decision in *R v Turner* [1970] judges were banned from indicating what sentence they would give if a defendant pleaded guilty. The ban was removed in *R v Goodyear* [2005]. Defendants can now request in writing an indication from the judge of their likely sentence if they plead guilty. Trial judges are allowed to indicate the maximum sentence they would give on the facts of the case.

It can be argued that plea bargaining offers benefits:

* for the defendant there is obviously a shorter sentence
* for the courts, police, and taxpayers there are financial savings made by drastically shortening trials. In fact without a high proportion of guilty pleas, the courts would be seriously overloaded, causing severe delays, which in turn would raise costs still further, especially given the number of prisoners remanded in custody awaiting trial.

Critics argue that the practice may place undue pressure on the accused and persuade inno-cent people to plead guilty and that the judge should be, and seen to be, an impartial referee, acting in accordance with the law rather than the dictates of cost efficiency. Plea bargaining goes against the principle that offenders should be punished for what they have actually done. It can lead to cases where people are punished more leniently than their conduct would seem to demand, and it may lead to quite inappropriate punishments. For instance, offenders who might usefully be given psychiatric help may never receive it.

 ✅ Looking for extra marks?

Be aware that if you are dealing with a scenario question where you are being asked to advise a par-ticular individual, take particular notice of the age of the suspect/defendant as this can have impli-cations at various stages of the criminal justice process, especially in relation to police powers, the location of any trial, access to the courtroom, and set-up of the court. In addition determine whether the young offender is a co-defendant with an adult offender, as this can have implications in relation to location of trial. You may also want to consider if the defendant has mental illness problems as again in relation to police powers there are safeguards for such suspects.

Key cases

✳✳✳✳✳✳✳✳✳✳

Case	Facts	Ratio/Held
Hayter v L [1998] 1 WLR 854	Two boys assaulted another boy and caused him actual bodily harm. After investigations the police cautioned the defendants but decided not to prosecute. The victim's father brought a private prosecution, but the magistrates dismissed the case as an abuse of process.	The High Court allowed the appeal by way of case stated and remitted the case for rehearing by a new Bench. The right of private prosecution was preserved by POCA 1985, subject to the procedural limitations in the Act and the court should not impose further constraints.
R v Gunning [1980] Crim LR 592	D was charged with theft. During the course of D's evidence in chief, the judge asked him 165 questions, compared with 172 asked by his own counsel.	The Court of Appeal quashed D's conviction, saying the judge had deprived D of the opportunity of developing his defence. The judge is not an advocate, said Cumming-Bruce LJ. Under the English system of criminal trials he is much more like the umpire at a cricket match. He is certainly not the bowler, whose business is to get the batsman out.
R (Da Silva) v DPP [2006] EWHC 3204	An innocent man was shot and killed by police officers who mistook him for a terrorist. The victim's family sought to challenge the CPS's decision not to prosecute any individual police officer for murder or manslaughter.	Their application failed. The court agreed that such a decision was in principle open to judicial review, but only where it was based on some unlawful policy, failed to comply with the Code, or perverse. In the instant case, the CPS felt that it would be unable to prove to a jury that the officers had not acted in self-defence. The case therefore failed the evidential test and the DPP's decision not to prosecute was lawful and rational.
R (Pretty) v DPP [2002] 1 All ER 1	A woman P suffering from motor neurone disease sought an undertaking from the DPP that if her husband were to help her die, as she wished, he would not be prosecuted under s 2(4) Suicide Act 1961. When the DPP declined to give such an undertaking, P applied for judicial review.	Rejecting her application, the Court of Appeal said the DPP had no power to give such an undertaking, which would be tantamount to a pardon for a crime not yet committed: his discretion to consent or refuse consent to a prosecution was to be exercised only after the crime had occurred. The House of Lords agreed that whilst the DPP might lawfully make general statements of policy, he could not lawfully grant immunity in respect of some future crime.

Case	Facts	Ratio/Held
Ricketts v Cox (1982) 74 Cr App R 298	Two officers were looking for youths responsible for a serious assault. They approached the defendant in the early hours of the morning. The defendant was said to have been abusive, uncooperative, and used obscene language, designed to provoke and antagonize the officers.	The magistrates found that the police acted in a proper manner and were entitled to put questions to the defendant; his behaviour and attitude amounted to an obstruction of the police officers in the execution of their duty. Appeal was dismissed.
Woolmington v DPP [1935] AC 462	D was charged with murdering his wife, and the trial judge directed the jury that once it was proved that D shot his wife, the onus was on him to show that it was an accident.	The House of Lords quashed D's conviction. Lord Sankey LC said there was a golden thread running through English criminal law that with very few exceptions the legal burden of proving any fact essential to a crime, including D's state of mind, lay upon the prosecution.

(?) Exam questions

Essay question

Critically evaluate the operation and role of the Crown Prosecution Service within the English legal system.

An outline answer is available at the end of the book.

Problem question

Jeff has been charged with a criminal offence.

1. Advise Jeff of the factors and tests the Crown Prosecution Service takes into account when determining whether to prosecute.

2. Jeff was stopped and searched by an officer on the basis of his racial characteristics and his known previous convictions. Evidence was obtained as a result. No record of the search was made. Has a breach of PACE occurred and what potentially may be the effect of this breach at trial?

3. During his detention and questioning, at no time was Jeff cautioned by any police officer. The officers in charge of the investigation and custody officer denied him contact with his solicitor or to have anyone informed of his arrest despite the offence being only of minor seriousness. The interview room was poorly lit, he was made to stand during the whole period of questioning, and denied any breaks for refreshment and sleep. He was questioned in an

Exam questions

oppressive manner by the officers for a non-stop period of 36 hours. The police have stated that they have a signed confession made by Jeff; however, no tape recording of the interview exists. Advise Jeff as to whether a breach of PACE has occurred and the potential effect of this at trial.

4. As Jeff's offence is of minor seriousness, a summary offence, advise him of the trial process in relation to such offences.

An outline answer is available online at <http://www.oxfordtextbooks.co.uk/orc/concentrate/>.

#6
Professional personnel

Key facts

- There is an increasing overlap of the work of barristers and solicitors.

- The postgraduate training of barristers and solicitors differs.

- Qualification as either a barrister or a solicitor remains expensive and demanding.

- The senior levels of both professions are dominated by white males.

- The debate over fusing barristers and solicitors into one profession has been addressed by extending rights of audience to both professions and allowing direct public access to barristers.

- Judges are principally selected from barristers and solicitors.

- There is a lack of diversity among judges.

- There is tension between guaranteeing judicial independence and the right of removal.

- The Constitutional Reform Act 2005 retains strict eligibility criteria and imposes a rigorous and extensive appointment process for judicial office.

- The office of Lord Chancellor breached the principle of the separation of powers.

- The Constitutional Reform Act 2005 resolves many of the conflicts by removing the right to sit as a judge and be a member of the House of Lords.

Introduction

The English legal system is almost unique in having not one but two distinct principal legal professions – barristers (organized and governed by the General Council of the Bar – known as the Bar Council) and solicitors (organized and governed by the Law Society). Formerly solicitors were 'Solicitors of the Supreme Court' but following the renaming of 'the Supreme Court' as 'the Senior Courts of England and Wales' under s 59 Constitutional Reform Act 2005, all solicitors have become 'Solicitors of the Senior Courts'. However, with increasing numbers in the professions, there is a blurring of the former sharp distinction between the roles exercised by these two professions. There are over 12,000 barristers in practice of whom about 45 per cent are female, although more women than men are now qualifying. At the higher levels, both professions remain dominated by middle-class white males. The legal professions are also important as for many years professional practice as a barrister or solicitor was a condition (and remains the principal route) to appointment as a judge. This chapter will first describe the training, roles, and structure of the two professions, and consider the challenges which an aspiring lawyer may encounter, before examining the extent to which the argument for fusion has been met. It will then consider the role and independence of judges and the qualifications required for appointment, before describing the processes of appointment and removal of judges. It will continue by observing that, logically (given that judges are principally appointed from legal practitioners), the criticisms against the gender and ethnic composition of the judiciary (the body of judges) reflect those against the senior members of the legal profession. Finally, it will consider the unique position of the Lord Chancellor.

The legal professions

Historically, each legal profession performed separate functions and had a monopoly in its own field. However, this is no longer the case and many commentators describe barristers and solicitors as branches of a single legal profession. These two branches reflect the results of nineteenth-century amalgamations and mergers of earlier professional organizations and societies whose work and functions overlapped; and currently this trend can be seen in the increasing similarity of the training and work of barristers and solicitors – advocacy before courts, tribunals, etc; drafting documents; and advice. In addition, now, a number of other specialist professionals work in law (eg legal executives) or legally related areas (eg trust and estate practitioners), and, paradoxically, these other specialist organizations have drawn strength from the increasing similarity of the work of the two legal professions. Three issues dog the legal professions:

1. *work practices*: the increasing similarity of work of barristers and solicitors, the limited similarity of training, the overlap between the two legal professions, and the issue of fusion

2. *entry and diversity*: the challenges and hurdles to entry into the professions, and the consequential issues of access to, and diversity in, those professions

3. *discipline and regulation*: disciplinary matters, the quality of legal services provided by the legal professions, and the extent to which they should be externally regulated.

Revision Tip

Many questions require a comparison of barristers and solicitors. As revision, place in two columns the characteristics of each profession. This will highlight the similarities and differences between each profession. You may even want to do this as you read this section.

Work practices

Solicitors

Currently there are over 145,000 solicitors qualified to practise of whom approximately 115,000 hold a current practising certificate; and over 45 per cent are female. Some solicitors may be employed by organizations like local authorities, large companies, or government organizations, but most solicitors practise either in partnerships or (less commonly) on their own (sole practitioners). There are wide-ranging variations in the type and size of practices: some large London-based practices have hundreds of partners, international offices, and advise on complex international commercial and corporate matters; but, in contrast, over three-quarters of all practices have four or fewer partners and only one office.

Barristers

In contrast, barristers are usually self-employed and share offices called 'chambers' and a clerk who manages the barristers' 'business'. Although this structure seems archaic, proposals to allow barristers to form partnerships have met with limited welcome. The majority of barristers are based in London but often travel to provincial courts. Other barristers may be employed in local and central government and in large commercial organizations. Barristers of whatever age are called 'juniors' unless they are Queen's Counsel (otherwise called 'silks') who are senior barristers (normally of at least ten years' standing at the Bar) and solicitors of similar seniority may now 'take silk', ie become Queen's Counsel. Each year, applications are invited for the creation of new silks, and a special selection panel (which includes non-lawyers) has replaced the Lord Chancellor in the process of selecting the new QCs. There are currently about 1,000 QCs of whom only about 100 are female. After taking silk, the barrister will be known as 'a Leader' in complex cases and may be assisted by junior counsel.

Barristers' work is allocated on the 'cab rank' rule – ie a barrister must accept the next case appropriate to their skill and competence, and for which an appropriate fee is offered. However, this rule gives way to a rule of non-discrimination for instructions received directly from a member of the public (with the result that a barrister can refuse work received in that way).

The legal professions

✳✳✳✳✳✳✳✳✳✳

Similarity of work

Until 1985, solicitors enjoyed a monopoly of all **conveyancing** work, but this monopoly has slowly been eroded by the establishment of licensed conveyancers and the provision of conveyancing services by financial institutions. Equally, barristers had a monopoly of the **rights of audience** in the higher courts, and lay clients could instruct barristers only through a solicitor. Traditionally, solicitors had a right to practise as advocates in the magistrates' courts and county courts but only in a limited number of instances before the higher courts, eg proceedings in Chambers. Thus, most of the work before the magistrates' courts and county courts was undertaken by solicitors and that before the higher courts by barristers. However, as a consequence of the Courts and Legal Services Act 1990 and the Access to Justice Act 1999, all barristers and solicitors now have rights of audience before all courts but must complete further training in order to exercise those rights. As a consequence many firms are ensuring that their solicitors complete this training and so are able to act as in-house solicitor-advocates rather than having to employ a barrister. Moreover, as the Access to Justice Act 1999 placed the majority of contractual and tortious cases in the county court where solicitors regularly appear, the volume of solicitor-advocacy has increased.

For many years, barristers were perceived as being merely advocates, ie they presented the case in the courts. Their additional roles were to prepare opinions (notes of advice) on complex cases for solicitors, to discuss cases with solicitors and the clients in **conferences**, and to prepare legal documents for the case which need to be filed with the court. To counterbalance the loss of the advocacy monopoly to solicitors, they were authorized to accept instructions directly from certain professionals such as accountants and engineers; and, since 2004, members of the public can instruct a barrister of at least three years' call directly to offer advice, prepare documents, or appear as an advocate.

Similarity of training

Following the Courts and Legal Services Act 1990 both branches of the profession were regulated by the Lord Chancellor's Advisory Committee on Legal Education and Conduct to maintain and develop standards in education, training, and performance. Under the Access to Justice Act 1999 this committee was replaced by the Legal Services Consultation Panel whose task is to develop and maintain standards in legal education and professional conduct.

Entry into either branch of the legal profession is now almost exclusively limited to graduates but not necessarily to law graduates. Graduates holding a Qualifying Law Degree are not required to pass the one-year course for the Common Professional Examination (also known as the Graduate Diploma in Law) before proceeding to vocational training, whereas those whose degrees are not Qualifying Law Degrees (eg in history) do have to undertake the Common Professional Examination before proceeding to vocational training. The syllabus of the Qualifying Law Degree and Common Professional Examination requires knowledge of legal skills and system plus study of the foundation subjects (constitutional and administrative law, contract, criminal law, equity, European law, land law, tort, and trusts). Whilst no minimum degree classification is required for entry onto the Legal Practice Course, the highly competitive nature of law results in most candidates having at least a 2:1 degree. Each profession has a different route for subsequent vocational and practical training.

Solicitor training

Prospective solicitors subsequently undertake a one-year full-time Legal Practice Course with one of the several providers available in England and Wales to acquire and develop practical skills such as drafting and advocacy as well as advanced legal knowledge. Some City firms have a bespoke Legal Practice Course for their trainees. Students then undertake a two-year training contract usually with a firm of solicitors. However, recruitment for training contracts may be effected at the end of a student's second year – perhaps two years in advance of the commencement of the training contract. During the training contract the prospective solicitor will undertake practical and further professional training including the 20-day Professional Skills Course. Having completed the training contract, application can be made for admission to the Roll of Solicitors. Once admitted onto the Roll, a solicitor must obtain a Practising Certificate in order to practise and there is an annual requirement for 16 hours of Continuing Professional Development; and, as previously mentioned the solicitor must undergo further training in order to exercise full rights of audience.

Barrister training

The Bar Standards Board (on behalf of the Bar Council) supervises the education system for barristers. Prospective barristers have to join one of the four Inns of Court in London: Inner Temple, Middle Temple, Gray's Inn, and Lincoln's Inn, in which students have to dine 12 times. **Dinners** are founded on the belief that dining students benefit from the wisdom and advice of established counsel also dining there; but in recent years Dinners have been accompanied by seminars, lectures, and presentations. Students may also attend a weekend course in substitution for Dinners. Students also have to undertake the one-year Bar Professional Training Course (until recently called the Bar Vocational Course) with one of the providers in England and Wales: this course covers some substantive law but also skills such as negotiating and drafting. Upon successful completion of the Bar Professional Training Course, the prospective barrister is then 'called to the Bar'. At present, in order to become eligible to practise, a barrister must then undertake pupillage, but there have been proposals to defer **Call** until the completion of pupillage, so that pupillage would be a prerequisite to being a barrister. Pupillage normally consists of two 'sixes': an initial period of six months training

The legal professions

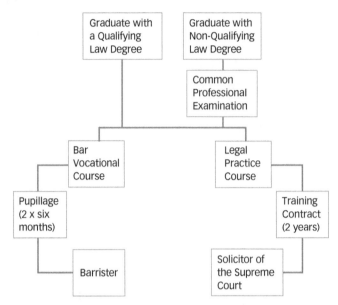

Figure 6.1 Routes for qualification

with a barrister followed by a further period of six months during which the pupil barrister may undertake some limited work. Pupil barristers are required to take various courses related to practice – eg advocacy and forensic accountancy. After completion of pupillage, a barrister must find a **tenancy** in chambers from which to start practising.

Overlap of functions and fusion

Historically, the roles of solicitor and barrister were quite separate – reflecting a nineteenth-century agreement over the rights of audience and direct access; but in the twentieth century this separation sustained an argument for fusion. The major criticisms of the separation of the professions were based on public attitudes and cost. Lay clients whose initial dealings were with the solicitor resented the case being passed to a barrister who was seen as remote; such clients did not appreciate that instructing an independent barrister provided an independent specialized opinion on the merits of the case and its prospects for success. The engagement of two practitioners was seen as an unnecessary expense, and Professor Zander likened the simultaneous use of both a barrister (for appearance before the courts) and solicitor (for preparing the case and instructing counsel) to using two taxis and having two meters running. The professional bodies resisted calls for fusion on a number of principles, eg the desirability of ensuring the availability to all of an independent bar, standards of advocacy and research, and judicial confidence.

However, the distinction between the two professions has become blurred by the reforms contained in the Courts and Legal Services Act 1990 and Access to Justice Act 1999. In principle, both professions now have coextensive rights of audience and are entitled to act as advocates in court at all levels; and there is direct public access to both professions, which can advise clients directly and draft court papers. As a consequence, the real differences between the two professions now lie in the extent to which each profession does in fact (rather than may) exercise those rights. Moreover, few solicitors will desire to exercise rights of audience before the higher courts when instructing a barrister might prove to be more cost-effective; and, in reality few individual clients (as opposed to major organizations) will know which counsel to instruct directly. Thus the calls for fusion have become muted.

Entry and diversity

Challenges and hurdles to entry into the profession

Qualification as either a barrister or a solicitor involves a considerable period of training and financial commitment in addition to that connected with obtaining a Qualifying Law Degree, and this is perceived to be a financial hurdle. Normally, entrants to either branch of the professions will have a degree (with the attendant fees and expenses) and, unless it is a Qualifying Law Degree, have passed the Common Professional Examination (which might cost in excess of £5,000 plus the costs of subsistence and accommodation).

Solicitors

A prospective solicitor is also faced with the costs of registration with the Solicitors Regulation Authority and attending a Legal Practice Course (for which there are about 11,000 places normally available but which can cost over £12,000) in addition to the subsistence and accommodation costs. However, a few large commercial legal firms offer financial assistance to graduates recruited onto their training contracts. Moreover, the Law Society specifies a minimum salary for trainee solicitors although many firms pay considerably more, and some larger firms pay more than £25,000. Upon completion of the training contract, many firms retain their trainees as salaried solicitors thereby providing some security and stability within the profession. Salaried solicitors may then progress to become associates and partners in private practice or work for large organizations, eg in the financial sector.

Barristers

A prospective barrister must meet the costs of registration with an Inn and attending the Bar Professional Training Course which can cost nearly £15,000 (plus the costs of subsistence and accommodation). Moreover, there is considerable competition to secure a place on, and to successfully complete, the Bar Professional Training Course. Typically, of 2,900 applications only 1,900 might be successful, and, of those, fewer than 1,700 candidates might pass. Moreover, success on the Bar Professional Training Course does not guarantee pupillage, for which there is also strong competition. Furthermore, a pupil barrister will not be able to take his own cases during the first six months of pupillage and cannot expect to earn significantly during the second six months of pupillage. Although a pupil is now paid at least £10,000 pa, it may take some years after Call before a barrister's earnings are sufficient to meet all expenses and provide a reasonable standard of living. The Inns of Court and many chambers do offer financial support (eg grants and loans) to assist student barristers and those commencing their practising career, but, there remains the problem that, even with such financial support, the Bar remains highly competitive, and many barristers encounter difficulties in finding a tenancy and establishing a practice.

After Call, a barrister has to complete at least 42 hours of continuing education in the course of the next three years, eg in case preparation, substantive law relating to practice, ethics, and advocacy. Nevertheless, the Bar Council is worried as it feels the best graduates may gravitate towards the security of training contracts with large firms of solicitors rather than go to the Bar where a successful pupillage does not guarantee a future or success as barristers practise on a self-employed basis.

Access and diversity

Membership of both branches of the legal profession is young (the average age is now around 40) and expanding at a very strong rate, having quadrupled since 1950 and trebled since 1970. In 1990 there were fewer than 55,000 practising solicitors, whereas now there are over 145,000 solicitors qualified to practise of which approximately 115,000 hold a current practising certificate. The Bar has experienced a similar growth: the number of barristers has risen from approximately 6,600 in 1990 to currently nearly 14,000.

The Law Society estimates that, annually, there are now over 25,000 graduates eligible to proceed into vocational training by virtue of either holding a Qualifying Law Degree or having passed the Common Professional Examination. However, a smaller proportion proceed to qualify professionally than was the case 30 years ago: during the period 1972 to 1979 approximately 60 per cent of eligible graduates proceeded to qualify as solicitors but in the period 1988 to 1991 the figure had fallen to approximately 50 per cent; and in 2008–9, there were nearly 8,500 new solicitors enrolled whilst only 5,809 new training contracts were registered.

Economic climate

Legal practice is a business, and the economic climate may affect the career opportunities. As mentioned above, recruitment for training contracts may be effected at the end of a student's second year – perhaps two years in advance of the commencement of the training contract – and where there is a subsequent downturn in the economic needs of the recruiting firm, it may be necessary to defer the commencement of training contracts. Clearly this can impact heavily on those who are carrying a significant debt. Similarly, on completion of the training contract, continuing employment with the training firm cannot be guaranteed, and many newly qualified solicitors do not proceed into practice. A further problem is that despite seemingly generous pay, the long hours of work drive many young lawyers with a few years' experience out of professional practice.

Gender

For some years, female law students have accounted for well over half the total number of candidates eligible to enter the professions, but at senior levels, both professions remain heavily male dominated. By 2008–9 females accounted for nearly 62 per cent of all solicitors' training contracts registered, but female solicitors average lower earnings than their male equivalents and are underrepresented at partner level. Similarly, the (predominantly London-based) Bar remains dominated by male barristers (being 70 per cent of all barristers in practice).

Revision tip

The composition of the Bar (and the Law Society to a lesser extent) has been criticized as favouring male, white, middle-class entrants. When revising the various elements of entry and training, ask yourself whether they are justifiable hurdles.

Discipline and regulation

The quality of legal services

The maintenance of the quality of legal services was traditionally entrusted to the professional bodies; and legal action against individual lawyers frequently proved difficult.

Causing loss to a third party

A solicitor's client could sue the solicitor in contract but, in contrast, as there was no contract between the lay client and the barrister, a claim would not usually lie in contract. Moreover, a solicitor's actions could affect a third party but the solicitor would not be contractually linked with that party, and so that third party would have no right of action in contract; thus claims had to be brought in negligence, which raised issues of public policy and remoteness. However, fairly recently in *White v Jones* [1995] the House of Lords revised its approach to claims in negligence against lawyers, so that where negligence has caused a loss to a third party (such as a beneficiary under a will) that person may be able to sue.

....

White v Jones [1995] 2 AC 207

Lord Browne-Wilkinson noted: 'In all these circumstances, I would hold that by accepting instructions to draw a will, a solicitor does come into a special relationship with those intended to benefit under it in consequence of which the law imposes a duty to the intended beneficiary to act with due expedition and care in relation to the task on which he has entered.'

....

Discipline and regulation

✳✳✳✳✳✳✳✳✳✳

Negligent advocacy

Another problem was that for many years the courts had refused claims in tort against a barrister or solicitor for negligent advocacy, eg *Rondel v Worsley* [1969] (House of Lords) and *Saif Ali v Sidney Mitchell* [1980] (House of Lords). However, in *Hall v Simons* [2002], the House of Lords thought that such an exemption could no longer be sustained.

....

Hall v Simons [2002] 1 AC 615 (House of Lords)

Lord Hoffmann noted: 'My Lords, I have now considered all the arguments relied upon in *Rondel v Worsley* [1969]. In the conditions of today, they no longer carry the degree of conviction which would in my opinion be necessary to sustain the immunity. The empirical evidence to support the divided loyalty and cab rank arguments is lacking; the witness analogy is based upon mistaken reasoning and the collateral attack argument deals with a real problem in the wrong way. I do not say that *Rondel v Worsley* [1969] was wrongly decided at the time. The world was different then.'

....

Thus, barristers and solicitors may now be sued for negligence in respect of advocacy and the conduct of litigation.

The Law Society, the Bar Council and the Clementi Report 2004

The **Courts and Legal Services Act 1990** had established a Legal Services Ombudsman to oversee the handling of complaints against legal professionals, and under the **Access to Justice Act 1999** could order payment of compensation. Matters warranting investigation (including unresolved complaints from clients) were passed to the Law Society's Office for the Supervision of Solicitors. Where its investigation showed a prima facie serious case (eg misconduct), the matter was referred to the Solicitors Disciplinary Tribunal which was able to impose a financial penalty, and ultimately could order that a solicitor be struck off the Roll. However, the Office for the Supervision of Solicitors was seen as insufficiently independent, and slow to act in less serious cases which formed the overwhelming volume of its work. It aimed to keep complainants better informed and to resolve issues at an early date, but achieved limited success and public confidence in the legal professions remained weak.

In 2004, the Clementi Report explored various ways of enhancing public confidence and recommended the separation of the disciplinary functions from the representative role of the Bar Council and Law Society and the creation of a new Office for Legal Complaints to handle complaints from consumers of legal services. In addition, it recommended a new regulator for legal services – the Legal Services Board – which could devolve regulatory and representative functions to separate legal bodies. As a result, the Law Society has separated its regulatory function (Solicitors Regulation Authority) from its representative function and similarly the Bar has separated its regulatory function (the Bar Standards Board) from its representative function. In addition both the Bar and the Law Society have enhanced non-lawyers' participation in complaints procedures and the Bar has a Bar Standards Board under a Complaints Commissioner and serious matters can be referred to the Senate of the

Inns of Court; and the Law Society has a Legal Complaints Service and serious matters can be referred to the Solicitors Disciplinary Council.

This was reflected in the Legal Services Act 2007 which created the Legal Services Board (whose membership is predominately non-legal) which will oversee the regulatory functions of the Bar and Law Society, and the Office for Legal Complaints. Further recommendations made in the Clementi Report were to encourage Legal Disciplinary Practices for lawyers from different professional backgrounds and allow non-lawyers to be involved in their management and ownership.

The result is that whilst the Solicitors Regulation Authority regulates the training, admission, and disciplinary functions many of which were formerly exercised by the Law Society under the Solicitors Act 1974, the Law Society's main function is now to represent the interests of solicitors. Where the complaint involves professional misconduct, it is passed to the Solicitors Regulation Authority.

The governing body for barristers is the Bar Council which undertakes a function similar to the Law Society in respect of representation, but exercise its regulatory and disciplinary role through a separate Bar Standards Board. Complaints against barristers are investigated by a Complaints Commissioner who may order compensation for poor service, and a Disciplinary Tribunal may hear serious cases of professional misconduct, and may ultimately disbar a barrister.

Judges

Judges are salaried officials appointed to decide impartially disputes between two individuals or the individual and the state. They are often categorized as either superior or inferior, as Figure 6.2 illustrates.

As shown in Figure 6.2, there is a hierarchy of judges. There are usually 12 Justices of the Supreme Court (formerly the 'Law Lords', ie Lords of Appeal in Ordinary), and then, in descending order, 38 Lord (Lady) Justices of Appeal (in the Court of Appeal) divided between the Criminal Division (headed by the Lord Chief Justice) and the Civil Division (headed by the Master of the Rolls who is also Head of Civil Justice); 3 other Heads of Divisions – Chancery, Family, and Queen's Bench Divisions; and 109 High Court (also known as Red or Puisne) judges who customarily receive a knighthood. The appointments system is necessarily complex because consistent with the theory of the separation of powers, once appointed, judges have to enjoy independence and be free from the threat of removal.

The independence of the judiciary

Judges apply the law to the facts as found, and must be unbiased between the litigious parties. In this function, they balance the rights and obligations of citizens *inter se*, and also between the citizen and the state – an area where the judges have to control the excesses of the executive (the Government). Although the judiciary cannot declare an Act of Parliament to be invalid, judges often find themselves in conflict with the Government, as has occurred

Judges

✳✳✳✳✳✳✳✳✳✳

Figure 6.2 Hierarchy of the judge

Judges of the Superior Courts	Court
Justices of the Supreme Court (formerly 'Law Lords', ie Lords of Appeal in Ordinary)	Supreme Court (formerly House of Lords)
Lord Chief Justice	Court of Appeal (Criminal Division)
Master of the Rolls	Court of Appeal (Civil Division)
Lord Justice of Appeal	Court of Appeal
High Court Judge	High Court & Crown Court
Judges of the Inferior Courts	**Court**
Circuit Judge	Crown Court and County Court
Recorder	Crown Court
District Judge	County Court
District Judge (Magistrates' Court)	Magistrates' Court

over the interpretation of the Human Rights Act 1998 and the Prevention of Terrorism Act 2005. According to the principle of separation of powers (the separation of the three primary functions of the state: legislature, executive, and judiciary) propounded by the French jurist Montesquieu, an independent judiciary is fundamental to a legal system.

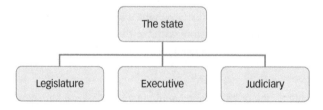

Figure 6.3

Until the recent reforms of the Constitutional Reform Act 2005, the role of the Lord Chancellor breached this principle of separation of powers; but more generally within the

English legal system, the principle is respected through the mode of judicial selection, the terms of **judicial tenure**, and limitations upon the removal of judges. The composition of the judiciary has been criticized, and to meet the criticism that the process of judicial appointments favours candidates from certain backgrounds, steps have been taken to widen eligibility for appointment and increase transparency in the selection process.

Judges need to be seen as independent (apolitical, unbiased, incorruptible, and free of the influence of the executive); thus the more important judges (superior judges and Circuit Judges – see Figure 6.3 above) may not be Members of Parliament, and judicial peers normally refrain from participation in political debates (other than on law reform) in the House of Lords.

Revision tip

To further your understanding on the subject of the separation of powers as well as the issue of political views in the judiciary, you may wish to refer to the following texts:

C de Montesquieu, *The Spirit of Laws* (originally 1748; later edition: George Bell, 1902), Book 11, Chs 6 and 7.

JAG Griffith, *The Politics of the Judiciary* (Fontana, 1997).

As part of this independence, all judges (including magistrates – s 31 Courts Act 2003) enjoy immunity from civil action in respect of their judicial activities conducted in good faith (*Sirros v Moore* [1975] (Court of Appeal)) even where the judge has acted mistakenly. Independence is reinforced by judicial salaries supposedly being sufficient to avoid corruption, and being paid from the **Consolidated Fund**; and by the complex procedure required for the removal of superior judges. The Constitutional Reform Act 2005 now requires the Government to uphold the independence of the judiciary.

This is important as some judicial decisions may have political dimensions or consequences, and in times of war and national emergency, judges have shown themselves to favour the executive's action (eg *Liversidge v Anderson* [1942] (House of Lords)). In his *The Politics of the Judiciary*, Professor JAG Griffith cites instances of the judiciary's evidencing pro-establishment views (eg *AG v Guardian Newspapers Ltd* [1987] (House of Lords) and *R v SS Home Office ex p Brind* [1991] (House of Lords)), and favouring interests on the political right (eg *Bromley London Borough Council v Greater London Council* [1983] (House of Lords)). He attributes these views to the judicial background of being upper middle class, having attended public schools, and having received an Oxbridge education. Moreover, this is reinforced by the socializing that occurs at the Bar. However, contrary to Griffith's assertions, recent governments (both Conservatives and Labour) have criticized the judges as impeding the intention of legislation.

Individual independence (ie lack of personal bias) is a more difficult notion; but natural justice requires that no one should be a judge in their own case (sometimes expressed in Latin as *nemo judex in sua causa*) and that a judge must withdraw from the case where he has a material, proprietary, or personal interest in the litigation. The test is whether

Judges

✳✳✳✳✳✳✳✳✳✳

a fair-minded observer would consider that there was a real danger of bias (*DG of Fair Trading v Proprietary Association of Great Britain* [2001]).

In looking at the judges, key factors include:

- eligibility
- the selection and appointment process
- tenure and dismissal
- diversity
- the revision of the role and functions of Lord Chancellor
- the transfer of functions from the House of Lords to the Supreme Court.

Figure 6.4

Judge	Eligibility	Appointment
Justice of the Supreme Court (formerly Law Lord, ie Lord of Appeal in Ordinary)	held high judicial office for two years or been a qualifying practitioner for fifteen years	by the Queen on the advice of the Prime Minister.
Lord Justice of Appeal	be a High Court judge or have held high judicial office for two years or been a qualifying practitioner for seven years	by the Queen on the advice of the Prime Minister
High Court Judge	have been Circuit Court judge for two years or have been a qualifying practitioner for seven years	by the Queen on the recommendation of the Lord Chancellor
Circuit Judge	have been a qualifying practitioner for seven years (or have been a Recorder or held another judicial office for three years)	by the Queen on the recommendation of the Lord Chancellor
Recorder	have been a qualifying practitioner for seven years	by the Queen on the recommendation of the Lord Chancellor
District Judge	have been a qualifying practitioner for five years	by the Lord Chancellor
District Judge (Magistrates' Court)	have been a qualifying practitioner for five years	by the Lord Chancellor

Eligibility

By the Courts and Legal Services Act 1990, the eligibility qualifications for judicial appointments were amended from membership of a particular branch of the legal profession to rights of audience before courts. Thus, the pool of potential appointees was expanded so that solicitors might be appointed directly to the High Court (as was Lord Justice Collins). The Tribunals, Courts and Enforcement Act 2007 further expanded that pool by amending these criteria to 'judicial-appointment eligibility condition' of various lengths as shown in Figure 6.4; but these are minimum lengths and most appointees' experience significantly exceeds these criteria. Moreover, as appointment is commonly predicated upon several years' experience of sitting judicially part-time, appointees will continue to be aged over 40.

Selection and appointment

Since the early 1990s judicial posts up to the level of Circuit Judge have normally been advertised, and more recently vacancies at High Court level have also been advertised, but the Lord Chancellor may also issue invitations to those eligible to become High Court Judges. Posts above High Court level are filled on invitation only, and although many judges are promoted to the higher (appeal) courts, there is no official judicial career or promotional path.

Selection process criteria

Traditionally three criteria (enumerated by Lord Hailsham, Lord Chancellor, in 1985) are applied to the process of selecting from qualified candidates:

* appointment is solely on merit
* no single view on any candidate is decisive
* no candidate should be appointed to permanent post without evidenced capability in a part-time capacity.

So, typically, a District Judge will usually have evidenced his ability by sitting part-time as a fee-paid Deputy District Judge for several years prior to appointment to permanent office.

The Judicial Appointments Commission staff collates factual information from the candidate as well as receiving references from referees nominated by the applicant as well as those it nominates itself so it will have the views of those closely involved with the work of the appointee. As part of the selection process for High Court appointments confidential **secret soundings** about candidates used to be made of senior practitioners and judges; and this process attracted considerable criticism because it favoured candidates with good contacts. This process has been amended but independent enquiries are still made and the candidates' files are reviewed.

Judges

✳✳✳✳✳✳✳✳✳✳

Criticism and reform

Many of these changes were in response to criticisms of the former system (eg the emphasis upon a candidate's advocacy experience and the influence of the comments and recommendations of the existing judiciary) as discriminating against women, ethnic minorities, and solicitors. In 2009 Jack Straw, then Lord Chancellor, established the Advisory Panel on Judicial Diversity whose report proposed steps to encourage applications from women and ethnic minority lawyers.

Reforms of the system of judicial appointments were sought for several reasons:

* the political influence (the Bar Council working party (and others) having criticized the political element of the role of the Lord Chancellor and the Prime Minister in the judicial appointments system)
* the secrecy surrounding the system which had placed considerable power in the hands of the civil service and favoured the 'old boy' system (as evidenced by the preponderance of applications emanating from barristers' chambers from where judges had previously come and exemplified by a media comment of Bridge LJ that the appointors look for 'chaps like ourselves')
* the stated objective of a more diverse judiciary which could be achieved by increasing the number of appointments of solicitors to the High Court, and of ethnic minorities, and women at all levels
* to challenge the tendency for judges to have been educated at public school and the older universities
* a strong candidate may often be able to earn significantly more in practice, even though judicial salaries may seem attractively generous.

The Peach Report

In 1999, the Lord Chancellor asked Sir Leonard Peach to review the process of judicial appointments. The Peach Report favoured maintaining the current system but also recommended:

* the creation of a Judicial Appointments Commission to investigate grievances and to audit the appointment process
* that nominees could give up to six consultees, which would shift the emphasis from a candidate's advocacy
* that candidates should attend one-day assessment centres and undergo psychometric testing.

The Peach Report did not recommend that 'secret soundings' be discontinued.

The Judicial Appointments Commission

In 2001, a Judicial Appointments Commissioner (Sir Colin Campbell) was appointed to review the operation of the appointments process, but not to advise on the actual appointments. He found that the system produced excellent judges but it lacked transparency and fairness. In addition, he found that many actual and potential candidates lacked knowledge of the process and this discouraged many potentially able candidates. Moreover, the Judicial Appointments Commissioner's 2003 Annual Report concluded that there was systemic bias that impeded sectors of the legal community from successful application for judicial office.

Following further criticisms and unease, the Constitutional Reform Act 2005 has underlined the separation of powers by establishing an independent Judicial Appointments Commission, all of whose members are appointed by the Queen. The Commission comprises 15 members as shown in Figure 6.5.

Figure 6.5

Number	Position held
6	Lay members (including the Chair)
3	High Court or Court of Appeal judges
1 of each	Circuit Judge, District Judge, barrister, solicitor, (lay) magistrate, tribunal member

The Judicial Appointments Commission applies the 'on merit' test as the sole criterion for appointment, and the selection and appointment is now conducted in a modern, open, and transparent manner, having regard to encouraging diversity among those selected for appointment. The Commission will propose one name only for each vacancy for appointment by the Secretary of State for Constitutional Affairs, so that a candidate could not be appointed without the Commission's recommendation. Before recommending a candidate for appointment, the Commission will have consulted with the Lord Chief Justice and another judge of similar experience. The Secretary of State can refuse, but only once, an appointment and request another name or ask for another to be reconsidered; but must accept the candidate thereafter proposed.

The appointments of the Lord Chief Justice, Heads of Division, and Lord Justices of Appeal continue to be by the Queen on the advice of the Prime Minister following a recommendation of a selection panel of two senior judges and two lay members of the Commission.

Appointment to the Supreme Court

The Constitutional Reform Act 2005 created a new Supreme Court (to replace the Judicial Committee of the House of Lords), and s 24 provides that the Lords of Appeal in Ordinary became Justices of the Supreme Court. The procedure for appointment is that the Lord Chancellor convenes a Commission which will report to him detailing who has been consulted and who has been recommended; he will then forward the name to the Prime Minister for appointment by the Queen.

Judges

****

Tenure and dismissal

Judicial tenure is the term used to describe the right of a judge to remain in office. For many years, there was no formal retirement age for a judge, but the current retirement age is now normally 70 although by s 11 Supreme Court Act 1981, the Lord Chancellor (the Secretary of State for Constitutional Affairs) may permit a judge to continue in office.

Similarly, for many years, there was no formal method of reprimand for a judge. In serious cases, the Lord Chancellor had issued a written reprimand such as that given to His Honour Judge Pickles who publicly described the Lord Chief Justice as a 'dinosaur'. Moreover (balancing the rule that courts will not look behind a parliamentary statute), there is a convention that individual judges are not to be criticized during debates in Parliament. By s 108(3) Constitutional Reform Act 2005, the Lord Chancellor and the Lord Chief Justice are jointly responsible for discipline including issuing disciplinary advice, warnings, and reprimands to a judicial office holder. In addition, suspension is now also available where necessary for maintaining public confidence in the judiciary, and the Judicial Appointments and Conduct Ombudsman will be able to review complaints concerning judicial conduct.

Dismissal of inferior judges

Whilst the judiciary needs to be seen to be independent, and free of fear of removal at the desire of the executive, the provisions for removal of a superior judge differ from those relating to an inferior judge. By s 17(4) Courts Act 1971 and s 22 County Courts Act 1984, the Lord Chancellor (but only with the agreement of the Lord Chief Justice) may dismiss inferior judges only for 'inability' or 'misbehaviour' or failure to comply with the conditions of appointment. Currently, 'misbehaviour' is considered to include drink-drive offences or offences involving dishonesty or moral turpitude – ie something morally and widely unacceptable. The only case of dismissal was that of His Honour Judge Campbell in 1983 who was convicted of evading customs duty on cigarettes and whisky. In 2000, the Lord Chancellor indicated that persistent failure to comply with sitting or training requirements, or sustained failure to observe standards reasonably expected were grounds for removal. In such a case, a nominated judge would effect an investigation but the Lord Chief Justice would have to agree with the decision.

Dismissal of superior court judges

Superior court judges enjoy security of tenure dating from the Act of Settlement 1700 during good behaviour (*quamdiu se bene gesserint*) and may be removed by the Queen only after a petition from both Houses of Parliament (by s 11 Supreme Court Act 1981, and s 6 Appellate Jurisdiction Act 1876). The only case where this was effected was in 1830 to Sir Jonah Barrington, a judge of the High Court of Admiralty in Ireland. However, usually a judge would prefer to resign rather than face dismissal. Where a superior judge is incapable (eg through ill health) of undertaking his duties or of resigning, under s 11 Supreme Court Act 1981 the Lord Chancellor can declare as vacant the office of that judge. Section 108(1) Constitutional Reform Act 2005 specifies procedures for the dismissal of a judge.

 Looking for extra marks?

A good answer will demonstrate the link between the judicial appointments process and judicial tenure.

Constitutionally it is important to have a judiciary independent of, and irremovable by, the Government. Consequently, the judicial appointments' process has to deliver appointments with a very high level of confidence which necessitates more extensive selection processes than in other professions.

Diversity

Prior to the Courts and Legal Services Act 1990 eligibility for appointment as a superior judge depended upon professional practice as a barrister, which favoured those with a privileged background. This favoured the image of judges as male, Oxbridge, and private-school educated, white, middle-aged, and middle class. Recent revisions, building on those offered by the Courts and Legal Services Act 1990 and the Tribunals, Courts and Enforcement Act 2007, should encourage candidates from the solicitors' branch of the profession which has the potential to encourage more female candidates and candidates from the ethnic minorities.

Section 64 Constitutional Reform Act 2005 requires the Judicial Appointments Commission to 'have regard to the need to encourage diversity in the range of persons available for selection for appointments' and the 2007 Act now authorizes the appointment of **Legal Executives** and **Patent Agents** to certain judicial posts. However, as indicated by the 2010 Report of the Advisory Panel on Judicial Diversity, there remains much to be done to improve the facility for part-time appointments (under High Court level) in order to attract candidates with family commitments.

The current eligibility criteria require all judicial appointees to have qualification and experience in law, so that a newly appointed judge is expected to rely heavily on previous experience, usually in legal practice, as preparation for judicial office. This implicitly assumes a link between the areas of practice and areas of jurisdiction, but, in fact, a judge may often be expected to determine cases outside his or her knowledge and experience. However, it should be remembered that judicial appointment invariably involves a preceding period in a part-time capacity as a deputy or assistant which allows the development of the candidates' judicial ability to be observed and discussed in appraisals.

Although at one time training was considered to interfere with judicial independence, the Runciman Commission (1993) recommended increased resources for judicial training, refresher training, peer appraisals, practitioner feedback, and increased awareness of race and gender issues. Now the Judicial Studies Board organizes some training of the judiciary, including a short initial residential course (three or four days), a continuation seminar once every three years, and training in major new areas of the law such as the Human Rights Act 1998 and the Civil Procedure Rules 1998. In addition, Recorders have to visit two penal establishments and attend Crown Court trials.

The Lord Chancellor

Historically, the Lord Chancellor's role was to protect the judiciary from the Government but, as indicated in Figure 6.6, his triple role offended the principle of the separation of powers (and, in particular, the independence of the judiciary) which was seen as essential to safeguard citizens.

As a result of critical comments, the Lord Chancellor no longer sits as a judge, and under the Constitutional Reform Act 2005, he will not have to hold a professional legal qualification (ie be a barrister or solicitor) – he will merely need to be qualified 'by experience'. Moreover, he may now be a member of the House of Commons. Section 3(1) Constitutional Reform Act 2005 asserts that 'all with responsibility for matters relating to the judiciary or otherwise to the administration of justice must uphold the continued independence of the judiciary', and s 3(5) reinforces judicial independence through the prohibition of influencing any particular judicial decision.

Figure 6.6

Member of the Executive	• Member of the Cabinet • Head of the Lord Chancellor's Department (now the Department for Constitutional Affairs) • Responsibilities include the Law Commission and state funding of legal services • Subject to removal by the Prime Minister • Responsible for courts, tribunals, and the Community Legal Service, Official Solicitor's Department, the Land Registry, and Public Trustee Office • Plays a major role in effecting senior judicial appointments – such as the Master of the Rolls – which in turn may have a major effect on the relationship of the judiciary with the executive
Member of the Legislature	• Speaker of the House of Lords • Member of the House of Lords
Member of the Judiciary	• President of the Supreme Court (Judicature Acts 1873–5) • Nominally President of the Chancery Division • May sit as a judge

The Constitutional Reform Act 2005 replaced the Judicial Committee of the House of Lords, ie the Law Lords, with a new Supreme Court, and transferred the Lord Chancellor's judicial function (re training, guidance, welfare, etc) to the President of the Courts of England and Wales (the former Lord Chief Justice Lord Phillips). By s 7, the President will also represent the views of the judiciary to the Government and Parliament.

Conclusion

The combined effect of the Courts and Legal Services Act 1990, the Access to Justice Act 1999, and the Tribunals, Courts and Enforcement Act 2007 has been to blur the former sharp distinction between barristers and solicitors, and so to quieten the calls for fusion of the legal professions. However, qualification as a barrister or solicitor remains a long and expensive process, and, as such, favours those with personal financial support. Both professions continue to receive criticism over their lack of diversity as exemplified by the continuing dominance of both by middle-class white males. Given that judges will continue to be appointed principally from eligible senior legal practitioners, it is unsurprising that the criticisms of a lack of diversity levelled against the professions are equally applicable to the judiciary which is also criticized as being 'old'.

In an endeavour to address tensions between guaranteeing judicial independence and the right of removal, the Constitutional Reform Act 2005 has retained strict eligibility criteria and a rigorous and extensive appointments process for judicial office.

 Key cases

Case	Facts	Ratio/Held
AG v Guardian Newspapers Ltd [1987] 1 WLR 1248 (House of Lords)	The courts granted an injunction to maintain the secrecy of the operations of the Security Service although the information was freely available elsewhere in the world.	The courts will prefer to protect actions which are claimed to be in the public interest.
Bromley London Borough Council v Greater London Council [1983] 1 AC 768 (House of Lords)	Bromley LBC sought to stop the Greater London Council from increasing the rates to allow lower public transport fares.	The additional rate was *ultra vires* because of the fiduciary duty to balance fairly the interests of ratepayers and transport users.
DG of Fair Trading v Proprietary Association of Great Britain [2001] 1 WLR 700	A party claimed bias, as one of the members of the court had once applied for a job in a company connected with the claim.	The test for a court's impartiality is whether a fair-minded observer would apprehend a real danger of bias.
Hall v Simons [2002] 1 AC 615 (House of Lords)	Claims were brought against solicitors for professional negligence in the conduct of advocacy.	The public policy of the immunity of advocates in earlier cases was no longer valid.

Exam questions

✳✳✳✳✳✳✳✳✳✳

Case	Facts	Ratio/Held
Liversidge v Anderson [1942] AC 206 (House of Lords)	An individual detained under a wartime order of the Secretary of State, made in good faith, challenged the reasonableness of the belief.	The courts will not question the reasonableness of the belief in matters which Parliament has entrusted to the discretion of the Secretary of State.
R v SS Home Office ex p Brind [1991] AC 696 (House of Lords)	The courts upheld the prohibition of a broadcast including direct speech from representatives of a proscribed terrorist organization.	The Secretary of State acted *intra vires* the wide discretion given to him by Parliament in issuing directions contravening the European Convention on Human Rights.
Rondel v Worsley [1969] 1 AC 191 (House of Lords)	Barrister unsuccessfully defended claimant on a charge of grievous bodily harm.	A barrister is not liable for professional negligence in the care and conduct of litigation prior to, or in court, as a barrister cannot refuse a brief.
Saif Ali v Sidney Mitchell [1980] AC 198 (House of Lords)	Barrister pursued a claim against the owner of the vehicle not the driver. When the error was discovered, the claim against the driver was unenforceable.	A barrister's immunity extends only to work before the court or closely connected work.
Sirros v Moore [1975] QB 118 (Court of Appeal)	A judge refused an appeal against deportation in the mistaken belief that he had no jurisdiction to hear the case.	Provided he is acting in good faith, a judge does not incur any civil liability for judicial acts taken in error.
White v Jones [1995] 2 AC 207 (House of Lords)	Solicitors failed to carry out a testator's instructions. Those who were to have benefited under the new will did not do so.	The responsibility of a solicitor to his client extends to intended beneficiaries.

 Exam questions

Essay question

To what extent does the judiciary represent modern society?

An outline answer is available at the end of the book.

Problem question

Arthur Brown instructed Kitchen & Smith (solicitors) to defend him in the county court in respect of a contractual dispute over the hire of some vehicles which were damaged during the hire period. John Smith, a partner in Kitchen & Smith, advised Arthur that a barrister should be instructed to represent Arthur, and suggested Robert Round. At the hearing, Robert failed to make several important legal points and forgot to question an important witness, and, as a consequence, Arthur lost the case.

Advise Arthur on the scope of the potential liability of Kitchen & Smith and Robert Round in negligence.

An outline answer is available online at <http://www.oxfordtextbooks.co.uk/orc/concentrate/>.

#7

Lay participation

- A layperson is an individual member of the public without legal qualification/training. Laypersons play a range of roles within the English legal system, primarily as members of a jury or as lay magistrates.

- There are two forms of magistrate: lay magistrate and District Judge (Magistrates' Court). They have very different characteristics but both have criminal and limited civil jurisdiction.

- A range of criticisms have been levelled at the use of lay magistrates; for example, influence of the Clerk to the Justices, composition of the bench, bias, lack of competence, and inconsistency in sentencing.

- The use of juries dates back more than 1,000 years. The right to jury trial is seen as a fundamental right, which protects citizens from harsh treatment by the state. Academics and legal professionals disagree over the effectiveness of such a mechanism.

- Within civil courts (High and county) the role of the jury can be twofold: to determine liability and level of damages awarded. Criminal juries (Crown Court) determine the guilt/innocence of a defendant who has been charged with a criminal offence (hybrid and indictable).

- Eligibility criteria for jury service is laid down within the Juries Act 1974. Serving as a juror is a civic duty and failure to attend, when requested to do so, can be punishable as contempt of court.

- A number of criticisms have been levelled at the use of juries: the influence of the judge when summing up, secrecy of jury deliberations, media influence, perverse verdicts, use of majority verdicts, and the composition of juries etc. Numerous reforms have been proposed over the years to limit and/or remove the use of juries.

Laypersons

A layperson is not legally qualified or trained. The legal system relies heavily on such people. Their importance lies in:

- ensuring accountability, the public seeing openly court procedures, thereby maintaining public confidence in the system
- providing the public with the opportunity to participate in the machinery of justice
- demonstrating that the law is understood not solely by lawyers. (Lawyers have to communicate in everyday language and explain legal concepts in a manner members of the public understand, ensuring that important issues are accessible to everyone)
- the fact that they are more democratic and decisions are made by people from a wide variety of backgrounds
- that they are less costly than legal professionals.

Laypersons can be involved in the administration of justice as:

1. lay magistrates
2. members of a jury
3. assessors – who advise the judge on technical matters in civil proceedings, aiding the judge to evaluate the evidence and make a final decision, per s 70 Supreme Court Act 1981 and s 63 County Courts Act 1984
4. coroners – appointed by local authorities to determine the cause of unexpected or suspicious deaths and accidents
5. tribunal members – who sit with a legally qualified chairman and assist with the decision-making process.
6. arbitrators – appointed by parties to adjudicate a dispute between them and to make a decision on the basis of the evidence and knowledge of the relevant area.

✅ *Looking for extra marks?*

In relation to examination questions on laypersons most students concentrate solely on the use of laypersons as members of a jury or as lay magistrates. However, you would gain extra marks by initially identifying a range of minor roles played by laypersons within the English legal system, eg arbitrators, coroners, lay assessors, tribunal members, etc, and providing information on their varied roles.

Revision tip

When dealing with any examination question on laypersons ensure that you can define the word and are able to provide a range of advantages and disadvantages associated with the use of laypersons generally.

Laypersons

****

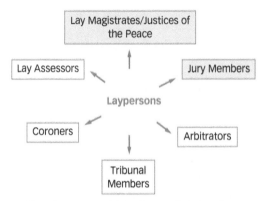

Figure 7.1 Laypersons' involvement within the English legal system

Magistrates

- Lay magistrates date back to 1195 when Richard I commissioned knights to preserve the King's Peace. They were granted power to investigate crime, arrest suspects, sit in judgment, and impose punishment.

- The quality of Justices of the Peace in London led to the development of stipendiary magistrates, professional magistrates who were paid and required to be legally qualified per the Middlesex Justices Act 1792. The Municipal Corporations Act 1835 provided for such appointments in towns.

- Lay and stipendiary magistrates used the same court buildings following the Justices of the Peace Act 1949.

- Following the Courts Act 2003, Her Majesty's Court Service, now manages the magistrates' courts on a national level. The country is divided into about 600 Local Justice Areas, each with a courthouse and Justices' Clerk where magistrates preside.

Magistrates' duties

Magistrates deal with 95 to 98 per cent of all criminal cases – 1.9 million cases in all. Magistrates are involved with preliminary issues in the remaining cases. Criminal jurisdiction includes:

- trying all summary offences and determining guilt/innocence – hybrid offences can be dealt with in the magistrates' court if the magistrates and defendant agree

- passing sentence on a defendant – sentences of 12 months for one offence, and £5,000 fine per s 154 Criminal Justice Act 2003 – magistrates may commit a person convicted of a hybrid offence to the Crown Court if they feel their powers are insufficient

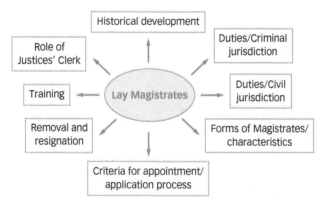

Figure 7.2 Lay magistrates/Justices of the Peace within the English legal system: issues to consider

- dealing with plea before venue hearings/mode of trial – if a defendant is charged with an offence triable only on indictment, or elects jury trial for a hybrid offence, the magistrates are still responsible for the initial hearing and for sending the case to the Crown Court for trial
- issuing applications for bail, arrest, and search warrants
- dealing with young offenders (aged 10–17 years) – Youth Court – bench consists of three magistrates, both genders, and under the age of 65 – restricted access to court and procedure is less formal.

The role of magistrates has increased:

- by many hybrid offences being downgraded to summary offences only – see Criminal Justice and Public Order Act 1994 (downgraded criminal damage below £2,000 to a summary only offence etc)
- by the CPS charging the lower of two possible charges (summary rather than hybrid) to ensure a conviction
- by many new criminal offences created being summary only offences.

Magistrates have civil jurisdiction to:

- hear appeals against a refusal to grant licences for the sale of alcohol per the Licensing Act 2003
- hear appeals against a refusal to grant licences for the operation of a Hackney cab
- grant licences for betting shops – Betting and Gaming Committee
- enforce debts owed to utility companies

- enforce demands for council tax and non-payment of television licences
- deal with issues affecting family/children – orders for protection against violence, adoption orders, emergency protection measures, etc, per the Children Act 1989 – Family Proceedings Court.

Revision tip

Ensure that you are aware of the actual criminal and civil jurisdiction of the magistrates' court and the various powers associated with magistrates. Questions on the operation of the courts and magistrates are common.

Forms of magistrate

There are two forms of magistrate:

- lay magistrates
- District Judges (Magistrates' Court).

Lay magistrates (Justices of the Peace)

Characteristics

- They are laypersons.
- Apart from certain preliminary matters, magistrates sit on panels of usually three, known as a bench – democratic decision-making.
- They are found sitting within all magistrates' courts.
- They are reliant on advice from Clerk to the Justices/Assistants.
- There are approximately 28,253 lay magistrates sitting nationally.
- They are unpaid, although eligible for expenses, loss of wages/travelling expenses per s 15 Courts Act 2003.
- They sit on a part-time basis (26 days).

Eligibility criteria and Application Process

- They must reside within a particular Local Justice Area or within 15 miles of it per s 10 Courts Act 2003.
- They must be aged 65 or under. Retirement age is 70 when placed on the supplemental list per the Courts Act 2003.
- They must be aged over 18.
- They must not be disqualified eg:
  - serving or recently retired police officers

- traffic wardens or civilian employees of police forces
- undischarged bankrupts
- close relatives of those already serving.

Figure 7.3 Application process

APPLICATION PROCESS
STAGE 1 Local Advisory Committees advertise vacancies in a range of publications. Individuals directly apply or organizations can nominate suitable candidates.
STAGE 2 An application form must be completed and the Local Advisory Committee identifies candidates who will be invited to a first interview. The Committee must ensure that the Bench broadly reflects the community which it serves, taking into account such factors as gender, ethnic origin, and occupation. An applicant must be able to demonstrate eg: • good character   • sound judgement • maturity and sound temperament   • social awareness • understanding and communication   • commitment and reliability
STAGE 3 If successful invited to a second interview where practical examples of cases that magistrates deal with will be explored.
STAGE 4 If successful the Local Advisory Committee will recommend appointment to Lord Chancellor. Appointment is made on behalf of the Queen per Justice of the Peace Act 1997 and Courts Act 2003. Local Advisory Committees consist largely of existing magistrates, who tend to favour the appointment of magistrates whose views are compatible with those of existing members.

Revision tip

In order to make revision more interesting, produce a range of different revision aids: wall charts, key cards, etc. Remember that even though it is a time-consuming process to produce revision aids you are actually revising the material as you prepare them.

Training

Magistrates undergo a training programme stipulated by the Judicial Studies Board and run by the Magistrates' Commission Committees. The training covers:

- basic law and procedure
- rules of evidence
- sentencing principles.

Forms of magistrate

✳✳✳✳✳✳✳✳✳✳

Training focuses on developing skills such as:

1. structured decision-making
2. communication
3. listening
4. awareness of community needs
5. problem-solving
6. team working.

All new magistrates have a mentor, who will support and introduce the magistrate to the bench and procedures involved. The early training involves observing/shadowing and reflecting on the court process with their mentor. After six formal sittings the magistrate will be ready for a first appraisal where any outstanding training needs will be identified.

Magistrates are kept up to date with changes in procedure via material and/or formal training. Extra training is required to sit:

- as chair of the bench
- within the Youth Court
- within the Family Proceedings Courts.

Removal and resignation

Magistrates can resign per s 11(1) Courts Act 2003. The Lord Chancellor can remove for incapacity or misbehaviour – s 11(2)(a); incompetence – s 11(2)(b); or declining or neglecting to take proper part in the exercise of functions as a magistrate – s 11(2)(c).

District Judge (Magistrates' Court)

Characteristics and appointment

- They were previously known as stipendiary magistrates per s 78 Access to Justice Act 1999.
- They are found within major cities when the workload dictates the need for a legally qualified magistrate.
- There are 106 District Judges (Magistrates' Court) appointed to a single bench with national jurisdiction per the Access to Justice Act 1999 (174 Deputy DJs).
- They sit on a full-time basis.
- They are paid a salary of £93,483.
- They are members of the judiciary and less reliant on the services of the clerk of the court.
- Under s 22 Courts Act 2003 and s 71(3)(c) Courts and Legal Services Act 1990 they must be a qualified barrister/solicitor of seven years' standing.

- They sit alone when hearing a case and will sit on complicated trials per s 26 Courts Act 2003.

Professional court users regard them as:

- quicker and more efficient
- consistent in decision-making and sentencing
- better able to control unruly defendants
- better at questioning CPS and defence lawyers.

Revision tip

Examination questions on magistrates are common; ensure that you are aware of the two forms of magistrate and provide information on their characteristics, highlighting differences and similarities. Also be aware of the problems associated with the replacement of lay magistrates and the perceived benefits.

✅ Looking for extra marks?

Examination questions that ask students to critically evaluate the use of magistrates within the English legal system are common. It would be advisable for students to read academic journals for supporting information and academic comment that may be used to make an examination answer more interesting/display understanding and support key issues raised within an answer. For example, an article that covers issues such as the powers of magistrates and Clerks to the Justices can be found within an article by Penny Darbyshire, 'A comment on the powers of magistrates' clerks' [1999] Crim LR 377, and comment on sentencing powers and court procedure can be found within an article by Andrew Herbert, 'Mode of trial and magistrates' sentencing powers' [2003] Crim LR 314.

Justices' Clerk

Every Local Justice Area has one Justices' Clerk appointed by the Lord Chancellor after consultation with the Lord Chief Justice per s 27 Courts Act 2003. Justices' Clerks delegate functions to assistants per s 27(7) Courts Act 2003 who must have a five-year magistrates' court qualification. Their role is to advise magistrates on law/procedure and ask questions in order to clarify issues per s 28(4) and 28(5) Courts Act 2003. Magistrates can ignore advice but must not blindly follow the advice per *Jones v Nicks* [1977]. The Clerk should not retire with magistrates when reaching their verdict.

....

R v Sussex Justices ex p McCarthy [1924] 1 KB 256

This case illustrates the appropriate role of the Clerk. The defendant was being tried in the magistrates' court on a charge of dangerous driving. The Clerk to the Justices was a member of a firm of solicitors who were representing the claimant in a civil case arising from the collision in the driving incident. When the magistrates retired to decide the case, the Clerk retired with them. Despite the fact that the Clerk did not take any part in the decision-making, the Divisional Court quashed the decision. Lord Hewatt CJ stated:

> it is not merely a matter of some importance but is of fundamental importance that justice should not only be done but manifestly and undoubtedly be seen to be done.

Under s 49(2) Crime Disorder Act 1998, Courts Act 2003, and The Justices' Clerks Rules (SI 2005/545), they may be required to undertake duties that could be ordinarily exercised by a single magistrate.

Composition

There is public perception that the magistracy consists of male, white, middle-class individuals with Conservative leanings but that they are more representative than District Judges (Magistrates' Court).

- Gender – women account for nearly half of new appointments and the numbers of male and female magistrates are now almost equal.

- Age – there are few young magistrates. Seventy-five per cent of new appointments are over 40 and 75 per cent of sitting magistrates are over 50. The average age is 57. Over 33 per cent of serving magistrates are in their 60s. It could be argued that longer experience of life brings greater wisdom but younger justices would bring understanding of the lifestyles of younger generations. In 2006 a 19-year-old, Lucy Tate, was appointed to a bench in Yorkshire. The Government wants more young magistrates per the White Paper *Supporting Magistrates' Courts to Provide Justice* (2005), to make benches more reflective of the community in which they operate.

- Occupation – they are drawn overwhelmingly from professional and managerial ranks. Forty per cent were retired from full-time employment. Only 10 per cent were from manual working occupations. Reasons for this include:
  - no obligation on companies etc to allow an employee time off to serve
  - employers unwilling to pay wages during their employee's absence – loss of earnings allowance is capped
  - the work pattern of the lay magistrates excludes certain groups of the population – only certain groups can actually spare the time to sit, eg retired persons, lecturers, senior managers, etc
  - the selection process being dominated by existing magistrates who appoint people with similar backgrounds to their own.

- Political affiliations – in 2003, 34 per cent were Conservative supporters, 26 per cent Labour, 40 per cent were supporters of other parties or non-voters.

- Ethnicity – there is variation in racial composition between local benches and the communities they serve. In 1987 the proportion of such magistrates was only 2 per cent. This percentage varied regionally. Following a number of Government initiatives, including major advertising campaigns and shadowing schemes, such persons now make up 6 per cent of the total number of serving magistrates per the 2003 *National Strategy for the Recruitment of Lay Magistrates*.

Local knowledge

Lay magistrates, living within the Local Justice Area, have local knowledge of particular problems in their areas and more awareness of local events, local patterns of crime, and local opinions than a professional judge unfamiliar with the locality. The following case illustrates this principle.

Paul v DPP (1989) 90 Cr App R 173

Here a man was charged with kerb-crawling under s 1 Sexual Offences Act 1985 after picking up a prostitute in his car. The court had to decide whether his actions were likely to cause nuisance to other persons in the neighbourhood. The magistrates took account of their own knowledge of the area as a heavily populated residential area in which many drivers looked for prostitutes, and convicted the defendant. Affirming the conviction, Woolf LJ said this was the sort of case that was particularly appropriate for trial by magistrates with local knowledge.

Cost

Traditionally it has been assumed that because lay magistrates are unpaid volunteers they are cheaper than legally qualified counterparts per a report, the *Judiciary in the Magistrates' Courts* (2000). Comparing annual salaries, expenses, etc, lay magistrates are cheaper. However, more indirect costs are associated with lay magistrates:

* slower than professional judges in hearing cases (one professional judge can handle as much work as 30 JPs)
* likely to make greater use of the court facilities and administrative support mechanisms, for recruitment, training etc.

However, judges are:

* more likely to impose a sentence of custody, upon a finding of guilt
* remand defendants to custody.

Appeals

Few defendants appeal against magistrates' decisions. Of those who do, many are against sentence, not against the determination of guilt. In 2003 the Judicial Studies Annual Report showed:

* Of 11,858 appeals made to the Crown Court only 2,811 were allowed.
* In 2,179 cases the decision/sentence was varied by the Crown Court.
* Of 96 appeals made to the Queen's Bench Divisional Court only 43 were allowed.

Forms of magistrate

****

Bias and competence

Magistrates are expected to act fairly, impartially, listen to the evidence, and not show bias towards either side.

R v Worcestershire JJ ex p Daniels (1996) 161 JP 121

Here a woman was convicted of failing to provide a specimen of breath and complained that whilst she gave evidence a magistrate was reading material and not paying attention to what she said. Quashing her conviction the court stated that it is important that justices give full attention to the proceedings; justices need not look at a witness constantly, but they should not appear to be engaged for any considerable time in some activity inconsistent with hearing the evidence.

Magistrates who repeatedly hear similar cases, often with similar evidence presented by the same prosecutors (and police officers) and who have previously seen a defendant, may become case-hardened and biased.

R v Bingham JJ ex p Jowitt (1974) The Times, 3 July, DC

A defendant was found guilty in a speeding case where the only evidence was that of the motorist and police constable. The Chair of the Bench stated:

> where the evidence is a direct conflict between a police officer and a member of the public. My principle...has always been to believe the evidence of the police officer...therefore we find the case proved.

The conviction was quashed on the grounds that the Chair's comments would cause any reasonable person to suspect that the defendant would not receive a fair trial.

✅ Looking for extra marks?

Ensure that you support the points that you make with relevant legal authority. This can be from a variety of sources, eg case law, statutory provisions, academic comment, law reform reports etc. Failure to provide such support would mean that it would be unlikely that you will achieve a pass mark for the question concerned.

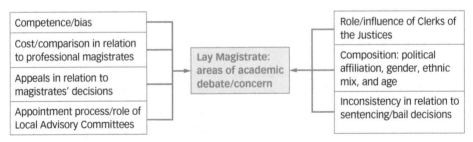

Figure 7.4 Areas of academic debate/concern

Inconsistency

There is inconsistency in the decision-making of different benches in relation to sentencing decisions. The Government's White Paper *Justice for All* set out differences found in the Criminal Statistics for 2001, for instance:

- *Burglary of dwellings*: 20 per cent of offenders were sentenced to immediate custody in Teesside, compared with 41 per cent of offenders in Birmingham

- *Bail applications*: magistrates in Hampshire granted 89 per cent of all bail applications whilst in Dorset only 63 per cent were allowed.

The Government has attempted to reduce inconsistency via sentencing guidelines and greater training. Under the Courts Act 2003 a Sentencing Advisory Panel has been established to further promote greater consistency in sentencing.

Revision tip

You should ensure that you have a good overview of the problems associated with the operation of the magistrates' court and lay magistrates generally as examination questions that ask for a critical analysis of magistrates and their role are common.

Proposed reforms

- Increase role and powers of Justices' Clerks and Assistants: *A Review of the Criminal Courts of England and Wales* (2001).

- Greater use of professional judges, District Judges (Magistrates' Courts): per the 1993 Royal Commission on Criminal Justice (a single District Judge could replace 30 lay magistrates) but this would be expensive, end the tradition of lay participation, and increase the risk of bias and case hardening.

- Auld LJ recommended, *inter alia*, that changes be made to the selection process – Local Advisory Committee membership should include individuals from minority groups, with legislation preventing employers from discriminating against employees who wish to serve: *A Review of the Criminal Courts of England and Wales* (2001).

- Increased involvement of lay magistrates – restructuring the criminal courts. A new Magistrates' Division would undertake the work of the court. The District Division would contain a mixed bench, a District Judge and two magistrates, and deal with triable either way offences. The judge in the case would decide issues of law but the bench would determine the issue of guilt or innocence: *A Review of the Criminal Courts of England and Wales* (2001).

Looking for extra marks?

Many reports have been produced which have analysed the problems associated with the operation of the criminal justice system. The Auld Report was the last comprehensive analysis. You would be advised to view this report, in particular the summary of those problems and recommendations: see Lord Justice Auld, *A Review of the Criminal Courts of England and Wales* (London: HMSO, 2001) <http://www.criminal-courts-review.org.uk/>.

Juries

The jury has been a feature of the English legal system for 1,000 years. In 1215 Magna Carta recognized a person's right to trial by 'the lawful judgement of his peers'. The right to be tried by one's peers is seen as the bastion of liberty against the state, one of the fundamentals of a democratic society. Lord Devlin stated that the jury is:

> The lamp that shows that freedom lives…The object of any tyrant would be to overthrow or diminish trial by jury, for no tyrant could afford to leave a subject's freedom in the hands of 12 of his countrymen. [Devlin, *Trial by Jury* (Stevens, 1956), p 164]

However, not all academics agree:

> juries are not random, not representative, but anti democratic, irrational and haphazard legislators, whose erratic and secret discussions run counter to the rule of law. [P Darbyshire, 'The lamp that shows that freedom lives: Is it worth a candle?' (1991) Crim LR 740]

✅ Looking for extra marks?

Examination questions that ask students to critically evaluate the use of juries within the English legal system are common. An article by Penny Darbyshire highlighted her experiences of jury service. Her comments/criticisms can be used in addition to those highlighted below. The article highlights the practical problems of jury service rather than mere academic concerns ('Notes of a lawyer juror' (1990) NLJ 1264, 14 September). In addition Peter Thornton has written an excellent article which illustrates the combined changes that have been made to jury trials over the past 50 years: 'Trial by jury: 50 years of change' [2004] Crim LR 683.

Revision tip

As soon as you have been made aware of the topics to revise, produce a revision timetable which detail, when, where, and what you are revising in each revision session. Plan the timetable around 30 minutes per session per topic.

Juries in civil cases

The use of civil juries declined after the nineteenth century; judges were given the power to refuse a case to be heard by a jury and insist that it be heard in front of a judge only per **Administration of Justice (Miscellaneous Provisions) Act 1933**. Juries hear less than 1 per cent of civil cases. They have a dual role:

1. determine liability
2. determine the damages awarded.

Per s 69 Supreme Court Act 1981 and s 66 County Courts Act 1984, juries are used *inter alia* within the **High Court** and **county court** when the case concerns:

- defamation
- malicious prosecution
- false imprisonment.

Jury trial is granted unless in the court's opinion the trial requires prolonged examination of documents, accounts, or scientific or local investigation, which cannot conveniently be made with a jury per s 69(3) Supreme Court Act 1981.

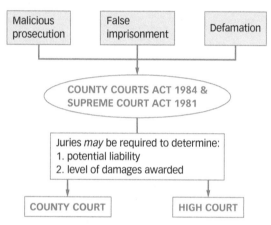

Figure 7.5 Areas of civil liability dealt with by juries

Oliver v Calderdale Metropolitan Borough Council (1999) The Times, 7 July

The trial judge rejected an application for jury trial by the claimant. The Court of Appeal upheld this decision, pointing out that there was no automatic right to jury trial. There was a presumption in favour but this could be displaced as the Supreme Court Act 1981 and County Courts Act 1984 only give a qualified right to jury trial.

It is rare for a jury trial to be granted in relation to other civil cases, eg personal injury. See *H v Ministry of Defence* [1991] in the key cases section.

Defamation

In the 1980s there were several high-profile cases in which juries gave extremely large awards of damages where untrue allegations were made by newspapers, eg £500,000 to Jeffrey Archer (sex with prostitutes). Until s 8 Courts and Legal Services Act 1990 the Court of Appeal was unable to change the award made by a jury where the level awarded was excessive. See *John v Mirror Group of Newspapers* [1996] in the key cases section.

Juries

****

In 1971, the Faulks Committee (*The Laws of Defamation*, Cmnd 5709 (HMSO, 1974)) recommended that the normal method for determining such cases should be by a single judge sitting alone.

Revision tip

When revising this topic area ensure that you have a good grasp of the venues where you may find a jury operating. Many students fail to mention the use of juries in the civil system and concentrate solely on criminal juries. By exploring their use in both systems you are expanding the potential areas of critical analysis which you can cover within any exam.

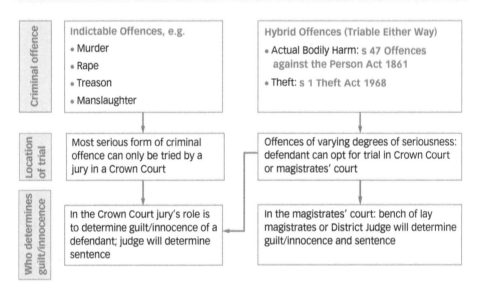

Figure 7.6 Forms of criminal offences dealt with by juries

Juries in criminal cases

Juries hear hybrid offences and indictable offences within the **Crown Court**. They determine the issue of guilt. The judge decides points of law and administers a sentence where the defendant has been found guilty. Juries actually operate only in a minority of cases, 2 per cent to 5 per cent of all criminal trials. However, a jury may still not be required to determine the issue of guilt, because:

- defendants may plead guilty prior to a jury being convened
- the CPS may withdraw its charges as new evidence shows that the defendant is not responsible, or it feels the case is too weak
- the judge may direct the jury to acquit where the prosecution's evidence has not made out a case.

Juries in fraud cases

There are only about 15 to 20 such trials each year. The Roskill Committtee on Fraud Trials 1986 found that fraud trials were long, expensive, and the evidence was too complicated for members of the public to understand. In 2001, the New Zealand Law Commission dismissed the argument that juries could not understand expert evidence, or difficult scientific or financial evidence. It suggested only a small proportion of trials were too long and perhaps too complex for a jury.

Auld LJ recommended that trial judges, in serious and complex fraud cases, should sit alone to hear such cases, or the case should be heard by a judge and two lay experts taken from a special panel (*A Review of the Criminal Courts of England and Wales* (2001)).

The Government enacted s 43 Criminal Justice Act 2003 which provides that on the application of the prosecution where the length and/or complexity of the trial would be unduly burdensome on jurors a case could be heard by a judge sitting alone.

 ✓ Looking for extra marks?

A range of articles which highlight the advantages and disadvantages associated with jury usage generally, and in particular fraud trials, can be found within R Rhodes, 'Juries in fraud trials' (1998) NLJ 239, 20 February; David Corker, 'Trying fraud cases without juries' [2002] Crim LR 283; and Sally Lloyd Bostocks, 'The Jubilee Line jurors: Judge only trial in long and complex fraud trials' [2007] Crim LR 255.

Eligibility criteria

Section 1 Juries Act 1974 sets out the eligibility criteria for serving on a jury. To qualify a person must be:

- aged 18 to 70: s 1(1)(a)
- registered on the electoral roll: s 1(1)(a)
- ordinarily resident in the United Kingdom, Channel Islands, or the Isle of Man for at least five years since the age of 13: s 1(1)(b).

A person may not serve if they are:

- a mentally disordered person: s 1(1)(c)
- disqualified from jury service: s 1(1)(d).

Originally under the Juries Act 1974 a wide range of persons were ineligible, disqualified, or could be excused as of right from jury service. The representative nature of jury selection was criticized by Auld. He believed that everyone should be eligible for jury service, except for the mentally ill – this would improve the representative nature of jury service by ensuring that all levels of society would potentially be represented on juries; that juries were deprived of the experience and skills of a wide range of professional people; and that their absence created the impression that jury service was only for those not important or clever enough to get out of it (*A Review of the Criminal Courts of England and Wales* (2001), pp 140–9). The Government accepted the proposal and enacted s 321 and Schedule 3 Criminal Justice Act 2003.

Since this enactment, members of the legal profession (including QCs) and the judiciary have sat on juries. However, use of legal professionals/judges could cause:

1. delays within the legal system, as many courts would be without a judge
2. a legally qualified juror influencing the rest of the jury
3. bias in favour of the prosecution.

....

R v Abdroikov and ors [2007] UKHL 37

The House of Lords in three appeals ruled that the prima facie presence of a police officer or law enforcement agent on a jury does not of itself make the trial unfair and would not lead a fair-minded person to suspect a real possibility of bias, primarily because bias of any individual juror can be mitigated by the other 11 members.

....

Prior to 2004, people in certain essential occupations had the right to be excused from jury service. Only full-time members of HM Forces can be excused from service per s 9(2) and s 9A Juries Act 1974 as amended by the Criminal Justice Act 2003.

The rules disqualifying people with certain criminal convictions from jury service remain under the Juries Act 1974 as shown in Figure 7.7.

Figure 7.7

Disqualified for life	Disqualification for 10 years
Imprisonment for a term of 5 years of more	Any term of imprisonment (including a suspended sentence)
Imprisonment for public protection	Community sentence
Life imprisonment or equivalent	
Those on bail are also disqualified.	

Jury service is a civic duty. Failure to attend is punishable as contempt of court, a summary offence per s 20 Juries Act 1974. Auld LJ noted that 15 per cent of potential jurors refused to answer the jury summons and that it was rare for courts to prosecute in such cases. He suggested that jury service should be more rigidly enforced (*A Review of the Criminal Courts of England and Wales* (2001), p 145).

Discretionary excusals and discharging a jury

Section 9(2) Juries Act 1974 provides the court with the power to excuse individuals who have a good reasons which make it difficult for them to serve, eg:

- too ill to attend
- suffering from a disability that makes it impossible for the person to sit as a juror
- being the mother of a small baby
- pre-booked holidays.

Under s 16 Juries Act 1974 the judge has a discretion to discharge a juror or the entire jury for, *inter alia*:

- illness
- misconduct, eg racial bias (see *Sander v UK* [2000] in key cases section)
- significant inadmissible evidence given to the jury
- the result of an external factor, eg media comments.

Disabilities and jury service

Those with disabilities other than that of a mental nature can serve by virtue of s 9B(2) Juries Act 1974 (inserted by s 41 Criminal Justice and Public Order Act 1994). However a judge has the power to excuse or discharge a juror when there is doubt as to 'capacity to act effectively as a juror' per s 10 Juries Act 1974 where:

- a disability will make it impossible to properly discharge duties
- command of English is not sufficient to follow the proceedings.

. . . .

Re Osman (Practice Note) [1996] 1 Cr App R 126

A deaf man O was called for jury service and informed the court before sitting that he would be unable to follow the proceedings without an interpreter. After questioning O the judge said it would be inappropriate to allow the interpreter to join the jurors when they retired to consider their verdict, and discharged O from jury service. The judge stated that the interpreter would have to attend the jury room and become a thirteenth person when only 12 were permitted. The fact that the interpreter would not be expressing personal opinions was not considered a sufficient safeguard.

. . . .

 Looking for extra marks?

An additional good source of information which details the courts' approach to individuals with disabilities and jury service in general has been compiled within an article by A Majid, 'Jury still out on deaf jurors' (2004) 154 NLJ 278. The article also suggests a range of mechanisms which can be used to assist those with certain disabilities, eg qualified interpreters could be appointed by the judge and given training as to the limits of their duties, eg not to enter into personal discussions within the jury room.

Selection of the jury

Section 1(1) Juries Act 1974 states, 'every person shall be qualified to serve as a juror in the Crown Court, the High Court and the County Courts'; as a result half a million people are called for jury service each year for two weeks. The selection process is undertaken nationally by the Jury Central Summoning Bureau (JCSB). Under the random selection process, many people are never called for jury service, whilst others may be called several times in a lifetime. Computers are used to produce a random list of potential jurors from the electoral roll database. Summonses are sent out with a set of explanatory notes including a form which must be returned, confirming that the person meets all eligibility criteria. From the resulting list a jury panel/pool is produced by the JCSB. This list is dispatched to the relevant court. It is necessary to call more than 12 jurors as many court buildings have more than one courtroom, so that several jury panels will be needed and it is not known how many of those summonsed are disqualified or excused from jury service.

Auld identified that the electoral roll did not truly represent the population. Many people failed to respond to the electoral roll form for many reasons, eg house moves or people declining to register in order to evade council taxes and official agencies. Some wished not to vote in order to send a protest to the Government or because of dissatisfaction with politics in general. He recommended a range of publicly maintained lists and directories should be used to make the jury more representative of society in general (*A Review of the Criminal Courts of England and Wales* (2001)). The Government rejected this proposal in its 2002 White Paper *Justice for All* (<http://www.criminal-justice-system.gov.uk/publications>).

Vetting

Vetting occurs when the names of potential jurors are passed by the prosecution to the Criminal Records Office to identify individuals who are disqualified from serving due to previous convictions. This is designed to avoid bias on the part of a jury member and remove the potential of such persons influencing other jury members. The process is limited by guidelines issued by the Attorney General.

The Court of Appeal in *R v Mason* [1981] stated that the vetting of previous convictions was necessary in order to ensure that disqualified persons do not serve was 'common sense'.

Challenges for cause/stand by

Challenges are made by any party if they can show good cause, eg the defendant might argue that a juror knows him personally. Jurors cannot be questioned before being challenged, per *R v Andrews* (1998).

The other possible method of objecting to a jury member is when the prosecution use the power to stand by, to serve only if no other juror is available. Attorney General guidelines state the power to stand by a jury is restricted to the following situations:

- where the juror is manifestly unsuitable and the defence agree with the exercise of the power
- in connection with jury vetting

Random selection and composition

The jury are theoretically supposed to be representative of society as a whole through the process of random selection. Despite this, a jury can consist of all men or all women or not contain any person from the defendant's ethnic minority group.

Following the recommendations made by the Royal Commission on Criminal Justice, Auld LJ recommended a right to alter the representation of the jury. The prosecution or defence could apply to the judge for the selection of a jury containing up to three people from ethnic minority communities (Auld, *Review of the Criminal Courts* (2001), p 155).

The measure was rejected by academics and the Government (in White Paper *Justice for All*, Cm 5563 (HMSO, 2001), para 7.29) on the grounds that, *inter alia*:

- it assumes bias on the part of excluded jurors when no prejudice has been proved
- ethnic minority jurors would be placed in a difficult position since they might feel they are expected to represent the interests of the defendant or victim
- it would place a burden on the courts to determine which cases require an ethnic minority quota.

Any suggestion that the principle of random selection be interfered with has been rejected by the courts:

R v Smith [2003] 1 WLR 2229

A black man was convicted of grievous bodily harm by an all-white jury following a violent incident in which the victim and all the witnesses had been white. There was evidence that the appellant and his companions had been racially abused in a nightclub by the victim and had suffered racial discrimination in the local area. He appealed on the grounds that a fair trial in such cases required a multi-racial jury and that this amounted to a breach of Article 6 European Convention on Human Rights. The Court of Appeal rejected this and dismissed the appeal. A judge has no power to empanel anything other than a random jury and this randomness was a key safeguard against the possibility that a juror might be prejudiced.

Judicial summing up and verdicts

After the closing speech for the defendant the judge will direct the jury on the law and remind them of the facts and evidence presented. In *R v Sanghera* [2005], the Court of

Juries

✳✳✳✳✳✳✳✳✳✳✳

Appeal stated that a short summing up was permissible provided it contained a summary of the points for and against the defence.

The judge will direct the jury to elect a foreman who will act as the chair for the jury deliberations and deliver the verdict within open court. The judge will direct the jury that they must reach a unanimous verdict, not to discuss the case with anyone outside the jury, and bring to the judge's attention any behaviour among the jurors which causes concern.

The jury is then placed in the charge of the jury bailiff who is given the responsibility of ensuring that jury deliberations take place at the correct time and when all jury members are present per *R v Hastings* [2003] and in secret per s 8 Contempt of Court Act 1981.

In 80 per cent of cases the verdict of the jury is unanimous. After two hours and ten minutes the judge could accept a majority verdict per s 17 Juries Act 1974, where at least 10 of the 12 jurors are agreed per Criminal Justice Act 1967. The foreman of the jury must announce the numbers agreeing and disagreeing with the verdict in court per s 17(3) Juries Act 1974.

Majority verdicts were introduced because:

- of the fear of jury nobbling (jurors bribed or intimidated by the defendant/associates in order to reach a not guilty verdict)
- jury acquittal rates were too high
- it avoided the problem of one juror with extreme or intractable views holding out against the rest, and reduced the need for expensive and time-consuming retrials.

'Despite the fact that most jurors...have prejudices, a majority verdict provides [a] safe-guard against...prejudice but in fact in the great majority of cases the verdict is unanimous' (Professor M Zander, 'The complaining juror' (2000) 150 NLJ 723). Majority verdicts are controversial because, if two jurors favour acquittal then the prosecution have not proved their case beyond a reasonable doubt.

If the jury are unable to reach a verdict they must be discharged via a *Watson* direction. It requires the jury foreman to state in open court that the jury cannot reach a verdict and the jury to be discharged per s 16 Juries Act 1974. When this occurs the defendant may face a retrial. This may not take place if:

- the prosecution choose not to continue proceedings
- the judge decides it is not possible to have a fair retrial and orders the proceedings stayed.

In addition to majority verdicts, to prevent jury nobbling *inter alia*:

- s 51 Criminal Justice and Public Order Act 1994 – this creates an offence in relation to jury intimidation/tampering.
- ss 44 and 46 Criminal Justice Act 2003 – where there is a risk of jury tampering in a case it can be tried by a judge alone on application of the prosecution. The first case where these provisions were utilized was *R v T and ors* [2009] (see key cases section).

An excellent academic overview of the case can be found within Rosemary Pattenden's article 'Case Comment *R v T*: Trial by judge alone' [2009] IJEP 355. Since this case, two further applications have been made under these statutory provisions by the Crown Prosecution Service.

Role of jury and relationship with the judge

The role of the judge is to direct the jury on the relevant law; the jury have to apply the law to the facts found and reach a verdict. The judge cannot direct a jury to reach a guilty verdict.

Bushell's case (1670) 124 ER 1006

B was a foreman of the jury charged with trying two Quakers accused of disturbing the peace via preaching. The jury refused to find the defendants guilty as instructed, in spite of being shut up without food or drink. Following their verdict the Recorder of London directed they be imprisoned for contempt. Vaughan CJ granted a writ of Habeas Corpus for their release stating: 'once the jury have given their verdict, the judge has no option but to accept it'.

In *R v Wang* [2005], the House of Lords stated the judge had been wrong to direct a jury to convict: 'It is for the jury, not the judge, to decide whether the defendant is guilty. There were no circumstances that justified a judge directing the jury to convict.'

A judge can order a jury to acquit. In *R v Young* [1995], Lord Parker CJ stated judges:

should be prepared to take the responsibility when appropriate, of saying to the jury that there was not enough evidence on which they could properly convict, and accordingly direct an acquittal.

Secrecy of jury deliberations

Jurors may have prejudices which can affect the verdict. The jury is not required to give reasons for its decisions, and there are suspicions that some decisions are based on irrelevant factors, eg personality of one of the barristers, prejudice in favour of or against the police, influence by the media, bribery or threats made by the defendant/defendant's friends, the way the defendant looks (eg race), or perhaps due to other non-justifiable reasons. Once the jury retire they are not allowed to communicate with anyone other than the judge and the bailiff. Section 8(1) Contempt of Court Act 1981 makes it an offence for anyone (juror or not) to disclose details of what was said in the jury room, or for anyone other than a juror to try to obtain such details, which includes 'votes cast, statements made, opinions expressed or arguments advanced'.

In *Attorney General v Seckerson and Times Newspapers Ltd* [2009] the Court of Appeal reiterated that 'initial voting' within the jury deliberation room and the 'reasoning of a jury verdict' were clearly matters that fell within s 8(1) provisions and that secrecy of jury deliberations were a 'fundamental part of the English [legal]...system and that numerous

Juries

****

previous authorities had indicated that this was the approved approach.' Also see *R v Young* [1995] concerning the use of a ouija board by the jury and *Attorney General v Scotcher* [2005] in the key cases section.

Arguments in favour of secrecy:

- ensures freedom of discussion in the jury room
- protects jurors from outside influences and from harassment
- enables jurors to bring in unpopular verdicts
- prevents unreliable disclosures by juries and a misunderstanding of verdicts.

Arguments in favour of disclosure:

- makes juries more accountable
- easier to enquire into the reliability of convictions and rectify injustice
- shows where reform is required.

The courts have been careful to ensure that the jury deliberations remain secret and will not usually entertain any appeal based on what happened in the jury room.

A key exception to this would be where irregularities come to the attention of the court before the verdict has been reached, ie when something can be done about it. The courts will not look into any alleged irregularities in the jury room once the verdict has been given per *Vaise v Delaval* (1785) (see key cases section). The Court of Appeal has, however, ruled that it is permissible to investigate any happenings outside the jury room which may affect the deliberations of the jury.

R v Mirza and ors [2004] 1 All ER 925

The House of Lords stated s 8(1) Contempt of Court Act 1981 was designed to prevent leaks to the press, and not inhibit the court from ensuring a fair trial. Where jury impropriety has been reported during the trial, the judge has a duty to investigate, make appropriate enquiries, and deal with any misconduct. This may include for example, racist comments being made in the jury room or ignoring the judge's direction not to discuss the case outside of the courtroom or bringing external material into the court. The common law rule prohibits any investigation once the verdict has been given and properly recorded, except perhaps where the irregularity is extraneous to the jury's deliberations or involves the jury being provided with information that it should not have had.

The Court of Appeal stated in *R v F* [2009] All ER (D) 162 (Feb) that the appropriate test was whether or not a reasonable person, an independent observer, would believe that there was a real risk that the jury during their deliberations had been influenced by something other than the legitimate evidence presented during the course of the trial.

A Practice Direction (*Crown Court: Guidance to Jurors* (2004) The Times, 27 February) clearly states:

> Trial judges should ensure that the jury is alerted to the need to bring any concerns about fellow jurors to the attention of the judge at the time and not wait until the case is concluded.

Publicity and media coverage about police investigations may influence jurors but the courts are unwilling to entertain this as a ground of appeal. In *R v West* [1996] 2 Cr App R 374 the Court of Appeal stated, 'to quash [a] conviction on the [above] ground…would mean that if allegations were sufficiently horrendous so as to…shock the nation, [defendants] could not be tried'.

Perverse verdicts/jury equity

The verdict is the jury's alone and they cannot be ordered to convict. They can ignore the law and bring in a verdict based on their own idea of fairness. This is seen as a protection against oppressive prosecutions in which the jury can rescue from the power of the state a defendant who, whilst technically guilty, does not deserve prosecution or punishment. This has become known as jury equity. However, it could be argued that this process leads to a perverse verdict which does not reflect the evidence and appears to conflict with the actual affirmation/oath undertaken by the jury which requires them to 'faithfully try the defendant and give a true verdict according to the evidence'.

R v Quayle and ors [2005] EWCA Crim 1415

In appeals involving the possession and use of cannabis for medical purposes, the appellants argued that the judge should have reminded the jury of their right to acquit regardless of the law. The Court of Appeal disagreed: the jury has a well-established power to return a verdict of not guilty whatever the law and however clear, but to require the judge to direct the jury in such a way would involve a positive invitation to the jury to act contrary to the law and take over the role of the legislative authorities.

McCabe and Purves in *The Jury at Work* (Blackwell, 1972) felt the proportion of apparently perverse verdicts was small with many actually being more attributable to:

* failure of prosecution witnesses
* the credibility of the defendant's explanation.

In a study, *Jury Trials* (Clarendon Press, 1979), Baldwin and McConville described jury trial as an 'arbitrary and unpredictable business'. They found 25 per cent of acquittals were questionable and found no evidence that juries acquitted people in the face of unjust prosecutions. Auld LJ was concerned with the situation where a jury verdict led to an acquittal despite the evidence:

> [practitioners] support…the right of the jury to ignore their duty to return a verdict according to the evidence and to acquit when they disapprove of the law or the prosecution in seeking to

enforce…juries…have no right to do so and it is an affront to the legal process…[Auld, *A Review of the Criminal Courts of England and Wales* (2001), p 168]

The Government did not accept Auld's recommendation that Parliament should clearly state in legislative provisions that juries could not acquit in contravention of the evidence or in defiance of the law.

....

R v Kronlid (1996) The Times, 31 July

The defendants broke into a British Aerospace hangar causing damage costing £1.5 million to a Hawk fighter jet. In a video they left in the cockpit explaining their actions they admitted breaking into the hangar and using hammers to damage the £10 million aircraft. They claimed a defence under s 3 Criminal Law Act 1967 that they were legally entitled to use reasonable force in the circumstances to prevent a more serious crime being committed. The jet was to be sold to Indonesia, where it would be used against the civilian population in East Timor fighting for independence. Their actions damaging the jet prevented the crime of genocide. The jury found all the defendants not guilty despite the evidence. It could be argued that by acquitting, it was a criticism of the British Government's position on the issue and the Indonesian Government.

....

✅ Looking for extra marks?

A recent research paper produced in 2010 by Cheryl Thomas in conjunction with the Ministry of Justice entitled *Are Juries Fair?* (Ministry of Justice Research Series 1/10) (<http://www.justice.gov.uk/publications/research.htm>) covered many of the issues/criticisms discussed above. Direct quotations from this paper and recent statistical analysis could be used to supplement information provided within your examination answer. This would demonstrate your research abilities, awareness of recent developments, and understanding of the subject area.

The research/report by Cheryl Thomas, *Are Juries Fair?* (Ministry of Justice Research Series 1/10) (<http://www.justice.gov.uk/publications/research.htm>), was an extensive analysis of the operation of juries within the Crown Court via:

- post-verdict surveys
- analysis of actual jury verdicts
- case simulations with real juries.

It analysed, *inter alia*, the consistency of jury verdicts, influence of media coverage eg via internet, understanding of legal process (judicial directions and reporting of improper conduct within the jury deliberation room), and racial bias. The study established *inter alia*:

- All-white juries did not discriminate against ethnic minority defendants – there was no more tendency to convict black or Asian defendants than white defendants.
- White jurors serving on racially mixed juries and on all-white juries had similar patterns of decision-making irrespective of ethnicity of defendant.

- However, jurors were more likely to convict a white defendant when he was accused of assaulting a black or Asian victim compared to a white victim particularly in more racially diverse areas.

- White jurors did not racially stereotype defendants as more or less likely to commit certain offences.

- Some jurors were more lenient towards a defendant of a certain ethnic group but the system of 12 jurors ironed out individual prejudices.

- Female jurors were more likely to be persuaded or opt themselves to change their vote than male jurors whilst jury deliberations were taking place.

- Most charges brought against defendants in the Crown Court are not actually decided by a jury – eg 59 per cent of all charges result in a guilty plea and thus no jury is sworn in.

- Only 0.6 per cent of all cases result in hung juries (where juries cannot reach a verdict).

- The jury conviction rate varied between the various courts surveyed – between 69 and 53 per cent.

- Juries were rarely discharged – less than 1 per cent of sworn juries.

- Some jurors were unable to follow the directions given to them by the judge – younger jurors were better at comprehending legal instructions.

- Despite judicial instructions 48 per cent of all jurors were unsure what to do if they suspected improper conduct within the jury deliberating room.

- 67 per cent of jurors wanted more information on how to conduct jury deliberations.

- 82 per cent of all jurors believed that the secrecy of jury deliberations should be maintained.

- 75 per cent of all jurors in high-profile cases were aware of media coverage in relation to the case before them.

- Most jurors only remembered reports they saw or heard during the time that their trial was going on – evidence of the so-called fade factor (the further away media reports were from a trial the more likely they were to fade from jurors' memories).

- 35 per cent of all jurors in high-profile cases remembered pre-trial coverage.

- Jurors in high-profile cases recalled media reports primarily from television/national newspapers. In standard cases local newspapers were the primary source of reports.

- 66 per cent of all jurors could not remember whether the reports were slanted towards guilt or innocence – those that could highlighted that the coverage was slanted towards guilt.

- 20 per cent of jurors in high-profile cases who recalled coverage found it difficult to put such reports out of their mind whilst serving.

- 26 per cent of all jurors in high-profile cases saw information on the internet pertaining to their case and 12 per cent stated they actually sought such information out in direct contravention of directions given.

Reforms

- The Government felt that many defendants manipulate the system when faced with a hybrid offence and plead guilty at the last minute in the belief that the delay may:
  - put pressure on the CPS to reduce the charge in exchange for a guilty plea
  - weaken the prosecution case as witnesses' recollection of events may deterioate and make a conviction less likely.
- This wasted considerable time and money, so an attempt was made to remove the right of defendants to opt for a Crown Court trial via the 1999 Criminal Justice (Mode of Trial) Bill. However, this was never enacted.
- Auld LJ proposed changes to the criminal court structure, which would impact on the use of juries. Three divisions would be created: Crown, District, and Magistrates' Division.
  - District Division would contain a mixed bench – a District Judge and two magistrates – dealing with hybrid offences.
  - Crown Division would operate in the same way as the present Crown Court but the jury would only be involved in determination of guilt in relation to indictable offences (Auld, *A Review of the Criminal Courts of England and Wales* (2001)).

Over the years various alternatives have been proposed to replace the full 12-person jury, *inter alia*:

- *Single judge*: used in relation to criminal cases before the Crown Court in Northern Ireland (terrorism-related offences known as Diplock Courts). Advantages/disadvantages:
  - quicker trials
  - easier for defendant to challenge a verdict – judge required to produce written decision
  - no involvement of laypersons
  - no protection against harsh prosecution decisions
  - judge might be biased, prosecution-minded, and case-hardened
- *Panel of judges*: advantages/disadvantages:
  - quicker trials
  - easier for defendant to challenge a verdict – judge required to produce written decision

- – no involvement of laypersons
- – prohibitive costs – salary of judges/training
- – judges might be biased, prosecution-minded, and case-hardened
- – lack of qualified judges and reduced availability of judges in other courtrooms
- *Mixed panel*: a judge and laypersons. Advantages/disadvantages:
  - – layperson involvement retained
  - – quicker trials
  - – laypersons on bench may merely rubber stamp judges view/decision rather than decide on the basis of the evidence provided
  - – layperson involvement would be significantly reduced
  - – in reality not likely to be much more efficient than present jury system.

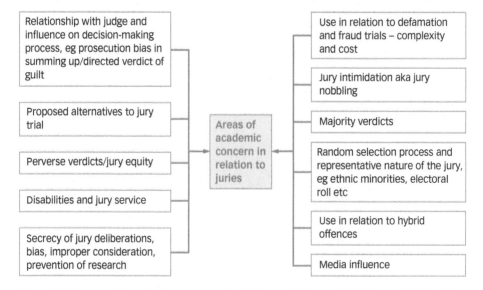

Figure 7.8 Areas of academic concern in relation to juries within the English legal system

Revision Tip

When revising ensure that you not only highlight the various proposed changes to replace/reform the use of juries over the years – mixed panel, judge only trial, mini juries, etc – but that you also cover the perceived advantages and disadvantages of such proposals. This critical approach to reforms is what will make your answer stand out.

Case	Facts	Ratio/Held
Attorney General v Scotcher [2005] UKHL 36	Shortly after a trial where the defendants had been convicted by a majority verdict, a dissenting juror wrote to the defendants' mother detailing the jury's deliberations and advising her to launch an appeal. The Attorney General brought proceedings for contempt of court.	The conviction was upheld. By writing to the defendants' mother he was disclosing the jury's deliberations to a third party who was not an officer of the court, and that contravened s 8(1) Contempt of Court Act 1981.
H v Ministry of Defence [1991] 2 All ER 834	A soldier, P, was left maimed through the negligence of an army surgeon. D admitted liability but disputed the level of damages. P sought a jury trial, but the judge refused.	P's appeal was dismissed. Damages for personal injuries should in almost all cases be assessed by a judge because of the need to ensure comparability; a judge would be able to match it to the standard tariff much better than a jury.
John v Mirror Group of Newspapers [1996] 2 All ER 35	The claimant sued for libel and was awarded £345,000 in damages.	The Court of Appeal allowed D's appeal and substituted £75,000 damages (Bingham MR). The time had come to allow the judge to indicate to the jury the level of award he thought might be appropriate; it would render their decision more rational and so more acceptable to public opinion.
Paul v DPP (1989) 90 Cr App R 173	A man was charged with kerb-crawling under s 1 Sexual Offences Act 1985 after picking up a prostitute in his car. The court had to decide whether his actions were likely to cause nuisance to other persons in the neighbourhood.	The magistrates took account of their own knowledge of the area as a heavily populated residential area in which many drivers looked for prostitutes, and convicted. Affirming the conviction, Woolf LJ said this was the sort of case that was particularly appropriate for trial by magistrates with local knowledge.

Case	Facts	Ratio/Held
R v Kronlid (1996) The Times, 31 July	The defendants broke into a British Aerospace hangar causing damage costing £1.5 million to a Hawk fighter jet. They claimed a defence under s 3 Criminal Law Act 1967 that they were legally entitled to use reasonable force in the circumstances to prevent a more serious crime being committed. The jet was to be sold to Indonesia, where it would be used against the civilian population in East Timor fighting for independence. Their actions damaging the jet prevented the crime of genocide.	The jury found all the defendants not guilty despite the evidence. It could be argued that by acquitting it was a criticism of the British Government's position on the issue and the Indonesian Government.
R v Quayle and ors [2005] EWCA Crim 1415	In appeals involving the possession and use of cannabis for medical purposes, the appellants argued that the judge should have reminded the jury of their right to acquit regardless of the law.	The Court of Appeal disagreed: the jury has a well-established power to return a verdict of not guilty whatever the law, however clear, but to require the judge to direct the jury in such a way would involve a positive invitation to the jury to act contrary to the law and take over the role of the legislative authorities.
R v T and ors (Twomey, Blake, Hibberd, Cameron) [2009] EWCA Crim 1035 (05 June 2009)	Concerned an armed robbery at Heathrow in 2004. The robbery netted £1.75 million pounds, the bulk of which had not been recovered. Charges against the defendants included, *inter alia*, possession of a firearm with intent to endanger life, possession of a firearm with intent to commit robbery, robbery, and conspiracy to rob. The defendants had originally been put on trial in 2008, but two trials had been stopped. The cost of the unsuccessful trials had been estimated at £22 million. The prosecution informed the court that approaches had been made to two members of the jury and the cost of giving a jury adequate protection would be approximately £6 million and use around 82 police officers. As a result the CPS applied for a judge-only trial per s 44 Criminal Justice Act 2003.	The Court of Appeal concluded that under these circumstances s 44 would apply and ordered that a retrial would take place without a jury determining the issue of guilt/innocence. This issue would be determined by a single judge. The cost of protecting the jury in a new case and the costs that had already been expended were far too high. Lord Chief Justice Judge stated: 'tampering was a significant danger [in this case] and that the protection measures did not sufficiently protect jurors from potential influence and ... [that the case involved] very serious criminal activity ... trial by jury was a hallowed principle, but the Act did allow a trial to be heard by a judge alone ... where it arises the judge assimilates all the functions of the jury with his own unchanged judicial responsibilities'.

Key cases

✳✳✳✳✳✳✳✳✳✳

Case	Facts	Ratio/Held
R v West [1996] 2 Cr App R 374	The defendant was convicted of murdering ten young women. Media coverage from the moment the bodies were discovered was intense and newspapers had paid witnesses to secure their story after the trial was completed.	The Court of Appeal rejected the appeal, that the media coverage had made it impossible for the defendant to receive a fair trial; the judge had given adequate warnings to the jury to consider only the evidence in court. To quash the conviction on the ground argued by the defendant would mean that if 'allegations were sufficiently horrendous so as to…shock the nation, [defendants] could not be tried'.
R v Worcestershire JJ ex p Daniels (1996) 161 JP 121	A woman convicted of failing to provide a specimen of breath complained that whilst she gave evidence, one of the magistrates was reading other material and not paying attention to what she said.	Quashing her conviction the court stated that it is important that justices give full attention to the proceedings; justices need not look at a witness constantly, but they should not appear to be engaged for any considerable time in some activity inconsistent with hearing the evidence.
Sander v UK [2000] Crim LR 767	An Asian man, D, was being tried on a charge of conspiracy to defraud. During the trial a juror, who was later segregated, wrote a note to the judge, raising concerns that other jurors had been openly making racist remarks and jokes. The judge directed the entire jury to 'search their consciences', put aside any prejudices, and try the case on the evidence. The judge then received two letters. One signed by all of the jurors which denied any racist attitudes and a second from a juror who admitted that he may have been the one making racist jokes. Despite the discrepancy between the letters, the judge concluded there was no risk of bias and refused the request to discharge.	D was convicted and appealed to the European Court of Human Rights per Article 6(1) European Convention on Human Rights. The court concluded the appellant had not received a fair trial. In the circumstances the judge should have discharged the jury as there was an obvious risk of racial bias. It was important for jurors to appear to an observer as being impartial.
Vaise v Delaval (1785) 99 ER 944	A defendant sought to set aside the jury's verdict in favour of the plaintiff, and produced affidavits from two jurors to the effect that the jury had resolved the case by tossing a coin.	The judge said he could not receive any such evidence from a juror: the verdict could not be impugned unless there was some external evidence of misconduct.

 Exam questions

Essay question 1

Critically evaluate the role of laypersons within the English legal system.

An outline answer is available at the end of the book.

Essay question 2

Academic Penny Darbyshire has descibed juries as:

> not random, not representative,…anti-democratic, irrational and haphazard legislators, whose erratic and secret discussions run counter to the rule of law'. ['The lamp that shows that freedom lives: Is it worth a candle?' (1991) Crim LR 740]

Critically evaluate the use of juries within the English legal system on the basis of the view expressed above.

An outline answer is available online at <http://www.oxfordtextbooks.co.uk/orc/concentrate/>.

#8
Provision of legal services

Key facts

- Barristers and solicitors have rights to appear in all courts.

- Barristers and solicitors now have similar liability for negligence in advocacy.

- Legal services are expensive.

- In civil litigation, the costs of the successful party are usually awarded against the unsuccessful party.

- The state has to impose some restrictions and tests on the provision of publicly funded civil legal services.

- Conditional fee arrangements offer 'no win, no fee' arrangements.

- The state is obliged to provide advice and representation in criminal cases.

Introduction

This chapter looks at the way in which legal services (whether criminal or civil, and whether or not involving litigation) are funded, and consequently the extent to which there is access to justice. One principal issue for the provision of legal services (both civil and criminal) is the quantum of public funding – as the Justice Secretary explained on 30 June 2010:

> Our legal aid system has grown to an extent that we spend more than almost anywhere else in the world. France spends £3 per head of the population. Germany; £5. New Zealand, with a comparable legal system, spends £8. In England and Wales, we spend a staggering £38 per head of population.

Another principal issue is the nature of the services provided (advice, professional **representation**, or both) in respect of criminal and civil law. In particular, the separation of the client and the funding source can create a conflict. More specifically, a demand-led provision risks imposing an uncertain and excessive burden on the public purse and therefore attracts much criticism in the current economic climate; in contrast, a budget-restricted provision provides financial certainty, but risks denying support for meritorious cases, and restricting provision in certain geographical areas. In addition, placing the choice of lawyer in the hands of the publicly supported litigant, without appropriate value-for-money safeguards, risks public funds not providing value for money or meeting needs or satisfying priorities. However, the subject matter also embraces a number of further diverse issues, such as who provides legal services, the nature of the services provided, and the parameters of demand on the public purse.

 *Looking for extra marks?*

Examination questions on this area are common, and most invite a critical consideration of the balance of those issues in either civil or criminal law (but rarely in both). A good response will offer a solid description of the funding of advice and representation for civil and criminal cases, exhibit an awareness of the economic and other tensions surrounding publicly funded legal services, and also be able to distinguish the principles and issues surrounding civil matters from those in criminal matters. The response could import material from other parts of the syllabus, eg it should demonstrate awareness that the Courts and Legal Services Act 1990 did not fuse the two principal legal professions (barristers and solicitors) but did end many monopolies and enabled various professions to offer advice and representation in civil and criminal matters. That Act aimed that 'the public has the best possible access to legal services and that those services are of the right quality for the particular needs of the client'. The Act did not assert that those unable to pay should receive the same quality of legal advice as those paying themselves, nor, directly, advocate a precise funding model.

Provision of services

The Access to Justice Act 1999 created the Legal Services Commission to replace the Legal Aid Board and to create, manage, and fund the Community Legal Service (CLS) for civil legal matters and the Criminal Defence Service (CDS) for criminal matters. The Act also allowed all lawyers to have full rights of audience before all courts. In an attempt to avoid re-litigating disputes, for many years, barristers (but not solicitors) were immune from claims in negligence in respect of their advocacy. However, in *Hall v Simons* [2000] the House of Lords underlined the principle of the equal rights of audience enjoyed by barristers and solicitors and allowed a barrister to be sued in tort for negligence in advocacy. In *Hall v Simons*, the House of Lords overruled the earlier decision in *Rondel v Worsley* [1967] that a barrister had no liability in tort for negligence in advocacy.

The 1999 Act further strengthened the powers of the Legal Services Ombudsman to make enforceable compensation orders against professional bodies and legal professional bodies.

Revision tip

Do remember to highlight that civil litigation offers opportunities for compromise and settlement by the parties, and consequently there is greater opportunity for the flexible approach offered by conditional fee agreements. However, as criminal litigation differs in nature and outcomes, such compromises are not really available.

Funding civil legal services

The aim

An effective legal system is essential to any civilized democratic community, and a key component within such a system is effective access to legal advice and to use the courts to pursue remedies. Without redress to courts, the rule of law is meaningless. However, the fact is that the provision of civil legal services involves the delivery of advice and litigation services by qualified and experienced personnel (eg barristers, solicitors, paralegals) for remuneration and in most cases the starting point is that the client pays for such advice and legal services at the point of delivery – as is the case with any other specialist service. The cost of bringing a civil action can be very high, particularly in the London area. One major consequence is that if the client is unable (or unwilling) to afford to pay for legal services, those services will not be provided; and the client is left without assistance to pursue a remedy, eg to recover damages in a personal injury claim. In practice, the cost of bringing or defending a case is out of the reach of most people without some assistance, but many 'ordinary' individuals with very modest savings fail to qualify for publicly funded assistance. However, most societies accept that the enforcement of civil legal rights should not be wholly dependent upon an initial ability to fund the litigation.

The 'costs rule'

Whilst in litigation the normal practice is that the courts will order an unsuccessful party to pay the legal **costs** of the successful party (as well as his/her own costs) and so, ultimately, it is the unsuccessful party who pays, this does not address the issue where the party is unsuccessful in litigation or where the legal services constitute only advice. The perennial systemic problem is to avoid financial and procedural issues forming a barrier to access to justice, whilst providing a funding mechanism that does not impose an unacceptable burden upon the state. This poses the additional questions as to the nature of assistance: should it be a consumer service free at point of use, and, if so, should it be self-funding by recouping its costs through post-litigation recovery of costs and other means?

Public funding

Public funding of legal services used to be provided by way of legal aid – a pillar of the welfare state. One of its initial objectives was to provide legal advice to servicemen in matrimonial proceedings, but its scope was extended to encompass other forms of civil litigation. The Legal Aid and Advice Act 1949 established a legal aid system, administered at various times by the Legal Aid Board and the Law Society, with the aim of establishing a comprehensive system of public funding mechanisms to remunerate lawyers for advice and civil litigation undertaken for those who would not otherwise be able to afford to have access to the justice system. The system embraced legal advice and assistance (widely used and commonly called 'the Green Form scheme' after the colour of the forms used) which funded an interview and advice within modest limits (but which, with approval, could be more extensive) without prior authorization from the Legal Aid Board. Ironically many claims under this scheme related to advice on other benefits. Civil legal aid was granted for representation in most, but not all, courts. To benefit from civil legal aid for advice, a client had to meet certain financial criteria, and the subject matter had to satisfy a characteristics test (ie that it fell within certain subject areas such as contested divorce). The case had to merit support – 'the merits' test – and the applicant had to meet 'the means' test – satisfying certain financial limits (applying disposable capital and disposable income tests similar to those currently applied). Such civil legal aid was awarded by the Legal Aid Board and subject to that Board's prior approval.

Financial limits

In respect of civil legal aid for litigation, a client had to meet certain financial criteria, and the case had to satisfy a merit test (ie that there was a realistic prospect of success). Once the Civil Legal Aid Board had awarded legal aid, there was no principle of a cap on the costs incurred in the conduct of the case by the lawyer to whom the case was entrusted. The only restriction was the costs approved by the court as being properly incurred by the solicitors in the conduct of the case. Thus, lawyers were paid on a case-by-case basis for the work they actually did. Where a legally aided case was successful, costs would normally be awarded against the non-legally aided party and accrue to the legal aid fund; in contrast, in unsuccessful cases, costs would not usually be awarded against the legally aided party – which was seen as somewhat unfair. The inevitable consequences were unacceptable – an imbalance in litigation and an unascertainable and limitless burden upon public funds.

Capping legal aid

The initial governmental response to spiralling costs had been the imposition of an overall cap on civil legal aid and this deprived many otherwise meritorious cases of funding. The position was further complicated by the criteria excluding most business disputes, however small the business might be, and whatever the consequences for the owners and employees might be. In practice, many firms of solicitors provided advice and undertook litigation without legal aid funding, in the knowledge that, if successful, costs would be awarded against, and recovered from, the other party (but that, if unsuccessful, the client would not be able to pay costs).

Legal aid was not a vote-catching service and imposed a heavy claim on the public purse and had to compete for public funding against other major pillars of the welfare state – the National Health Service and education. Towards the end of the last century, there was a marked rise in the volume of divorce and employment disputes and of smaller cases meeting the criteria; as a consequence, the cost of Civil Legal Aid more than doubled in five years (from £685 million in 1991 to £1,400 million in 1996) despite tighter controls of the means test criteria which in 1995 excluded 10 million from eligibility. The principal problem remained the soaring cost of public funding of cases which by 2006 had touched £2 billion annually.

Conditional fee arrangements

This rise in cost coincided with the White Paper entitled *Modernising Justice* (1998) and Lord Woolf's inquiry into the civil justice system and recommendations for its modernization. As indicated in the chapter on civil process, he had identified civil litigation as being costly, lengthy, complex, and uncertain; and these problems applied whether the case was funded privately or by civil legal aid. In his final report, *Access to Justice*, Lord Woolf argued that these issues arose from the lawyers' control of litigation and consequently he recommended a number of key reforms (including the overriding objective that the courts deal with cases 'justly' and judicial case management). In respect of funding litigation, paragraph 46 proposed the exploitation of **conditional fee agreements** (CFAs):

> In the future, insurance could have a larger part to play in funding litigation. This could apply both to parties' own costs and to liability for the other side's costs. A rapid increase in the availability of insurance is important to greater access to the courts. It is also important to the legal profession. However the ability to assess the risks involved is important if insurers are to increase their involvement. Certainty as to costs and moderation in their amount is critical to insurers offering affordable terms.

Historically, the laws of champerty (against a third party benefiting from litigation in which he had no legitimate interest) had prevented lawyers from receiving a share of the damages from litigation which they conducted. Although champerty is no longer a crime, solicitors cannot enforce such agreements. The 1989 White Paper *Contingency Fees* had proposed that a lawyer could receive a proportion of the damages recovered; but following criticism the principle was not pursued. Section 58 Courts and Legal Services Act 1990 had originally established the principle of conditional fee agreements. The principal requirements were that it was a written agreement between a person providing **advocacy** or litigation services and his client that that person's fees and expenses were to be payable only in specified circumstances.

This 'no win, no fee' basis denied lawyers' fees if unsuccessful but allowed a lawyer to 'uplift' his normal fee through a supplement of up to 100 per cent (with a voluntary cap of 25 per cent of the damages recovered). One problem was that where a litigant under a CFA was successful, s 58(8) provided that the costs order in his favour 'shall not include any element which takes account of any percentage increase payable under the agreement'. Thus, a successful CFA litigant risked having to pay the 'increase' element out of the damages awarded. However, s 27 Access to Justice Act 1999 revised and amended these provisions by allowing for a costs order to include the payment of any fees payable under a conditional fee agreement which contained a success fee. Thus a successful CFA litigant can agree a fee (and success fee) with his lawyer; if the case is successful, a litigant can recover the full success fee – ie he is no longer prevented from recovering all his costs (including the 'increase' element). However, where a CFA litigant is unsuccessful, the norm remains that the court will usually order an unsuccessful party to pay not only his own legal costs but also those of the successful party, so whilst the CFA relieves the unsuccessful litigant of liability for his own costs ('no win so no fee'), he does remain liable for those of his opponent (who may also have a CFA). This risk is usually addressed by the litigant taking out an insurance policy which will pay the opponent's costs if the litigant is unsuccessful; and in many but not all cases, the client will be required to pay the premium on the policy although it should be recovered in the costs ultimately awarded to be paid (s 29 Access to Justice Act) – assuming the case is successful.

The Court of Appeal's decision in *Thai Trading Co v Taylor* [1998] confirmed that a firm can undertake work on a no win 'less than full fee' basis; but there remains concern that firms activities on 'no win, no fee' cases are insufficiently regulated.

Problems of conditional fee arrangements

CFAs have allowed professional representation even where previously none was available through legal aid (eg where the client failed to satisfy the financial tests) and have proved to be popular. Litigants do not have to pay in advance, worry about possibly huge legal costs, or suffer delay pending the award of legal aid. Nevertheless, they are not without both theoretical and practical problems, as the decision to enter into a CFA is made by the litigant and his legal adviser who has to evaluate the case in order to determine its chances of success for the success fee calculation and the completion of the costs insurance proposal. This requires the legal adviser to invest significant time and effort in evaluating the claim and ascribes to the legal adviser the role of both gatekeeper and financial stakeholder in the litigation at only a preliminary stage of the litigation. Whilst this may deter legal advisers from undertaking speculative litigation only to (have to) abandon it at a later stage through lack of merit, it does place a substantial financial burden on the legal adviser which cannot be recovered without litigation. Moreover, expenses called 'disbursements' (eg medical or other expert reports) are often incurred and payable as a case progresses; and even assuming success, the legal adviser will receive repayment of these and his remuneration only upon completion of the litigation (rather than by interim payments as occurred under legal aid funding) which impacts on the legal adviser's cash-flow. Moreover, the courts have ruled that the increased fee in a CFA should not exceed 100 per cent of the costs otherwise recoverable. In practice, therefore, a legal practice must average a success rate superior to 50 per cent to remain viable.

Policy revisited?

Usually a successful party is entitled to have his costs paid by the unsuccessful party, although this rule may be amended where there has been a payment into court or an unreasonable refusal to attempt alternative dispute resolution (ADR; see chapter 4).

In January 2010 Lord Jackson published a controversial report critical of the current rules on costs which, for some types of litigation, he found to be 'excessive or disproportionate' and criticized 'the present system for achieving costs protection for claimants [as] the most bizarre and expensive system that it is possible to devise'. His proposed reforms include:

- retaining CFAs but capping the success fees at 25 per cent and making them payable by the client (not the party 'losing' the case)
- allowing US-style **contingency fees** (whereby lawyers receive a percentage of no more than 25 per cent of the awarded damages)
- fixed costs on fast-track cases
- the defendant will continue to be liable for the successful claimant's costs but unsuccessful claimants will not liable for the defendant's costs.

✅ Looking for extra marks?

Civil legal aid was expensive and not a 'vote-catcher' but, as Lord Jackson identified, CFAs remain problematic – not least because they conflate the responsibility of evaluating the prospects of the litigation with the responsibility of financing it. Remember, this has not reduced the cost of litigation: CFAs have merely shifted the costs onto legal practices and litigants (and their insurers). Contingency fees shift onto legal practitioners further risk and responsibility for case evaluation. The fear is that contingency fees will discourage lawyers from accepting risk-laden cases but encourage claims for higher levels of damages.

Relevance of ADR

The encouragement of ADR, though a rigid application of the costs rules (see chapter 4), risks forcing litigants unwillingly into ADR under threat of an adverse costs order. Whilst ADR should be encouraged, this risks distorting litigation decisions. Evidence shows that some legal practices have been unable to meet the financial and practice demands generated by CFAs and ceased to offer litigation services, thereby effectively inhibiting some local communities from accessing justice. Some trade unions and many domestic and motor insurance policies provide that the insured has access to a panel of legal advisers at the cost of the insurer.

Revision Tip

Remember that ADR was traditionally external, and an alternative, to litigation – and remains so – but also it now has become part of the litigation process.

Other civil litigation and advice

The corollary of CFAs is that legal aid (in civil areas) is no longer available for:

- small value claims – as the costs may exceed the value of the claim
- most tribunal hearings
- defamation
- personal injury matters
- matters relating to wills
- company law or commercial cases
- disputes relating to land.

As CFAs are not suitable for all disputes, the Community Legal Services Fund continues to fund some types of case, although the funding is limited. The nature of some court **proceedings** (eg family law, welfare law, housing, medical negligence, and human rights) makes CFAs unsuitable and such proceedings were excluded by s 58(10) in the earlier Courts and Legal Services Act 1990. An additional factor was that some litigious cases (such as medical negligence cases) require a substantial amount of investigation to evaluate the probability of success (or otherwise) of a claim, and so were also unsuited and excluded from CFAs.

For such civil and family cases, the CLS has replaced legal aid and the means and merit tests have been replaced by 'likely success rate'. In each case it is for the litigant to justify that his case should be funded. Section 8 Access to Justice Act 1999 requires consideration of a number of matters including:

- the likely cost of funding (ie the cost of the case) and the benefit obtainable (ie the value of the asset to be recovered or retained)
- monies available in the Community Legal Fund
- the importance of the matter to the individual (eg dispute about his home)
- other services available (eg mediation or a CFA)
- probability of success (there needs to be a realistic chance of success)
- public interest.

Only a limited number of services – principally involving children – are available without having to meet the personal financial criteria ('means test'). This requires the litigant to demonstrate that he meets the financial criteria for disposable income (income available

Provision of services

✳✳✳✳✳✳✳✳✳

after deduction of essential living expenses) and disposable capital (including the net value of the home above £100,000 ie after deducting any mortgages and expenses). A litigant's income and capital must fall below the minimum threshold to qualify for publicly funded assistance; and a litigant who exceeds the maximum threshold (which is set at a low level, currently £8,000) will receive no publicly funded assistance; and one whose income or capital falls between the minimum and maximum limits will be required to pay a contribution to the cost of the case. The legal services provided may vary from straightforward advice to undertaking complex cases in the High Court.

Problems with this system

The system is proving problematic for several reasons:

- some believe the 'success' test has been set too high
- low rates of remuneration for firms undertaking publicly funded work, so:
  - the number of firms undertaking such work (3,500) is lower than under the legal aid system
  - some geographical areas have no legal practitioner offering to undertake publicly funded work
  - many geographical areas have no legal practitioner offering to undertake publicly funded work in certain areas
- funds are distributed on a regional basis which risks one region having surplus funding and another being unable to fund any further cases
- disjunction of funding and need
- high-cost cases remain centrally funded on a case-by-case basis through specific contracts
- the Community Legal Services Fund imposes a statutory charge on all damages recovered in publicly funded litigation and so a litigant may not retain the full amount of the damages awarded.

Provision of legal advice

A significant part of the legal aid budget was expended on the provision of legal advice (ie without litigation ensuing). Under the Access to Justice Act 1999, the former Legal Aid Board was replaced by the Legal Services Commission which was charged with establishing and running the CLS and distributing legal aid. By s 4 Access to Justice Act 1999, the CLS receives and distributes resources to provide legal services for individuals. Section 4(2) lists those services very broadly as:

- the provision of general information about the law and legal system and the availability of legal services

- the provision of help by the giving of advice as to how the law applies in particular circumstances
- the provision of help in preventing, settling, or otherwise resolving, disputes about legal rights and duties (which might include professional representation in court)
- the provision of help in enforcing decisions by which such disputes are resolved
- the provision of help in relation to legal proceedings not relating to disputes.

This duty is currently discharged through competitively tendered contracts with approved organizations including professional legal practices and some specialist not-for-profit organizations such as the Citizens Advice Bureau and Law Centres. Each contract covers one specific area of law (eg immigration, welfare, or housing law) and is awarded on the basis of meeting specific performance standards. Advice (and in some cases representation) is provided by specialist advisers (but who may not hold professional legal qualifications). The Legal Services Commission has explored other methods including websites and an expert system (*Project Eagle* was a computer system which would have produced advice on the law and procedure from responses to specific questions); but in most cases the complexity of law and the variables justify individual advice.

Pro bono provision

Some organizations (such as the Bar Council's Free Representation Unit and some university law schools) also offer free legal advice (and, occasionally, representation) *pro bono publico* (for the public good), although, in some instances, this provision may be in with legal aid from the Community Legal Service.

Evaluation

Lawyers used to be paid on a case-by-case basis for the work undertaken, but in order to limit the overall value of claims on the public purse, the provision of these legal services is delegated to specific legal practices and organizations which demonstrate meeting specific standards and performance levels. However, there are budgetary limitations imposed. Now lawyers bid for a contract to undertake work in a certain area or work for a certain period of time. If successful, they enter into a contract with the LSC for the provision of these legal services. The result has been a 12 per cent fall in the number of certificates issued for family matters (ie number of cases accepted) between 2000–1 and 2001–2, and a 30 per cent fall in certificates in other areas. Moreover, the various schemes have not been without problems as there is evidence of some overcharging by some firms.

It is for society to decide the extent to which it is willing to support (particularly financially) the delivery of a civil justice system as a public service in the same way as the NHS provides care universally and free at point of delivery. Moreover, the present system presumes that everybody should have access to the civil justice system, but not necessarily an entitlement to use that justice system at nil cost.

Funding criminal legal services

✳✳✳✳✳✳✳✳✳✳

Revision tip

Take care to distinguish the provision of legal services in civil matters (where the parties stand to gain or retain benefits) from that in criminal matters where the state needs to ensure the delivery of justice by according to the accused effective legal advice and representation.

Funding criminal legal services

An effective system to provide legal advice and assistance to those accused of a crime is not only essential to any civilized democratic community, but also a key right now guaranteed through the Human Rights Act 1998 and the European Convention on Human Rights. England and Wales operates an adversarial system, requiring each party to advance its evidence and legal propositions; the court has very limited power to consider other evidence and law. Article 6 of that Convention provides for the right to a fair trial and in particular Article 6(3(c) states the right of anyone charged with a criminal offence:

> to defend himself in person or through legal assistance of his own choosing or, if he has not sufficient means to pay for legal assistance, to be given it free when the interests of justice so require…

Criminal legal aid

Under the Legal Aid Act 1988, criminal legal aid covered the costs of preparing and presenting a defence in criminal cases and was administered by the courts usually through the court clerk's office with a right of appeal to the Law Society. In effect, this provides state-provided legal advice and defence advocacy and is a demand-led provision without a fixed budget. Despite governmental steps to restrict the right to jury trials, public funding for cases in the Crown Court rose by 125 per cent between the reporting year 1995–6 and 2004–5. Lord Carter's report, entitled *Procurement of Criminal Defence Services: Market-based reform* (2006), proposed greater competitive bidding for criminal contracts and the use of fixed fee contracts. One anticipated advantage would be to avoid the headline-seizing public funding payments of over £1 million to certain barristers, and the redistribution of the funds to lower-paid practitioners; but such proposals risk removing half of existing firms from undertaking such work, and thereby reducing the availability of their advice and representation.

Advice

Paralleling civil legal aid, there was both a 'means test' and a 'merits test' (although with criteria different from those used in civil legal aid). Since 1999, all defendants (ie those arrested and held in custody) have access to publicly funded advice, assistance, and representation if it is 'in the interests of justice'. The means test remains for advice and assistance but this single 'interests of justice' test replaced the means and merits tests for representation and this reflects the norms accepted in a civilized society.

The most common provision of advice is through the Duty Solicitor Scheme that pays accredited personnel to give free advice to those arrested and held at the police station. It is the custody officer who has to inform those arrested of the Duty Solicitor Scheme and its availability through the Defence Solicitors' Call Centre which can also offer a limited telephone based advice service. The Duty Solicitor Scheme also provides free professional advice at the magistrates' court.

Tests for criminal legal aid

The Legal Services Commission also provides publicly funded legal representation for defendants if it is 'in the interests of justice'. Historically, these legal services were delivered through criminal legal aid, with no more than a limited financial contribution payable by the accused. Now the provision of publicly funded legal representation requires the application of five tests:

- the accused risks losing his liberty or livelihood or suffering serious reputational damage
- the determination of any matter arising may involve consideration of a substantial point of law
- the individual may be unable
  - to understand the proceedings brought against him
  - to state his own case
- the case may involve witness evidence
- it is in the interests of another person that the accused be represented.

Costs orders

In contrast to civil litigation, if the client is unable to afford to pay for legal services, the requirement is that the state will provide those services at its expense. Although the court may make a costs order (eg against the defendant upon conviction), such orders are not common (and seem to be of a lower value) in criminal matters than in civil matters. The need to provide legal aid and assistance in criminal matters imposes an extensive and potentially unlimited burden on the legal aid budget – a factor that contributed to the restriction of civil legal aid.

Controlling costs

Previously, anyone accused of a crime could seek legal advice and representation from a chosen legal practice; and the court would formally grant legal aid provision subject to the accused satisfying a means test of assets and a merits test of the case. Whilst the amounts claimed by that firm for the various aspects of the work undertaken would, as in civil matters, be subject to ultimate approval by the court, the difficulty was that once legal aid had been granted, the total amount claimable was rarely subject to any other control, so that the cost of criminal legal aid was both unrestricted and uncontrolled at the point of use.

In an endeavour to address these problems, the Access to Justice Act 1999, established the Legal Services Commission (in place of the Legal Aid Board) to establish and manage, *inter alia*, the Criminal Defence Service – in effect a state-funded counterbalance to the Crown

Funding criminal legal services

✳✳✳✳✳✳✳✳✳✳

Prosecution Service – to fund the defence of those accused of crimes. The Criminal Defence Service employs a staff of defence lawyers – the Public Defender Service – but may also contract with independent legal practitioners to provide this service.

The Public Defender Service

The Public Defender Service has been piloted by the Legal Services Commission, and is seen to have the advantage of a more comprehensive and cohesive overview of the costs of providing a publicly funded defence service as well as providing high-quality value-for-money criminal defence services. In fact, it has been found that it is often cheaper to instruct a private lawyer than to employ lawyers and several offices have been closed.

Legal advice and assistance is not provided by the CDS wholly free of charge. At the end of the criminal case, but not necessarily dependent upon the defendant being found guilty, the court assesses the defendant's means to determine whether or not an order for the recovery of some or all of the defence costs should be made. The criteria are similar to those applied for eligibility for civil legal aid. Moreover, in 2003, as a reaction to criticism that wealthy defendants facing motoring offences had received free representation, the Government introduced means testing of all criminal legal aid and assistance for defendants in the magistrates' courts, but not the Crown Courts.

Of course just as in civil litigation, an individual may, if he so wishes, choose to instruct any lawyer on the basis that the individual himself will pay for the lawyer's services, but CFAs are not allowed in criminal legal proceedings.

Evaluation

Criminal legal aid used to pay private legal practices on a case-by-case basis for the work undertaken in approved cases; but this open liability to provide legal assistance and representation inevitably created a parallel open liability upon the public purse, and there were reported instances of lawyers receiving large fees for such work. Under current provisions, the delivery of these legal services is entrusted to salaried lawyers and to specific legal practices and organizations which demonstrate meeting specific standards and performance levels within budgetary limitations. Now lawyers bid for a contract to undertake work in a certain area or work for a certain period of time. If successful, they enter into a contract with the LSC for the provision of these legal services.

Whilst it is accepted that under the European Convention on Human Rights, the legal system must ensure an effective defence service for those accused of a criminal act, the state is obliged to fund such a defence only if the accused does not have 'sufficient means to pay for legal assistance'; and so the principal issue is the level of those means. It is for society to decide the level of means at which the delivery of legal advice and representation should be free of charge – as the Justice Secretary warned on 30 June 2010:

> We are always going to have to provide legal aid for criminal cases. But it must be means tested.

Quality assurance

Separating the choice of lawyer from the public funding source exposes the risk of poor-quality legal services. From 1994, the Legal Aid Board operated franchises – a quality assurance scheme – on a voluntary basis in several areas of law. Legal practices which met certain quality assurance criteria were given authority to undertake relevant cases, and so the Legal Aid Board assumed the function of quality control.

 **Key cases**

Case	Facts	Ratio/Held
Hall v Simons [2000] 3 WLR 543	Solicitors were sued for negligence in litigation and sought immunity analogous with that of barristers.	There was no longer a public policy justification for exemption.
Rondel v Worsley [1967] 3 WLR 1666	A barrister was negligent in preparing documents for a case.	As a barrister was not employed and could not sue for his fees, he was not liable in negligence.
Thai Trading Co v Taylor [1998] 3 All ER 65	It was not illegal for a solicitor to agree with his client not to charge for litigation services if the client was unsuccessful; but if successful could recover only the ordinary disbursements and profit costs.	There is a distinction between contingent fees and conditional fees; but public policy should not prevent a solicitor waiving fees if the case was unsuccessful.

 **Exam questions**

Essay question 1

Has the Access to Justice Act 1999 improved access to justice or merely saved public money?

An outline answer is included at the end of the book.

Essay question 2

Critically distinguish the state's provision of legal services in criminal matters from that in civil matters.

An outline answer is available online at <http://www.oxfordtextbooks.co.uk/orc/concentrate/>.

Outline answers

Chapter 1

Essay answer 1

Students should:

- Highlight that following the enactment of the **Lisbon Treaty** the European Court of Justice is one of the six main European Union institutions. Students should briefly highlight those other institutions: Commission, Parliament, Council etc.
- Highlight the location of the ECJ – The Court is situated in Luxembourg.
- Highlight the basic composition and appointment requirements to this court – It has 27 judges appointed by the Member States for six years; appointments are renewable. Such individuals will have previously held high judicial office within Member States, eg in relation to the UK members of the new Supreme Court or former Lords of Appeal in Ordinary.
- Highlight the role of the Advocate Generals – There are 8 Advocate Generals who produce opinions on the cases assigned to them assist the judges. The opinions will highlight the relevant issues and suggest potential conclusions.
- Indicate that the Court delivers a single judgment with no indication on the number of judges who dissented.
- Highlight that the Court can hear proceedings against Member States brought by other Member States or by the Commission alleging breaches of EU law.
- Highlight that the Court can also hear proceedings against EU institutions brought by Member States or other EU institutions because, for instance, Treaty powers and procedures have been misused and abused.
- Highlight a range of cases that have been resolved as a result of intervention by the ECJ, or where fundamental principles of EU law have been established, eg *Van Gend en Loos v Netherlands* [1963] CMLR 105, *Leonesio v Italian Ministry for Agriculture and Forestry* [1973] ECR 287, *Van Duyn v Home Office* [1974] 1 WLR 1107, etc.

- Indicate that **Article 267 Treaty on the Functioning of the European Union** (formerly **Article 234**) provides that any court or tribunal of a Member State can refer a question on EU law to the ECJ. The preliminary reference procedure promotes uniformity of interpretation throughout the EU.
- Highlight that in relation to this procedure the case in the domestic court is adjourned until the ECJ directs the English court on the correct interpretation to be implemented. The domestic court must then apply the ECJ's ruling to the facts of the case before it.
- Indicate that such a reference must be made if the national court is one from which there is no further appeal, eg the UK Supreme Court (the former House of Lords).
- Indicate that the UK has been bound by the decisions/rulings of the ECJ since it joined the European Union on the 1 January 1973 following the passing of the **European Communities Act 1972** under **s 2**.
- Highlight that in *HP Bulmer Ltd v Bollinger SA No 2* [1974] Ch 401 Lord Denning stated that in relation to UK courts to save expense and delay no reference should be made where:
  - it would not be conclusive of the case and other matters would remain to be decided
  - there had been a previous ruling on the same point
  - the court considers that point to be reasonably clear and free from doubt
  - the facts of the case had not yet been decided.
- Indicate that a Court of First Instance with limited jurisdiction was established in 1988 under **Article 225 EC Treaty** in order to assist and reduce the workload of the ECJ. It is now known as the General Court following changes made by the **Lisbon Treaty**. Also, in order to hear disputes between the European institutions and its civil servants a new Civil Service Tribunal has been created.

Outline answers

✳✳✳✳✳✳✳✳✳✳

Chapter 2

Essay answer 1

To answer this question you will need to:

- Explain that this is secondary or subordinate source of law.

- Define what is meant by the phrase delegated legislation – that law-making powers are passed from Parliament to other organizations and individuals to create the law on its behalf – highlight various examples of Parent Acts/Enabling Acts that do this, eg the **European Communities Act 1972**, etc.

- Identify and deal with each organization that can create delegated legislation and the various forms that this delegated legislation can take. Again highlight relevant Enabling Acts and highlight the scope of law-making powers – highlight various forms of delegated legislation that have been created under various Enabling Acts.

- Identify the perceived advantages and disadvantages associated with this form of law.

- Highlight the various methods that Parliament has at its disposal to control delegated legislation, eg parliamentary questions, affirmative, negative resolution processes, duty to consult, etc.

- Highlight the method by which the courts can control delegated legislation – judicial review within the Queen's Bench Division – highlight the grounds for a potential challenge and the various powers the court has at its disposal, eg granting compensation, etc.

- Support the various grounds of challenge with relevant case law, facts, and decisions.

Conclude answer with an overview of the content you have provided and the adequacy of control methods via the courts and Parliament.

Chapter 3

Essay answer 1

This question would involve coverage of the following issues:

- Explain how the common law operates and the requirements needed for precedent to operate effectively, law reporting, settled court hierarchy, etc.

- Provide information on the binding and non-binding elements of a judgment and provide relevant terminology. Comment on the fact that it is sometimes difficult to identify the key elements in a judgment and explain why.

- Explain with the use of relevant terminology how the doctrine of judicial precedent operates within the court system. Ensure that mention is made that courts are generally bound by their own previous decisions and by decisions made by courts above them in the hierarchy but only where the facts of cases/legal principles raised are similar. Begin with the influence of the European Court of Justice and decisions of the European Court of Human Rights, then deal with the domestic courts.

- Explain how historically the issue of precedent has operated within the House of Lords, from pre-1898 to date, with case illustrations. Ensure that the **Practice Statement** is highlighted and relevant cases where it has been used. Highlight why the operation of precedent has changed in the House of Lords. Comment on the fact that the House of Lords may not change the law simply because the court feels it is wrong; provide some case illustrations and judicial comment.

- Highlight the operation of precedent in the Court of Appeal, that it is bound by decisions above it in the court hierarchy, and that it is usually bound by its own decisions in both divisions but there are exceptions.

- Highlight issues in relation to EU law and human rights law and the operation of precedent. Illustrate this area with a case/judicial comment that highlights the UK courts' approach to these issues. Ensure that you highlight relevant statutory provisions.

- Provide comment on the operation of precedent within lower courts. Comment on the academic debate as to whether we need two senior appeal courts and the advantages and disadvantages of the doctrine in overview.

- Explain that if a case raises novel issues then a judge may be able to create new law, known as original precedent – note that the question of whether the judiciary do create the law and should create the law has been commented upon by members of the judiciary and academics. Comment on these views. Highlight cases such as *R v R*, etc.

• Explain the meaning of distinguishing and that this can potentially be used to avoid a previous precedent of a court – that courts have the ability to distinguish cases irrespective of court position etc. Illustrate with cases.

• Explain the meaning of binding precedent and persuasive precedent. Illustrate the operation of the principle with a few cases.

• Conclude with a few sentences relating the information back to the original information provided within the question and that precedent is to a limited extent flexible, not suitable for major reforms in the law, and relies on a case actively being taken to the superior courts before precedent will develop, or on a judge willing to depart from earlier case decisions etc on the basis of distinguishing etc. This can depend on the view of the judge/s of their constitutional role within the English legal system.

Chapter 4

Essay answer 1

In principle, ADR and the litigation process are separate and mutually exclusive. Some contracts will include an ADR clause (often committing the parties to arbitration), and the courts readily support the application of such clauses. Even in the absence of such provision, litigators will often explore the benefits of ADR through negotiation with a view to settling cases outside the court process.

To reduce the unnecessary use of the courts, the Woolf reforms, as embodied in the CPR, encourage the use of ADR both prior and subsequent to commencement of litigation. Such encouragement is usually by varying the usual costs order (normally the costs of the successful party are ordered to be paid by the unsuccessful party). The refusal by one party of the suggestion by the court or other party to use ADR risks an adverse costs order so that the refusing party bears all the costs irrespective of success in the substantive claim. *Burchell* and *Dunnett* highlight the court's residual right to exercise this power and set out common tests for its application.

The policy now strongly promotes ADR without and within the litigation process; and whilst parties cannot be forced into ADR, failure to

use ADR risks adverse costs orders which can exceed the value of the underlying claim.

Chapter 5

Essay answer

This question would involve coverage of the following issues:

• Highlight the problems associated with the police being responsible for detection, investigation of crime, and the decision to prosecute, eg cracked trials, lack of evidence, wasted court time, the cost to the criminal justice system, etc.

• Highlight comments/reforms proposed by law reform agencies and pressure groups and compare with the actual way the agency was eventually set up.

• Highlight the problems associated with the CPS when it was set up, eg lack of funding, inability to retain and attract lawyers, relationship with the police, etc.

• Highlight the contents of the Glidewell Report and the changes made to the agency in response to the report. Also highlight recommendations by Auld LJ in his *Review of the Criminal Courts*.

• Highlight the evidential and public interest test, factors taken into account by Crown Prosecutors when utilizing their discretion to prosecute, and involvement of prosecutors in relation to the charging of suspects.

• Provide an overview of personnel within the agency: DPP, Crown Prosecutors, Associated Prosecutors, Chief Crown Prosecutors, Higher Court Advocates, Duty Prosecutors (CPS Direct), and relationship of agency with the Attorney General.

Chapter 6

Essay answer

As a preliminary point, one must question the extent to which the judiciary needs to mirror the social, political, economic, etc, composition of modern society. It should be argued that the important issue is that society has confidence in the judiciary by seeing the judiciary as being

Outline answers

✳✳✳✳✳✳✳✳✳

independent, unbiased, and appointed solely on merit.

There are three elements of judicial appointment (meeting the minimum statutory criteria, application for consideration, and selection) and each of these elements filters appointees and implicitly reduces the population from which an appointment might be made. First, not everyone meets the statutory eligibility criteria. Candidates should briefly set out those criteria (details relating to appointment at a particular level would attract additional marks) and explain that they are based on seeking appropriate legal knowledge and independence in judgement, and thus are predicated on professional legal qualification and practice. Obviously, these eligibility criteria not only exclude many sectors of society but also skew judicial appointments towards those who have successful legal practices which may further favour eligible candidates from certain sectors of society.

Secondly, there is an issue of candidate confidence in making an application for appointment. Many potential candidates are reluctant to seek judicial office lest, if unsuccessful, doubt might be cast over his/her reputation as a legal practitioner. This favours applications from eligible applicants who also know successful candidates. Thus, a barrister in chambers from where previous applications have been successful is likely to have more confidence of a successful application than a barrister from chamber which has no such 'track record'.

Thirdly, and leading on similarly from the point above, the selection process is thought to favour those candidates who have specific knowledge and experience of court practice. This implicitly excludes many very able practitioners whose court experience is limited.

However, the **Tribunals, Courts and Enforcement Act 2007** seeks to adjust this skew by extending the eligibility criteria beyond membership of the two branches of the legal profession; but it is suspected that the expectation of knowledge of legal practice will perpetuate favouring candidates from certain sectors of society.

Chapter 7

Essay answer 1

This question would involve coverage of the following issues:

- Define the word 'layperson'.
- Provide an overview of the advantages and disadvantages associated with the use of laypersons generally within the English legal system.
- Identify minor roles played by laypersons within the English legal system and provide information on their area of work.
- Identify the two major roles played by laypersons within the English legal system as juries and as magistrates. Provide an overview of these two roles.
- Provide a range of criticisms in relation to magistrates: consistency in sentencing, case-hardening, bias, role/influence of clerk of the court, comparison with their legally qualified counterparts, etc.
- Provide a range of criticisms in relation to juries: media influence, majority verdicts, bias, composition, influence of the judge, etc.
- In conclusion, provide an overview of recommendations in relation to juries and magistrates and provide a brief critical analysis of these. For instance, highlight in relation to juries, removing right to trial by jury in hybrid cases, alternatives to jury trial (single judge as in Diplock Courts, panel of judges, mixed bench (laypersons and judge)), and smaller jury panels. In relation to magistrates, explore the expanding use of District Judges, the role of the clerk, impact of the potential removal of the right to jury trial for hybrid offences. Also explore the proposed changes in the court structure under the Auld Report.

Chapter 8

Essay answer 1

Prior to the Act, legal aid was the main method whereby individuals who were unable to afford to fund their civil case might be supported.

However, as this funding constituted an increasing burden upon the public purse, steps had already been taken to limit that burden by imposing various requirements and restrictions on legal aid eligibility. As a result fewer individuals were able to pursue their cases.

The Act amended a number of rules and provided methods (eg CFAs) to allow individuals to pursue litigation other than at the expense of the state. By removing legal aid from most cases, it has saved money; but it has also allowed litigants who would otherwise have been ineligible under legal aid, to pursue their cases. Thus, it has both allowed access to justice and saved public money.

Glossary

Advocacy Arguments (usually oral) addressed to the court.

Arraignment This is when the charges, listed on the indictment are formally put to the defendant in the Crown Court by the court clerk and the defendant will be asked to enter a plea.

Associated prosecutors Members of the Crown Prosecution Service who can undertake certain forms of prosecution in the magistrates' court, following advice from a Crown Prosecutor.

Attorney General Law Officer of the Crown. Represents and advises the Government on legal issues. Responsible for laying report on the operation of the CPS before Parliament. Can be asked questions by Parliament on the report but not on individual cases dealt with by the CPS.

Bail Process by which the court or police decide whether a suspect/defendant should be released into the community until a trial date or further questioning is required. If bail is refused then defendant will be detained, remanded in custody, until the trial date.

Bench When more than one lay magistrate sit together to hear a case they are referred to as a Bench.

Call The act of a student barrister being 'called' to the Bar of his Inn of Court after successful completion of his vocational stage training (currently the Bar Vocational Course).

Caution Two meanings:

- a formal warning/reprimand administered by the police to an individual who has committed a crime – a measure to divert the individual from the criminal justice system – usually used only in relation to minor criminal offences
- the warning given to suspect when being arrested and interviewed by the police.

Chief Crown Prosecutor Member of the Crown Prosecution Service who has the responsibility for the day-to-day operations of a Crown Prosecution area.

Clerk to the Justices Responsible for the administration within the magistrates' court. Provides advice on legal procedures, eg sentencing issues etc, to magistrates.

Codes of Practice Written document created by the Home Secretary under the **Police and Criminal Evidence Act 1984**, which provides police officers with further information/guidelines on how their powers under the Act are supposed to be utilized. Breaches of the Codes can result in disciplinary action and evidence obtained being rendered inadmissible.

Common law Judge-made law, developed on a case-by-case basis, incrementally. Developed in early history from local customs. Also referred to as case law. Developed through the doctrine of judicial precedent.

Community penalties Form of criminal punishment that can be served in the community, hence the name, eg probation, etc.

Conditional bail Form of bail where conditions are attached in addition to the one that requires defendants to surrender for trial, eg agreeing to keep away from certain places and/or people, surrendering passport, etc.

Conditional fee agreement An agreement under which the successful lawyer receives a fee greater than that usually awarded; but if unsuccessful, no fee at all.

Conferences Meetings between a barrister and his instructing solicitor (with or without the client present).

Consolidated Fund The general account receiving/paying parliamentary sums without the need for a specific parliamentary vote for each transaction.

Contingency fees Fees payable only on success but which are a percentage of the compensation recovered.

Conveyancing The transfer of houses and land between parties.

Glossary

✱✱✱✱✱✱✱✱✱✱

Costs The fees and other expenses paid to lawyers for their advice or services.

County court First-instance court that deals with low value, non-complex civil cases.

Cross-examination Process by which a lawyer can question an opposing party's witnesses or even the defendant etc in order to enhance his/her clients case by establishing the witness is not accurate or truthful in response to answers given to the court.

Crown Court Criminal first-instance court, hears indictable offences/triable either way offences – jury determine guilt/innocence of accused. Judge administers sentence.

Crown Prosecution Service The primary agency responsible for prosecuting individuals who have committed criminal offences within England and Wales. Also determines the charge that is placed against the defendant on the basis of evidence provided to the Service by the police.

Crown Prosecutors Members of the Crown Prosecution Service who determine the decision to prosecute and can undertake the prosecution of offenders within the courts.

Custodial sentence A form of sentence administered by the courts. Most severe form of punishment. Defendant is detained for instance in a prison to serve a term set by the court.

Custody officer A member of the police force who is responsible for the well-being of suspects placed in their care during police detention.

Dinners Dinners held at each of the Inns of Court to assist barristers (and student members) in getting to know each other.

Director of Public Prosecutions Head of the Crown Prosecution Service. Can undertake criminal prosecutions in his/her own right. Role was in place before the creation of the CPS. Must produce a report on the operation of the CPS, which must be placed before Parliament by the Attorney General.

Distinguishing Process where a judge attempts to determine material differences between the case before him and an earlier case in order to not be bound by the earlier case decision.

District Judge (Magistrates' Court) Legally qualified magistrate, has different characteristics from their lay equivalent, eg sits to hear cases alone, appointment process etc. Presides over cases within the magistrates' court.

Equitable maxims Decisions of equity were not based on previous case decisions but determined on the facts of the particular case before the court. Therefore, there was no particular certainty in relation to the operation of equity and the application of its remedies. Maxims are basically the principles upon which equity operates. They are designed to provide some certainty/predictability in relation to the operation of equity.

Equity A form of law based on principles of natural justice and fairness. Developed in order to remedy the defects of the common law in relation to availability of writs and remedies etc. Operates on a discretionary basis.

European Court of Human Rights Court that hears infringements of the **European Convention on Human Rights and Fundamental Freedoms**. Prior to October 2000, if there was an infringement of such rights an individual citizen would have to take the case to this court to have the rights enforced. Now domestic courts have the power to uphold the Convention rights after inclusion into UK law by the **Human Rights Act 1998**.

European Court of Justice Court of the European Union which is responsible for hearing actions between Member States, between institutions and the Member States, and between EU institutions themselves. Also responsible for ensuring uniform interpretation and application of European Union law throughout the Member States via the preliminary reference procedure.

Examination in chief The process within the courtroom where a lawyer for the prosecution or defence will ask questions of their own witnesses.

Extrinsic aids Devices external to an Act of Parliament which can be used by a member of the judiciary to interpret statutes, eg Hansard.

Hearing The oral submissions in the litigation before the court, tribunal etc.

High Court First-instance civil court hears complex cases and high value claims. Three divisions: Family, Queen's Bench, and Chancery.

Hybrid offences Also known as triable either way offences. Offences of varying degrees of seriousness which may be heard in the Crown Court or magistrates' court.

Inadmissible evidence Evidence which is not admitted into the trial proper. This may be because the evidence has no probative value, eg hearsay evidence, or has been obtained in an improper manner. Admissibility of evidence determined in a *voir dire*.

Indictable offences Most serious form of criminal offences, eg murder, treason, rape, piracy, which can only be dealt with in the Crown Court.

Intrinsic aids Devices internal to an Act of Parliament which can be used by a member of the judiciary to interpret statutes, eg long title, schedules, etc.

Judicial precedent The foundation of the development of modern common law/case law. Process by which members of the judiciary follow previous case decisions where facts are similar.

Judicial review A higher court's supervision of a tribunal's procedure.

Judicial tenure The terms on which a judge holds office.

Jurisdiction Area of work, eg a magistrates' court has dual jurisdiction as it can hear criminal cases and undertakes minor civil work. A magistrates' court has local jurisdiction, it hears cases which involve matters within the geographical area within which the court is situated.

Jury equity/perverse decisions Cases where the jury reach a verdict in perceived contradiction to the evidence presented by the prosecution.

JUSTICE Law reform pressure group specializing in issues related to the criminal justice system.

Lay magistrate A layperson, ordinary member of the public without legal experience who sits within magistrates' courts determining eg the guilt/innocence of defendants, sentencing issues, etc.

Layperson A member of the public without legal experience and knowledge who plays a role within the English legal system.

Legal executives Members of the Institute of Legal Executives who are qualified by that Institute's professional examinations and training. Legal executives may have rights of audience in some courts.

Legal Services Commission Government agency responsible for administering legal aid, legal representation, etc.

Limitation period The period within which litigation must be commenced.

Magistrates' court First-instance court which has primarily criminal jurisdiction but also some civil jurisdiction.

Majority verdict Verdict where those in favour of a particular verdict outweigh those opposing. Only certain majority verdicts are allowed in relation to the Crown Court.

Mitigating circumstances Circumstances particular to a defendant, which are taken into account by the courts when determining sentence. These circumstances may result in a reduction of sentence, eg first offence committed, previous good behaviour, cooperation with investigative authorities, etc.

Nolle prosequi An order of the Attorney General which prevents a prosecution taking place.

Obiter dicta Latin phrase literally means 'things said by the way'. Hypothetical issues a judge may refer to in the course of a judgment. Not binding but may be followed in subsequent cases which raise the hypothetical legal issues.

Original precedent The first decision on a particular legal problem which is novel in nature.

Patent agents A practitioner registered as a patent agent (see also **Copyright, Designs and Patents Act 1988**). Patents are exclusive rights to use or authorize the use of a design.

Glossary

✻✻✻✻✻✻✻✻✻

Practice Directions Instructions issued by the court concerning the conduct of cases generally or a particular case.

Pre-action Protocols Standard steps which each party should effect prior to issuing a claim or prior to a hearing.

Preliminary reference procedure Procedure used by domestic courts within European Union Member States to obtain a uniform interpretation of European Union law from the European Court of Justice.

Proceedings Steps to start or pursue a case in court.

Public interest test One of the two tests administered by the Crown Prosecution Service when deciding whether an individual should be prosecuted for a criminal offence.

Quantum The amount of money awarded by way of damages.

Ratio decidendi Latin phrase literally meaning 'reason for the decision'. The binding element of a judgment, which must be followed where subsequent cases have similar facts and raise similar legal issues.

Remand Where a person has been refused bail he will be placed in custody until the trial takes place.

Representation Appearing on behalf of a client.

Right/s of audience The right to appear as a lawyer in a particular court.

Royal Assent Monarch (at present the Queen) gives formal approval to a bill becoming an Act of Parliament.

Royal Commission Official government law reform agency – makes proposals for changes in the law in the form of a report.

Secret soundings Enquiries made of professional practitioners and bodies about a prospective judge.

Settlement Out-of-court agreement of a claim.

Sentence Pronouncement of the court, which highlights a form of punishment that is to be imposed on a defendant convicted of a criminal offence.

Sentencing Process determined by a judge or magistrates where a punishment will be imposed on a defendant who has been found guilty of committing a criminal offence.

Statutory interpretation Process by which the courts, through the common law, remedy the defects, interpret ambiguous words and phrases etc, contained within a statute in order that it can be properly enforced.

Summary offences Minor criminal offences that can only be heard in the magistrates' court.

Tenancy A place in a set of barristers' chambers.

Triable either way offences Offences of varying degrees of seriousness which may be heard in the Crown Court or magistrates' court; aka hybrid offences.

Trials on indictment A trial that takes place before the Crown Court.

Tribunal A panel authorized to adjudicate on specific matters.

Ultra vires Acting beyond powers given.

Vetting and challenges Procedures whereby members of a potential jury can be removed from serving.

Voir dire A trial within a trial. The jury are removed from the courtroom; the judge determines the issue of admissibility of evidence based on representations made by advocates.

Youth Court Special court within the magistrates' court, which hears criminal cases involving young offenders. Magistrates must be specially trained to hear such cases. The general public and media are prevented from attending the court when in session.

Table of cases

Table of cases

****

Table of primary legislation

✱✱✱✱✱✱✱✱✱✱✱

Table of primary legislation

Table of primary legislation

✳✳✳✳✳✳✳✳✳

Table of secondary legislation and codes

✳✳✳✳✳✳✳✳✳

Table of secondary legislation and codes

Table of European legislation

Index

Index

✳✳✳✳✳✳✳✳✳✳

Index

Index

****

Index

✳✳✳✳✳✳✳✳✳

Questions & Answers

keeping you afloat through your exams